THE FICTIONS OF SATIRE

THE
FICTIONS
OF
SATIRE

By Ronald Paulson

THE JOHNS HOPKINS PRESS
Baltimore, Maryland

To Maynard Mack

ACKNOWLEDGMENT

A certain interdependence must be confessed between this essay and the author's *Satire and the Novel* (New Haven, Conn.: Yale University Press, 1967). Although separate and independent works, completed at different times, they were originally conceived as a single whole dealing with the development of fictive techniques in satire. *The Fictions of Satire* places its emphasis on satire, *Satire and the Novel* on the eighteenth-century English novel, but in a sense the one is an introduction to, and even includes a few passages that also appear in, the other (in the sections on picaresque and the "Quixote Fiction"). In this book I am interested almost exclusively in practice; in the other, where critical dicta importantly influence practice, I consider in some detail theories of satire and comedy in the eighteenth century.

For some of the material of this book I have drawn on essays previously published. Parts of Chapter I, "The Central Symbol of Violence," "Relationship: The Fool and the Knave," and "Picaresque Narrative: The Servant-Master Relation," have appeared in different form in *Rice University Studies,* LI (1965) under the title "The Fool-Knave Relation in Picaresque Satire." Sentences and occasional paragraphs, especially of sections of Chapter II entitled "The Satirist and the Satirist-Satirized" and "The Fictions of Tory Satire," have appeared in reviews published in the *Journal of English and Germanic Philology.* Part of Chapter III, "Swiftean Romanticism: The Satirist as Hero," was originally published as "Swift, Stella, and Permanence" in *ELH A Journal of English Literary History,* XXVII (1960).

My first thanks go to the University of Illinois and the American Philosophical Society for grants that enabled me in the summers of 1960 and 1961 to begin thinking about the subject of satire. Since then, other grants from universities and learned societies that contributed directly to other projects have incidentally offered moments in which I could return to it. Rice University generously provided a typist for the final draft. Jack Stillinger read much of the manuscript in a very early form and helped me in the many ways to which his friendship has long accustomed me. I must also thank, once again, Maynard Mack, who read both parts of the original manuscript, and to whom I have dedicated the finished product as an overdue token of gratitude and esteem.

TABLE OF CONTENTS

THE FICTIONS OF SATIRE

I. RHETORIC AND REPRESENTATION

C
Introduction

ontemporary definitions of satire usually join two terms: "wit or humor founded on fantasy or a sense of the grotesque or absurd" for one, and "an object of attack" for the other; or fantasy and a moral standard; or indirection and judgment. One is a wild, not quite stable comedy; the other a moral condemnation. Both are attitudes or tones, although implied is "an object" to be acted upon. Put into Aristotle's correlation, satire can be said to study an ugliness in a manner that is not itself painful, and its approach consists of denigration or attack.[1]

To the extent that satire presents, and so represents, its "object," it is related to other mimetic forms. But to the extent that satire attacks, it is rhetorical—the *vituperatio* of *laus et vituperatio*—and there is a persuasive end in sight. However much mimesis or representation is involved, the generic end is rhetorical. As Swift wrote to Gay following the success of *The Beggar's Opera* in the eventful spring of 1728: "The *Beggar's Opera* has knocked down *Gulliver;* I hope to see Pope's *Dulness* [*The Dunciad*] knock down the *Beggar's Opera,* but not till it *has fully done its job*" (my italics). The "job"—Swift later

---

[1] Northrop Frye, *The Anatomy of Criticism* (Princeton, N.J.: Princeton University Press, 1957), p. 224; Ellen Leyburn, *Satiric Allegory: Mirror of Man* (New Haven, Conn.: Yale University Press, 1956), p. 7; Aristotle, *Poetics* 5, 1.

3

refers to it as the "task"—is a *sine qua non* of satire.[2] Satire imitates, presents, explores, analyzes the evil (the term I shall use instead of Aristotle's "ugly"), but it must at the same time (1) make the reader aware of a pointing finger, of an ought or ought not, that refers beyond the page to his own life, or—and this is not always the same thing—(2) take a moral stand, make a judgment, and place or distribute blame. The first can develop into an extremely elaborate rhetorical structure; the second requires only that the object be made to appear evil or ridiculous, not neutral or acceptable. The element of judgment is acutely described by David Worcester as a "closeness of pursuit" and an "intensity of condemnation";[3] by the comparative intensity of these qualities satire is distinguishable from the freer, more careless and permissive world of comedy. Satire has a certain specific business to do, and it does it. Clearly Worcester's distinction leaves a great deal to opinion, but it does designate in comedy a residuum of pure exuberance. There is always a strong sense of efficiency in satire: nothing is done without a purpose. It has no time for loitering and highjinks.

But if comedy is the pure substance which satire uses for its own businesslike ends, we might wonder if satire is anything more than a tone attached to certain forms and subject matters. Without an article "satire" refers more to a tone than to a form. It is not at all the same thing to say that Pope wrote satire and to say that he wrote *a* satire. The latter introduces ideas of form and convention as well as of tone; but a novel, or a play, or a poem, can be satire without being *a* satire, and the adjective "satiric" is much the most popular form of the word. Following is a typical view of satire's form, or non-form: "One thing satire, as a form, is incapable of doing: it cannot provide the plot for a novel. Traditionally, satire has always borrowed its ground-plan, parasitically and by ironic inversion, from other

[2] Letter to Gay, 28 March 1728; to Pope, 10 May. See *The Correspondence of Jonathan Swift,* ed. Harold Williams (Oxford: Clarendon Press, 1963), III, 278, 286 (I have modernized for purposes of clarity in this instance).

[3] *The Art of Satire* (Cambridge, Mass.: Harvard University Press, 1940), pp. 37–38.

forms of ordered exposition in art or in life. . . ."[4] Historically, the satirist has often had to be on his guard and hide his satires beneath the sheep's clothing of a commonly accepted form. Whether the satire appears to be a children's tale or sheer nonsense, it offers both the author and the audience an opportunity to take it that way—for self-protection. Moreover, an object of satire is best attacked through a generally understood form that is perverted to convey the satiric message. Satire's purpose ordinarily is not to create something new but to expose the real evil in the existing. In the troubled England of the seventeenth century, this could best be done through a happy form like the nursery tale or a pious one like the liturgy or a hymn, under which is revealed an unexpected impiety. The effect is almost always one of surprise: that an old conventional form could contain such depravity, or that an ordinary, accepted commonplace of experience could mean something hitherto unsuspected. It is therefore true that satire is partly defined by its use of commonly accepted forms, both as a false face for itself and as a cogent demonstration that what we ordinarily think of as good or real may be only a masquerade.

Nevertheless, while adopting the forms of other literary genres, satire finds some forms more congenial than others. The liturgy and the hymn, the almanac and the petition, offer an unlimited series for portraits and vignettes—a shape as well as an allusion. Satire enjoys the episodic forms, the collection of stories or anecdotes, the list, the large dinner party or the group conversation, the legal brief, the projector's pamphlet, the encyclopedia, and the calendar. When it assumes a less accommodating form it always exploits only those aspects that serve its own end; when it does not find those aspects in the form parodied it superimposes them.

Formally speaking, satire is as concerned with exposition as it is with attack; if attack helps to describe its tone, exposition suggests the kinds of form it employs. Some forms, adopted

[4] Frederick J. Stopp, *Evelyn Waugh: Portrait of an Artist* (London: Chapman and Hall, 1958), p. 201.

from comedy and oratory, are used for their expository value only, not as an allusion to anything else. Other forms are parodied by an allusion here and there while their structures are wholly abandoned. Nobody would mistake *Gargantua* or *Don Quixote* for romances or *The Satyricon* or *The Dunciad* for epics. In the last of these Pope parodied not the epic structure but the epic paraphernalia, the action and conventions of a particular epic, *The Aeneid*. His borrowings point, however, to one basic fact of satire's form: *The Aeneid* is invoked to suggest the ideal in the past by which Pope judges the present. In Pope's case, or Petronius', the parody does not ridicule what is parodied but uses it as a standard of excellence; with Rabelais or Cervantes the parodied is exposed as a false ideal against the real complexity of experience. The form implicit in these satires simply opposes two portraits, of the good and the bad. Parody telescopes both elements into a single symbol.

Satire's own structure is most clearly visible in its primitive shape, the curse drawn from fertility ritual—probably the source of the idea that satire is a tone independent of a form. The vatic figure who encouraged fertility was accompanied by a satirist who exorcised the elements that could prevent fertility. The curse naturally contrasted forces of sterility with creative and fertile images such as sun, rain, and male and female generative organs. The effect of the curse was creative through denigration of the sterile. In this way a simple A-B (thesis-antithesis) structure is present in the earliest satire. (A), the false, by itself, without the awareness of (B), the true, could not be regarded with indignation or with any but a neutral or perhaps a melancholy emotion. In *The Dunciad,* for example, (B) is only implicit in the epic allusions and the normative form of the couplet; in some cases it is only implicit in the corruption itself, as a decadent literature contains within itself the ideal of a sound one.

Satire's structure is essentially a setting or frame for showing off something. In general the satiric form is anything that will serve to expose a succession of different aspects of a single subject, the object of denunciation; with a small niche reserved somewhere for an indication of the good to which it is opposed.[5]

Without the simple opposition provided by the curse or parody, a fiction must be constructed in which a villain combats a hero, with the impression emergent that evil is either the victor or simply more prevalent, but at any rate the *subject*. Northrop Frye's description of the comic and satiric actions is useful because it puts a matter heretofore stated in terms of tone in terms of a fiction. "The intensity of condemnation" which, according to Worcester, was a distinguishing characteristic of the satiric tone, is restated in Frye's terms as the fact that satire excludes more people from its society of the blessed at the end than does comedy. Frye sees comedy in general as concerned with the conflict between two societies, a true (or good, or normal) and a false (or evil, or absurd). But while comedy focuses on the conflict itself and the victory of the true society over the false, satire focuses on the massive presence, if not the victory, of the false society, with the true either overwhelmed or just emerging into the light of day.[6]

As a mimetic art, then, satire imitates a vice or folly. The tone of exorcism, we might say, manifests itself in the intimidating list of the curse and its angry exaggerations of defects on the one hand, and its projected hypothetical situations of discomfort and pain on the other. But one complication should be noticed at the outset. As the derivation of the curse itself suggests, the indication of a contrasting good may be embodied in the satirist himself, and very often we find the writer of satire imitating the secondary subject of the satirist—his character, his perceiving, his chastising, and the language of his vituperation. The dualism of satire's subject is responsible for some of its most interesting and ambiguous as well as some of its least fortunate products.

I would suggest that if satire originates as rhetoric, or attack,

[5] See Mary Claire Randolph, "The Structural Design of Formal Verse Satire," *Philological Quarterly*, XXI (1942), 368–84. Maynard Mack offers a useful interpretation of the two-part form in his essay, "The Muse of Satire," *Yale Review*, XLI (1951), 80–92.

[6] Frye, *Anatomy of Criticism*, pp. 180–85, 223–39.

it only matters—or survives as literature—as mimesis, exploration, and analysis. Like comedy or tragedy, satire is a form which gives a compelling poetic representation of a certain area of experience. Roughly speaking, if tragedy explores the upper range of man's potential in relation to the limitations of society, custom, or his own nature, satire explores his lower potentials. To map a part of this area as it emerges in satire's fictions will be the aim of the present study.

The first chapter outlines the general areas of subject matter taken by satire and the fictions in which they are embodied. It also broaches the questions of how attack—or ridicule or condemnation—relates to imitation in these fictions, how rhetoric relates to representation, and the imitation of the satirist to the imitation of the satiric object. I rely heavily on classical examples both because the Romans developed the fictions that were the most important and influential for all subsequent satirists in the western tradition and because an understanding of their satires is, for modern readers, relatively uncomplicated by historical context. The second and third chapters take up the evolution of a single image of evil—a single fiction—to meet the needs of a particular historical period, the English Augustan Age. The old fictions—first seen in formal verse satires, then adapted to prose narrative satires—now reappear in new guises, contributing to the particular image of evil constructed by Dryden, elaborated by Swift, and contradicted by Addison and Steele. These chapters are not intended as an account of the Augustan Age, or even of its satire, but only of its central satiric fictions, how they were constituted, and the satiric world they projected. A history of satire could be written by tracing its different images or versions of evil and the different (or sometimes repeated) fictions used to express them. This essay is a tentative gesture in that direction, with the limitation of a bias toward a single period.

The final chapters also indicate the mimetic drift of satire in the eighteenth century away from formal satire—satires that are called "Satire I" or "Satire II" or otherwise draw attention to themselves as satires—toward what I take to be the typical satire of the Swift period, which in fact pretends to be something else. This satire is specifically a fictional construct, both in the sense that it pretends to be something it is not, and in the sense that it produces stories, plots, and character relationships. This is the satire, it seems to me, that points the way to, and gradually merges into, the satiric novels of Fielding, Smollett, and Sterne, in which the representational qualities appear in a new relationship with the rhetorical.

The Central Symbol of Violence

What we remember from a satire is neither character nor plot per se, but a fantastic image, or a series of them. At the center of almost every satire there is an image which, if effective, the reader cannot easily forget: the copulation of an ass and a woman (Apuleius' *Metamorphoses*), a fanatic leaping into a bonfire (Lucian's *Death of Peregrine*), the drowning of half the populace of Paris in a flood of urine (Rabelais' *Gargantua*), the sawing off of a man's head (Waugh's *Decline and Fall*). In the field of cannibalism alone there are such incidents as the projected cooking and eating of children (Swift's *Modest Proposal*), the eating of a pet spaniel and a tutor (Byron's *Don Juan*), and the eating of a fiancée (Waugh's *Black Mischief*). In Juvenal's Satire XV Egyptians devour an enemy soldier, and in Petronius' *Satyricon* the heirs of Eumolpus must eat his body before they can share his suppositious estate. At the center of Nathanael West's *A Cool Million* is the dismemberment of the hero and the repeated rape of the heroine, and in *Gulliver's Travels* there is the threat of blinding or mastication.

Such a scene is, of course, in one sense a poetic strategy. The satirist uses cannibalism as a metaphor for aggression. But poetry is incidental result rather than intention; more to the point, these scenes represent the characteristic fictions through which the satirist conveys his subject matter: the corruption of an ideal and the behavior of fools, knaves, dupes, and the like.

(1) *Corruption.* The corruption or degeneration of the nor-

mative or ideal is conveyed by a static image, usually related to the Theophrastan "character." Behind the copulation of beast and bestial woman is the normal relationship between man and woman. The woman in Juvenal's Satire VI who has become a gladiator is juxtaposed with the feminine ideal; the rakehell is measured against the statues of his heroic ancestors (Satire VIII); or the pretender to social status against the proper social values (Horace's Satire I.9). In Pope's *Dunciad* unreason and wretched writing ("Dulness") are simply placed alongside the great literary works of the past.

(2) *Consequences.* But while the corruption of an ideal is almost always at least implicit, it only rarely appears as the sole subject of the satire. The basic polarity of an ideal (usually in the past) and a degenerate present provides a useful frame for the argument of a satire; but the only comment it has to offer is, "Alas, what a falling away!" A merely static contrast cannot demonstrate other areas of satiric subject matter, folly and knavery on the part of the degenerate. In order to portray these subjects the satirist must present (or at least imply) an act of some kind, for example, the copulation of ass and woman, which is shown to be the conseqeunce of the woman's lust.

Satire characteristically judges by consequences rather than by causes or motives, which are too slippery; the final standard is an objective one like success or failure. (The satirist is, in fact, fond of showing up the subjective standard of motive or intention by the concrete fact of its consequence.) The satirist who wishes to convey his indictment by a fictive rather than a discursive structure must (if his indictment is very severe) employ a physical encounter which ends in violence. The scenes noted above are all shockingly violent concatenations of action and consequence; they are, in effect, symbolic actions that convey the central meaning of the satire. Peregrine's self-immolation proves his self-consuming folly, as the eating of children, spaniel, tutor, and fiancée demonstrate the eaters' cannibalistic viciousness.

Punishment is the most extreme, and at the same time most common, consequence in satire. The satirist can show the consequences of folly in the punishment of the guilty (Peregrine burned), or he can show the guilty in the process of punishing, or persecuting, the innocent (the savage treatment of the hero and heroine in *A Cool Million*). The latter paradoxical situation is obviously the more popular one with a satirist: its attack is less direct and less optimistic than the straightforward administration of justice. The punishment of the innocent, however, while producing a striking momentary effect and an appropriate atmosphere, tells us nothing about the victim and relatively little about the punisher. Punishment of people with varying degrees of guilt can permit elaborate analysis and exposition of the public as well as the private aspects of a character.

In Apuleius' *Metamorphoses,* Lucius is punished for his spiritual and physical lusts by being turned into a symbol of lust, an ass, and thereafter frequently threatened with gelding. What follows for him is, in fact, one long punishment. But the same befalls the subsidiary characters: the robber Lamachus puts his hand through a keyhole in order to lift the bar inside. The owner of the house nails the housebreaker's hand to the inside of the door (a suggestion of crucifixion, the punishment for robbers); in order to make their escape the robbers cut off Lamachus' arm at the elbow (the offending member is removed). Elsewhere Thelyphron loses his ears and nose as a consequence of his excessive self-confidence. The evil boy who has tormented Lucius is eaten by a bear, a murderous slave is crucified, a murderous woman is condemned to copulation with an ass, the eunuch priests are carted off to jail, the robbers are rolled off a cliff, and the wicked sisters of Psyche are plunged to their deaths. The adulterous husband, whose wife takes revenge by throwing herself and her child into a well, is eaten by ants (as by the lusts that drove him to adultery). If we may judge by Apuleius, the satirist seldom bothers to punish the totally innocent, and the first feeling of persecution is quickly followed by its opposite, a suspicion of justice.

The implications of the device of punishing the guilty are clarified by a survey of its sources. A satire is said to "pillory" or "lacerate" or "blister" the person it attacks. The convention of punishing a knave within the satiric fiction was probably first based on the belief that by a pre-enactment of his wishes the satirist could somehow coerce nature into making the fiction real; in this sense, punishment is a vestige of satire's origin in ritual and magic. Certainly one source is the primitive satirist's curse which enumerates the poxes and floggings he wishes to see descend upon his enemy. The satirist who wants to materialize the curse (and perhaps recall some of its vigor) must describe a physical chastisement of the villain. The ancient satirist Archilochus asks that his enemy be shipwrecked: "Shivering with cold, covered with filth washed up by the sea, with chattering teeth like a dog, may he lie helplessly on his face at the edge of the strand amidst the breakers—this 'tis my wish to see him suffer, who has trodden his oaths under foot, him who was once my friend."[7] Helplessness and isolation are not an arbitrary revenge; they describe the character of the turncoat who has cut himself off from human loyalties.

The curse itself derives from the idea that external appearance should correspond to inner reality, a diseased body to a diseased soul, and so (some satirist must have inferred) the marks of punishment will suggest the quality of the soul within that merits such punishment. A pox is both a painful punishment for transgression and an externalization of an internal corruption. As in the case of Lucius, punishment adjusts the false appearance until it does correspond to the inner reality. It fastens on the delicate spot, exaggerating it, inverting it, or in some way distorting it.

These punishments represent very literally a rhetorical stance transformed or objectified into an image of evil. By contrast, the commonest of literary punishments, in which the culprit is simply roasted in hell fire or whipped unmercifully or submerged in excrement, is more an objectification of the satirist's disgust than

---

[7] The quotation is from the Strassburg Fragment (97A), trans. G. L. Hendrickson, "Archilochus and the Victims of his Iambics," *American Journal of Philology*, XLVI (1925), 115. Satiric punishment is also perhaps related to the "elaborate ritual of the defeat of winter known to folklorists as 'carrying out Death'" (Frye, *Anatomy of Criticism*, p. 183); and to God's punishment of sinners, which carries a sanction that no civil punishment could (see, e.g., *Isaiah* 3:16-17; 28:14-22).

of the evil man's sin. When Ezra Pound (*Cantos* XIV and XV)
describes his usurers covered with filth, he is attempting to make
us share his own feelings about them by giving us an objective
correlative which presumably excites in us similar feelings. The
result is that the image lacks cognitive particularity. As too often
happens, the punishment is decorative and tells us very little
about the person or crime punished.

In all of these instances, however, the satirist has attempted to
convey a truth about his sinners which is not apparent on perusal
in ordinary circumstances. Only in hell—or in the agony of
punishment—is it possible to see that they *are* (spiritually)
splitting open with their excess, or that their sin is actually con-
suming them, not they it. Even Pound's newspaper and banking
barons appear in the "last squalor, utter decrepitude" in hell
because that is their reality—the reality their money and power
prevent us from seeing. The poetic justice of these punishments
is irrelevant to the satiric effect; but their symbolic appropriateness describes an inner state that cannot be exposed simply by
showing the knave in action tormenting the innocent.

Carried far enough, the image of punishment leads to the
belief that the manner of one's dying defines the man; or, as
Kenneth Burke has noticed, we say not that a man is "by nature
a criminal" but that "he will end on the gallows."[8] In the picaresque satire *La Picara Justina* (1605), the heroine gives us
accounts of the violent deaths of her many ancestors, each symbolic of the ancestor's crime. For example, her gluttonous
mother stole steaks and puddings; when she was finally caught,
"for fear of a discovery, [she] cramm'd in half a yard of
Pudding, which being thrust down too hastily, stop'd up the
Passage, so that there was no moving forwards or backwards,
nor could she Speak or Breathe." The merchant interrogated
her, "but she could return no answer; and the best of it was,
that a long piece of *Pudding* hung out at her Mouth, so that she
look'd like a *Bear* in *Heraldry,* Arm'd and Langued."[9] In her

---

[8] "The Imagery of Killing," *Hudson Review,* I (1948), 162.

[9] Francisco de Ubeda, *La Picara Justina* (1605), in *The Spanish Libertines,*
trans. Capt. John Stevens (London, 1709), p. 20.

suffering and death she creates the satiric image (almost an escutcheon) that sums up her essential character. Punishment and death are terminal actions that round off tidily the vicious actions they conclude. They obviate potentialities and establish a fixed, complete portrait. Justina's mother brings about her own end, demonstrating neatly that, as with a glutton whose gluttony only increases his appetite, the crime is its own punishment.

Punishment thus conveys a definite admonition: this is the consequence of your foolish act, this is the effect of X's evil act; or, beware! this is what you could look like or what X does in fact look like. There is also, of course, a strong element of the therapeutic in punishment: besides the lash and the strappado, the purge and the scalpel define the distemper as they remove it.[10] But if satire is essentially a study of evil, we can interpret punishment of the guilty as a way to present the psychological reality of the vice, its ethos; while punishment of the innocent presents the objective effects of the vice. One is concerned primarily with the criminal, the other with the crime (and sometimes with the suffering of the innocent, which may lead out of satire into sentimentalism).

In many satires, we may note in passing, the punishment is also objictified in the satirist's image of himself as a surgeon or public executioner—with the effect of drawing the reader's attention away from both persuasion and presentation to the interesting image of the performer and his operations.

(3) *Distance*. A determining factor in the effect of the satiric symbol is the distance maintained between the reader (and the author) and the satiric fiction that is being presented. At one extreme is an ironic, oblique presentation, about which the reader, as a member of an elite, feels rather superior. If in some sense he is the ordinary, lethargic backslider, he is distinct from the evil tendencies the satirist presents. The satirist's irony, which goes over the head of the guilty party, is understood by

---

[10] Mary Claire Randolph has discussed this subject in "The Medical Concept in English Renaissance Satiric Theory: Its Possible Relationships and Implications," *Studies in Philology*, XXXVIII (1941), 125–57.

the intelligent and morally-aware reader. The other satiric approach, in effect, rubs the reader's nose in the dirt of which it is trying to make him aware. It forces him by intimate sensuous contact to suffer such revulsion that he will see a truth he has overlooked, change his ways, or campaign against the evil in question. In Gulliver's fourth voyage there are the filthy Yahoos, and in Juvenal's famous portrait of Messalina (Satire VI) we smell and feel the sheets, see her feverish body and its gestures.

The satiric scene, however, is ordinarily carefully distanced from the reader. Imagine the death of Prendergast in *Decline and Fall* full of blood and Prendergast's agony: as opposed to Waugh's account, held at arm's length by the secondhand source who is inserting the information into the verse form of a hymn being sung at chapel. One is reminded of the difference between the cartoon submitted to *The New Yorker* which showed one fencer slashing off the other's head with blood spattered everywhere, and the printed drawing (the caption, "Touché") by James Thurber, executed with the very minimum of detail. Sensuous detail is almost entirely absent, and the act is kept as abstract as possible while remaining suggestive. Swift's babies are hypothetical and unparticularized; their fate is particularized in the extreme (fricasseed, put in a ragout, made into gloves for ladies) but applied to abstractions.

The discrepancy created by ironic understatement, as has often been remarked, may make the horror greater; but the distancing, or the remove at which we witness the act, also keeps us from losing ourselves in the horror. The butchery of Prendergast or of babies, we are reminded, is not itself the main point of the image, merely a metaphorical notation for the real one. Whereas, as the sensuous immediacy of the action increases, the image becomes more a thing for its own sake in which the reader is immersed. The satirist, in short, demands decisions of his reader, not feelings; wishes to arouse his energy to action, not purge it in vicarious experience.

The detachment demanded by satire, however, is different from that we feel when we witness a farce, for example an animated cartoon of the cat and mouse, Tom and Jerry. The satiric image has to be taken seriously in a way altogether different from its cousin, the farcical image of Jerry squashing Tom's head between millstones. Or better, take the example of Titania kissing Bottom the tailor (transformed into an ass) in *A Midsummer Night's Dream.* Here the reader is so detached from the characters that the comedy is, as Meredith would say, very pure. To be satire there would have to be (among other things) a great deal of impurity—the reader would have to grimace when the lovely, deluded queen kissed the hairy mouth. The satiric image lacks the complete abstraction of the comic: a certain disgust, a certain physical involvement of the reader is always necessary. One way this seriousness of involvement is maintained is by the basic causality that is stressed in satire's world: when a head is sawed off, the man dies; but also by introducing enough physical details to be suggestive without breaking the abstraction of the idea. Waugh does imbed in the hymn two details about Prendergast, his screams and their duration: "Poor Prendy 'ollored fit to kill / For nearly 'alf an hour." The balance is a delicate one between contemplation and arousal.

(4) *Corrective.* As its ritual origin shows, the satiric fiction is a throwback that has not yet completely transformed sexual orgy into the more genteel comic resolution of romantic marriage. The leather phalli are still in view, and the conflict presented between the forces of fertility and of barrenness is much less veiled—and also much more obviously a conflict, with the author clearly on the side of fertility. If punishment (as curse) is one aspect of its action, copulating, eating, and defecating are others. In Aristophanes' plays the phallic costume constantly reminds the spectator of the norm behind the play, of the characters' shared humanity, of their true and basic motives and desires beneath fashion and hypocrisy. Thus in *Lysistrata* Aristophanes shows the women's refusal to sleep with their husbands (the frustrated phalli much in evidence) as an analogue to the barrenness caused by the war—spiritual as well as material. Sexuality is Juvenal's most basic symbol for life and human relationships, all of which spiral down toward sexual perversion. Horace uses sexual passion to represent all kinds of excess in

his Satire I.2, and many satirists from Rabelais to Rochester make sexuality a microcosm of their world. Juvenal's (or Petronius') attack on the sterility of perversion suggests that his satire still carries a vestige of the fertility ritual. Copulation is one of the most basic, natural, unavoidable acts of men, offering a universality that few other examples can have; it reminds us, when we become proud, of our ties with the animal. The eating and excreting of food, even more basic acts, are the other favorite symbols of the satirist. Both love-making and eating make the gratuitous, romantic, or perverse easily apparent.

Animal functions contribute still another important characteristic of satiric violence: the sense of release, which is the motive force behind Aristophanes' plays. Aristophanes' action is presented as a fantastic explosion of energy, only in the most general sense sexual. In the midst of a long, hopeless war one citizen makes a private peace with Sparta and sets up his own small, independent, and prosperous state within Athens; another travels up to Olympus on the back of a dung beetle to secure the goddess Peace; two other citizens, disgusted with the present state of affairs in Athens, found a city of birds between earth and heaven and intercept the burnt offerings to the gods. Aristophanes' action may be a parody of the miraculous or magical event at the center of romances; in a more important sense it derives from the mythos of the fertility ritual, showing a hero trying to bring the moribund society of the present—made so by continued war or political stagnation—back to life. The plot consists of a revolutionary plan that is acted upon to solve the insoluble problem faced by the Athenians.

When the violent importation of one situation into an alien one is related to moral values it becomes universe-changing, order-disrupting, attitude-mixing, a reversal of values; and if the emphasis is on the disruption as a corrective and the thing disrupted as wrong, the result is revolutionary satire. The effect is to shatter the world of custom and convention, to break open the coffin in which Athens has immured itself.

But this is to see the revolutionary plan in too simple a way. At best it is a fantastic if not ridiculous plan, which by its madness shows up the situation against which it reacts. It says: Things are so impossibly terrible that this, fantastic as it is, is the only answer. The "plan" is not a serious proposal but a ridiculous alternative that indirectly illuminates the nature of the problem. The facts that the hero is unheroic and buffoonish —a parody of epic and romance heroes—and that his antagonist is only an alazon are also part of the comically hopeless situation as Aristophanes dramatizes it. The heroes of Marathon are now old and decrepit, eager for the status quo, the government is dominated by fools, and the duty of resuscitation is left to the most ordinary citizen.

There is also, we should notice, a sense in which Aristophanes' most revolutionary satire is in fact conservative. The analogy of ancient fertility ritual is useful to explain the conservatism that underlies even revolutionary satire, as a self-justfication if not a pose. The old god or king died or was killed in ritual combat, but the new god who defeated or replaced him was not new in the sense of *different*. He was the same man restored to his youth, and the new killed and replaced the old simply because age had hardened his arteries, softened his brain, slowed him to a walk, and induced impotence. In terms of Frye's mythical categories, the new, true society is always a return to an older society (usually visualized as a Golden Age in the past), whose place has been usurped by an intermediate, aging, and false society. Depending on the emphasis—whether it is on the nonconformity and deviation of the false society from old norms, or on its rigidifying of the old ways—the satire can be conservative or revolutionary, its aim to attack release or to use it as a foil to stultification.

The Aristophanic exuberance can serve two antithetical purposes in satire. The more common use is to interpret the outburst of energy as the chaos of uncontrol, of vicious individualism. The emphasis on eating, defecating, and making love, which in Aristophanes is almost a comic ideal in itself, in the Roman satirists—particularly in Juvenal—becomes the multiplicity of disorder, sinking from gluttony to cannibalism, from unrestrained to perverted lusts. These satirists see the world as a simple, stable social order with forces at work trying to undermine or overthrow a beautiful status quo—or perhaps the overthrow has already taken place and the satirist looks back with nostalgia to the time of order. The result is less an imitation of exuberance than of overripeness, rottenness, a sinister often horrible quality. This quality is altogether lacking in the work of the satirist who sees the world as per se a place of complexity and disorder. His satire is offensive, clownish, seeking the new which may open unsuspected possibilities for individual fulfillment and shading off into comedy. A satirist who believes that his society is stuffy, overordered, and convention-ridden employs revolutionary satire, and a satirist who sees his society as chaotic, individualistic, and novelty-seeking tries to rein it by using a defensive satire.

Thus to the demonstration of folly and knavery, can be added a further function of the violent symbol of action and consequences: to serve as a corrective. Looking again at some of those violent actions with which this section began, we can classify them according to their intention. Basil Seal's eating of his fiancée in *Black Mischief* is evil, its purpose being to reveal in a dramatic image the truth about Basil, that he is indeed a cannibal (the same is true of the heirs of Eumolpus and the English and Irish landowners in the *Modest Proposal*). On the other hand, Gargantua's drowning of half the population of Paris in a flood of urine, however fatal to the Parisians, is good because Paris has become moribund, dry, and parched. The sawing off of Prendergast's head, while not in itself good, does serve to point up Prendergast's withdrawal from all human commitments by having him sawed on for half an hour by the most committed of men, a homicidal maniac. The act also, of course, reflects back on the prison warden with his narrowly progressive penal theories. The dismemberment of the protagonist of *A Cool Million* is largely a commentary on the vicious society, but partly also on the naïve protagonist himself.

The dual use of the violent image points to the conclusion that it is essentially equivocal and is exploited as such. Being a rhetorical form, satire invariably engages in casuistry and inconsistency—often at the expense of the coherence of its fiction.

The significant characteristic of the satiric symbol is its flexibility; it can be used in more than one way at the same time and to catch as many different—often contradictory—facets of falsity or evil as possible. Its absence of consistency is a complement of its flexibility; it is operative less as a device of verisimilitude than as a device to "catch the conscience of the king."[11]

The evil represented, then, is either an excessively disordered or an excessively ordered society, with its opposite used as a foil or, sometimes, as a complement (both of them wrong). The contrast can extend to illusion and reality, affectation and plain-speaking, rebellion and complaisance—any set of extremes between which the satirist takes one or neither side. These extremes are the areas imitated by the satirist. They are ordinarily represented, however, with one doing something to the other, or to itself. The action, reaction, or interaction is finally the object represented.

Relationship: The Fool and the Knave

The consequence of an action in satire can be either the effect it has on other people, or the repercussions it brings upon oneself. In either case the fictions used by satire are essentially relationships between people. Plots may be borrowed, but certain relationships—between the bad, the foolish, the good—are indigenous to satire. Even the static emblematic image of punishment usually involves the punisher as well as the punished. Without a situation in which one man exploits or injures another, knavery cannot be demonstrated; and to demonstrate folly he must himself be discomfited. A knave is only finally a knave by virtue of his impingement on the lives of others; a fool's actions are not foolish unless they are ineffectual or bring down upon

[11] It might even be argued, with Sheldon Sacks, that if we accept the idea that every part of a satire ideally contributes to the generic aim of ridicule, there can be no expression of an ideal as such. Ideals are present only to set off the evil, and tell us nothing of the satirist's positive values. See Sacks' *Fiction and the Shape of Belief* (Berkeley and Los Angeles: University of California Press, 1965), pp. 8–9.

him unpleasant consequences. The satirist even goes so far as to suggest that the knave is less a knave when his villainy fails or back-fires, or when he is punished; these consequences may turn his knavery into folly.

It is possible for a fool to appear alone in a satire: a single glutton, his health worn away, his character undermined, his money gone, can exemplify folly. But a knave can never appear without a victim in sight. There must be a dupe, or a fool, or an innocent for him to prey upon, otherwise he becomes himself a fool expending his energy on air. An Iago can be evil in soliloquy because tragedy looks at the inner life as an independent world. But a satiric Iago, without an Othello, would be a fool spinning bootless plots. In his sixth satire Juvenal writes primarily about women, not about marriage, but he can define their evil only in terms of marriage or some similar relationship. In the central part of the satire, where the women are without an object of aggression, he exposes only their folly: here they are drunken Venuses unable to control themselves, the prey of eastern superstitions, oracles, and charlatans. But once their husbands and stepsons, slaves and neighbors, are back in the picture, their folly again turns to cruelty and destructiveness, progressing from infidelity toward murder.

The distinction between Horatian and Juvenalian satire is largely one of focus on fool or knave: Horace focuses on the fathers who are hated, while Juvenal focuses on the sons who kill their fathers. The fictions they employ are therefore basically different, and since most subsequent satire derives from one or the other, they should be clearly distinguished.

Horace gives his attention almost exclusively to fools. There is no real knave in his world because one of his assumptions is that deviant behavior brings its own punishment, that those who give the appearance of being knaves are in fact fools. Punishment, the most frequent consequence of action in his satires, turns crime into folly, apparent knaves into fools. Anyone (says Horace) is a fool who fails to see his own best course of action, who mistakes a false for a real good. Accordingly, Horace shows the miser the unpleasantness that results from burying one's money in the ground and spending sleepless nights worrying about it, when, in spite of all his care, the money that has been hoarded will be run through in no time by his heir (Satire I.1). When the miser drives his son away, it is he and not the son who suffers; he is an exploiter not of others but of himself. The adulterer in Satire I.2 is not wicked, only foolish, and his foolishness is proved by his fate at the hands of irate husbands and loyal servants.

Even such a monster as the witch Canidia is shown to be a fool rather than a knave. In Epode V she buries an innocent boy up to his neck and starves him to death (food is placed just beyond his lips), her aim being to transfer his longing to the man who has not returned her love. Although she destroys the boy, we are given ample evidence that she will not get her man; her witchcraft has not worked in the past and will not work now. The boy's curses point to an ironic similarity between the hopeless passivity of his position and that of his tormentor's. Though immediately destructive, and in that sense evil, Canidia is in the long run ineffectual, as she was earlier in Satire I.8 when Priapus routed her and dispelled all her factitious incantations by a single vulgar and natural gesture. Even the worst knaves, Horace shows, finally turn out to be fools. The detection of folly at the heart of apparent knavery, as much as the light carefree tone, explains the difference between the satire of Horace and Juvenal. As Plato phrased it, "ignorance in the powerful is hateful and horrible, because hurtful to others both in reality and in fiction, but powerless ignorance may be reckoned, and in truth is, ridiculous."[12]

In Satire I.9 Horace presents the basic situation of his kind of satire: a bore pursues and unmercifully bothers the speaker ("Horace"), trying to break into the charmed circle of Maecenas, Virgil, Horace, and their friends. The outsider only succeeds in making a fool of himself, and solid Roman society shakes its head in disapproval. The bore seeks social status, Canidia seeks love, and Nasidienus (in II.8) tries to give a

[12] *Philebus* 49, in *The Dialogues of Plato,* trans. B. Jowett (New York: Random House, 1937), II, 384.

fashionable dinner; while the insider, who understands the nature of society, affection, and hospitality, points out wherein the upstarts fall short. The outsider is outside because he is a fool, and will remain so until he adjusts to the proper standards of conduct.

The ridiculing of an outsider from the security of a conservative, order-conscious society is one of the most pervasive conventions of satire. Horace, however, characteristically extends his satire to one insider, himself. The actual subject of Satire I.9 turns out to be as much the discomfiture of "Horace" as the aggression of the bore who annoys him. Otherwise there would be no reason for Horace's inclusion of the vignette concerning the friend who refuses to extricate him from his comic dilemma. Horace too, unable to adjust to this threat from outside, is something of a fool; he is satirizing himself—and all people who cannot cope with bores—as well as the bore. Horace's satire is essentially self-oriented, and in the satires that Eduard Fraenkel and other Horatian scholars consider most characteristic (those that lead to the *epistolae*) he identifies himself with the subject, his "I" with the admonitory "you." He finds the folly in himself and uses himself as an example of the universal folly: "If I am foolish, and admit it, perhaps you had better examine your own conduct." He claims to walk about the streets of Rome questioning his own actions and motives, seeking self-improvement. The fools he observes are important only insofar as their folly illuminates his problems.

For Juvenal evil is a potent and destructive force, and it lacks the comic element that accompanies impotence. He is much more concerned with the effect of aggressive behavior than with its repercussions on the foolish agent. The story of the patron who sends away his dependents, gorges himself on a huge banquet alone, and has a stroke in his bath afterward (Satire I), is an exceptional situation in Juvenal. In his later satires, as he adjusts himself to the benevolence of the Emperor Hadrian, he does deal (though by no means frequently) with retribution for the wicked. In Satire XIII punishment is shown to be an inevitable accompaniment of crime, whether it is imposed by a judge or by the criminal himself. But most often—in those satires which we think of as characteristic—Juvenal is concerned with a relationship between two people, and with the effect of one person on another. One is the evil man who, unlike Horace's harried characters, is unfazed as he pursues his merry, wicked way; the other is either a fool or an innocent.

To understand Juvenal's kind of satire it is necessary to relate his use of the fool-knave relationship to his use of the static contrast of an ideal and its corruption. Discussing Juvenal's rhetorical structure, W. S. Anderson has shown that his satire ordinarily moves from a statement of a paradox (Rome no longer Roman, or sexual perverts with pious faces) to the splitting of the paradox into polar opposites of good and evil (Roman values versus the corrupted city, or piety versus perversion).[13] The truth of the paradox lies in the fact that the society of the present does not repudiate the old forms but rather conceals its own perversion behind them, paying virtue the compliment of hypocrisy. Juvenal begins with amazement or fierce indignation at the paradoxical situation he sees before him, and then shows why it is paradoxical by separating the ideal from the corruption of the ideal. As Anderson suggests, Juvenal's practice is the reverse of Horace's typical method, which is dialectical: Horace begins with a thesis (wild spending), follows with an antithesis (stinginess), then resolves his extremes with a compromise (the ideal of moderate spending). Moderation is not ordinarily a Juvenalian ideal. He opposes black to white instead of settling for Horace's intermediate shade. Roman values, and the past in which they were effective, are Juvenal's positive pole; the foreigner-infested present, with its mercenary values, is his negative pole. All that lies between must gravitate to one pole or the other.

My description might suggest that Juvenal's satires are simpler than Horace's; they are not. In order to see their complexity and originality we must regard them as fictional rather than

[13] "Studies in Book I of Juvenal," *Yale Classical Studies,* XV (1957), 89.

rhetorical structures. Juvenal only displays his positive pole from time to time as a sort of obbligato; he achieves his complexity not in his contrast of good with evil but in his portrayal of the various aspects of evil contained in the negative pole.

The series of metonymies Juvenal uses to represent un-Roman Rome consists of social relationships between husband and wife, father and child, friend and friend, emperor and adviser, patron and dependent—all of which serve Juvenal as paradigms for the degeneracy he attacks. Each relationship at one time had been an ideal, involving reciprocal respect, duty, and responsibility, and each had once been associated with the traditional coherence and solidarity of Roman society. In Satire III the failure of the relationship between the patron and his dependent is generalized to the failure of all relationships, climaxing in the case of the man who is beaten up by rowdies or crushed into nothingness beneath a load of marble. The breakdown extends to crumbling or burning buildings and (for Codrus) sheer starvation.

The relationship Juvenal uses most tellingly is the typically Roman one between a patron and the poet or scholar who is his dependent (or client). The ideal behind the patron-dependent relationship stood ready to hand for Juvenal in the satire of Horace, where the solidarity of the Maecenas circle—the ideal relationship between the patron and his dependent—served as the norm by which the deviant behavior of bores, misfits, and other outsiders was measured. In the satire of Juvenal the situation of Roman society has become reversed: the satirist, the upholder of standards, is himself outside society as it now exists. The forces of chaos and vice are in control, and so they exclude the deviant satirist, the maintainer of old values.

In the patron-dependent relationship, then, the good dependent, who upholds the old social standards, is simply driven out. There is no room for him. In Satire I, where the patron and his dependent are introduced to embody Juvenal's attack on avarice, the old relationship has deteriorated to the point that money is all that holds the two parties together and financial support is merely a dole. In Satire III the old dependent is thrown out of the patron's house and his place is taken by the pliant foreigner or the "foreign" Roman. He therefore becomes the positive ideal of the satire, and the negative pole becomes *both* the corrupt patron and the corruptible dependent who has filled the gap.

Juvenal's fiction enables him to portray two kinds of satiric subject matter at once: the folly of one party and the knavery of the other (with a third, the degeneration of the ideal relationship, implicit in the background). The dependent who accepts the false values of his corrupt patron is a fool (as is proved by the brutal treatment he receives for his trouble), and the patron who imposes them, exploiting his dependent, is a knave. Satire V demonstrates the reciprocal quality of the guilt Juvenal exposes. The speaker is addressing a poor dependent, Trebius, who has accepted the corrupt values of his patron, and for whom the *summum bonum* is now a good meal. Trebius deserves the humiliations he receives from his patron, for he has allowed wealth to enslave him; and Juvenal points relentlessly to the consequences—the stinking eel from the sewers of Rome and the undrinkable wine, as opposed to the exquisite repast served to the host. But the satire also catches the patron. If Trebius has sacrificed his self-respect and his freedom, Virro has set himself up for a tyrannous exploiter of his fellow Romans. The standards of Trebius and Virro are precisely the same, the only difference being that Virro has the money. In a digression Juvenal remarks that if only Trebius happened to become rich the tables would be turned—then Virro would become *his* dependent. Both members of the relationship must adhere to the perversion to make it flourish in its full degeneracy. Without a toadying dependent the corrupt patron would cease to exist.

Satire IX picks up Virro again and offers a savage parody or *reductio ad absurdum* of the patron-dependent relationship in the association of the homosexual with his pathic. Again the dependent, Naevolus, is essentially the fool in the relationship: he is not strictly speaking a homosexual himself (as we gather from his relations with Virro's wife) but allows himself to fall in with Virro's desires simply for the money involved, just as Trebius did in Satire V. Like Trebius he is mistreated and discarded in

favor of more alluring rivals. But Virro, too, is something of a
fool. In a sense Naevolus is exploiting his unnatural desires, both
by taking his money and by doing Virro's sexual duty to his wife
(all Virro's children are in fact Naevolus'). Virro is driven by
perverted lust, Naevolus by avarice—and so they interact as
fool and knave, knave and fool.

The fool has become more specifically a dupe in Satire III
("Rome"), in which the ideal is the true Roman Umbricius,
who is fleeing from an un-Roman Rome to the provinces, where
there may still be something of the genuine Roman values left.
Opposite Umbricius is a squalid alliance between the present
money-mad Romans and the foreigners who are exploiting them.
Like the dependents in Satires V and IX, these Romans, because
they accept the false values of the foreigners, are fools rather
than innocent victims; here they are used as dupes by the foreigners who wish to advance themselves socially to the position of
"true" Romans.

Even in those Horatian satires of Juvenal's later years that
focus on the bitter consequences of folly, the fool's behavior is
used as a reflector of knavery. To wish for wealth or power, he
says in Satire X ("The Vanity of Human Wishes"), is folly:
look at the consequences to yourself. In Horace's satire a consequence would be to grow fatter and fatter, or perhaps to become a tyrant and therefore be hated by one's sons. In Juvenal
what begins as the repercussions of folly ends as the effects of a
knave's evil. The man who foolishly wishes for riches can expect
to be murdered by scheming relatives or wiped out (his fortune
confiscated) by an envious king; the mother who wishes for a
beautiful daughter can expect to see her raped. While admonish-
ing fools, the satire also attacks the knaves who batten on human
follies. Juvenal's emphasis is on the folly (and this emphasis
distinguishes Satire X from his earlier satires), but the evil is
always present—the fool is never without his knave.

The first conclusion to be drawn from the satires of Horace
and Juvenal is that a satiric relationship tends to diffuse guilt.
Horace too is a fool in his satires; in Juvenal's the guilt extends

to the persecuted fool as well as to the knave. Satire populates the world not with knaves and innocents but with knaves *and* fools or other knaves, one reason being, of course, that normative people have no prominent place in satire. Here, however, we must make a crucial distinction between the satiric scene and the character who observes and frames it. Horace's speaker is morally a part of the scene, but Juvenal's is separate and personally unstained by contact with bores. The role of the satirist himself is as different in their satires as is the composition of the scene he observes.

Like all subsequent satirists, both claim that their satire is the result of circumstances beyond their control. The satirist does not want to write satire, but he must. The fiction invented to convey this impression relies, like the rest of the satire, on consequences and relationships. The Juvenalian persona says that his satire is literally forced out of him by knavish surroundings or by a knave's behavior. Faced with such evil, "difficile est saturam non scribere."

Horace, we have seen, writes primarily because of what he is himself. Satire is simply an expression of his turn of mind, a consequence of his own character. At its most Juvenalian, it follows from Horace's Venusian ancestors, who guarded the Roman border against barbarians, as Horace does figuratively now. But most of the time he claims his satire as a weapon of personal defense, not, like Juvenal's, a sacred weapon. In neither case does the satirist have any control over his writing, but Horace's satire is in a sense a lack of control over himself, almost an eccentricity, and so is ridiculous. It must be apologized for because it is an excessive reaction, not consonant with the moderation Horace advocates, and not necessary for ideal men like Maecenas.

Juvenal keeps himself rigorously separate from the folly and the knavery he portrays. He purposely reduces the character of his persona to an abstractness far beyond Horace's: he is merely a bundle of old Roman virtues, including significantly the military, which offers an explanation for his outbursts of indignation. Roman discipline appears in the alternative periods of control—

sometimes arrived at by a change of tone, sometimes by a simple splitting of his persona, in the militant spirit of "Juvenal" and the more controlled performance of Umbricius (Satire III). This abstractness sets aside the Juvenalian persona as a point of view and an ideal and little more.

Horace uses his persona as the central fact of his satire, making of him a complex figure of Everyman rather than an ideal; this Everyman addresses himself to other ordinary citizens in order to share his self-knowledge. His satire is aimed at the reader, who is the object of his attack, and it advises him of his follies. Juvenal ordinarily addresses himself to those few like himself who are weathering the storm, but never to the fools or knaves. His attack is therefore aimed at someone other than the reader (at *les autres*), and if any advice is involved it is advice to the reader to *écrasez l'infâme*. He has thrown up his hands in despair over the reformation of the evil (a rhetorical pose, of course, and an effective one), and he can only warn the good to keep away.

In the works of Horace and Juvenal we can distinguish two modes of satire. One we can call admonitory and subjective, the other presentational and objective. Horatian satire is most interested in outlining a practicable code of conduct. Through the opposite extremes of examples to be avoided the Horatian dialectic at length points the way to just how one *should* act in certain circumstances, and leads indirectly to spiritual autobiography or to ethical essays like those of Montaigne. The Juvenalian gives only the sketchiest advice as to a way of conduct: the ideal of the past offers little but a signpost from which the reader can take his bearings in the labyrinth of Juvenal's fictional embodiment of evil. What we remember is the presentation of the masculine wife and her effeminate husband, the homosexual and his pathic, the city with a Clytemnestra in every street and houses toppling on unwary pedestrians—in short, the complex and fantastic world that results when evil is dominant *and* regarded by an isolated, agitated, good man.

This "good man," insofar as the reader is made to associate with him, is a rhetorical device, parallel to Horace's "you."

Although Horace and Juvenal are usually (with justice) regarded as extremes of detachment and involvement, there is a sense in which both immerse their readers. Horace—to borrow an image used earlier—rubs his reader's nose in his own dirt; Juvenal rubs his reader's nose in someone else's. With Horace the reader's experience is to feel complicity in the guilt; with Juvenal it is to feel repugnance at the evil. Satire always strives toward one or the other of these experiences: oneness with, or separateness from, the evil; complicity and guilt, or outrage; action directed toward oneself, or toward others; punishment of the guilty, or persecution of the innocent. Ultimately, as representation, they amount to the imitation of the foolish or evil man experiencing himself, or of the morally sensitive man experiencing folly or evil.

To the extent that it materializes the "you" and "I" of his satire, Horace's admonitory stance can become a representation of man's lower potentials as he recognizes them and struggles upward or slides downward. Rhetorically, Horace makes the reader identify to some extent with the deviant (though remaining distinct enough to judge him); as representation, he involves the "I" and the "you" with each other, combining subject and object. The result can be either self-discovery or self-revelation.

The other—Juvenalian—kind of satire is less closely allied to the essay than to the epic. or tragedy, even to the lyric, or to other presentational as opposed to argumentative (or persuasive) arts. While it operates from a moral viewpoint, and so is informed by indignation, its main purpose is to present and explore the nature of evil as it plays upon a poet's sensibility: two movements which appear sometimes separately and sometimes together.[14] As the people on the satirist's side dwindle and he is

[14] Edward Rosenheim (*Swift and the Satirist's Art* [Chicago, Ill.: University of Chicago Press, 1963], p. 15), divides satiric purpose into two types, persuasive and punitive; the latter does not attempt to urge the reader to any action but merely displays the vice and analyzes it. It is misleading, however, to call this punitive, with all of its connotations of chastisement. "Presentational" seems to me a more useful term, although a fictive punishment is sometimes a part of this presentation.

left alone, and the enemy becomes bigger, more terrible, and more powerful, the satire moves to another area, indicated by Plato, where the situation is no longer comic at all, and yet it is satiric.[15] When the deluded fool has the power to enforce his illusion on others the situation is no longer ridiculous, but it may still be satiric. Juvenal believed this to be a transition from comic to tragic satire. To the commonsensical Horatian satirist, however, it might seem to be a movement in the direction of melodrama. In the practice of some Juvenalian imitators it became a movement away from the satiric object toward the isolated and suffering satirist-observer, and so toward sentimentalism.

Fiction as Device: Lucian

As some of our examples have indicated, a satiric fiction can be a metaphysical fact and/or a device of exposition. At one extreme the fiction is consistent on its own terms, a symbol or an allegory complete in itself. It is an artifact without any direct relationship (certainly not a shifting one) to an audience. At the other extreme, the fiction as device is casuistic, its consistency changing with every moment. In the greatest satire the two possibilities combine; more often they lie far apart. The ingenious and influential satire of Lucian of Samosata offers us a particularly interesting example of this division. Because he was in some ways the great virtuoso among satirists, and because his works were influential on all later satirists (especially, for our purposes, Swift), we must deal in some detail with his fictions and the uses to which he put them.

The Observer-Object Relation. The typical Lucianic fiction has a protagonist asking questions—probing appearance, idealization, myth, or custom. The approach is through the many small points and barbs of dialogue rather than the sweep of a narrative; it is strongly Socratic, or at any rate cynic (since Lucian shows no love for Socrates). Lucian's protagonist begins

---

[15] See the *Philebus* 49, Jowett trans., II, 384.

on earth with the pseudo-oracles: the Alexanders and Pythag·
orases, the charlatans and the sophistical philosophers. Occasionally, as in the *Nigrinus,* he believes that he has found the
answer and that his quest is fulfilled, but the reader soon sees
that he has accepted a false solution. Having exhausted mundane
oracles, in desperation the protagonist sets off on a supermun-
dane journey—either up to Olympus *(Icaromenippus)* or down
to Hades *(Menippus).* There he questions the gods themselves
or the dead; if the gods, he only manages to throw them into
confusion, revealing their shoddy pretentions to omniscience; if
the dead, he sometimes gets a worthwhile point of view. The
dead are the only objective observers; that is, if they have been
dead long enough to shake off human prejudices (to which the
gods are clearly not immune).

When the quester is not a Menippus, he is a Cyniscus, a
Damis, a Diogenes, or even Lucian himself; or he is a god like
Charon who comes up from Hades to look around and clarify
certain points that have bothered him; or he is Justice coming
down from Olympus to earth. Even when there is no protagonist—when the dialogue is between two or more of the gods
whom the protagonist ordinarily questions—we are aware of the
inquisitive author who has moved down into Hades or up to
Olympus to overhear them and seek an answer.

Lucian's protagonists are like Aristophanes' in being questers
after the great "All," after true philosophy. But while Aristophanes' heroes went straight to their own private solutions,
Lucian's try all the doors on earth, all the so-called philosophers,
and even in Olympus and Hades they go indefatigably from one
witness to another. Aristophanes focused on the solution; Lucian
focuses on the quest and on the witnesses and their testimony.
He is interested in the separate encounters, knowing that there
is no solution but only the people who offer false solutions. To
the extent that Lucian himself sees life as a meaningless ramble,
the pilgrimage is an ironic symbol of his meaning. To a very
great extent, however, he uses the pilgrimage as merely a device
of satiric exposition, a clever refurbishing of the catalogue form
of Horatian and Juvenalian *satura.*

The Lucianic cosmos is an elaborate mechanical structure that has less moral than technical significance. It consists of a heaven populated by gods, an earth, and a hell where all mortals go, some to be punished. Heaven is made up of humans whose ridiculous aspirations can be largely fulfilled; earth is all aspiration weighted down by body; and hell is all body, all flesh, the phoniness and the aspiration gone. The questing protagonist can accordingly pass from one world to another, comparing, using one as a standard by which to judge the other. His pilgrimage can offer views of man from far above and far below. From the enormous height of Olympus man is a mite, wars are fought for a few inches of land *(Dialogues of the Gods);* from the position of death, all the actions of the living appear futile and foolish *(Dialogues of the Dead)*. Lucian is always seeking new viewpoints from which to see man's folly, to see through his pretensions: that of the cock who can penetrate locked houses and who has passed through the bodies of many different men including Pythagoras himself, or of the scurrilous cynic Diogenes, or of the selfish misanthrope Timon. The character of the observer does not matter, only his point of view. He can be good or evil, separate from or part of the satiric object—whichever offers the more striking insight.

The God-Man Relation. As Juvenal explores the patron-dependent or husband-wife relation, Lucian devotes himself to the god-man relation. The gods, and in particular Zeus, think most persistently about sacrifices—the sign of man's loyalty to them. But the gods' part of the arrangement has long been shirked, and there is no justice, no causal relationship between prayers and results. The more penetrating folk (Lucian's protagonists) point to the disorder of experience, bringing this empirical reality to bear on the logic of the myths concerning the gods. They show that Fate is on the one hand superior to the gods, preventing them from answering prayers that were not foreordained for fulfillment anyway; on the other hand, that Fate is superior to man, who therefore bears no responsibility for his misdeeds, so there is no reason to sacrifice to the gods or to obey their laws. Consequently (as dialogue after dialogue point out), sacrifices have fallen off and man's duty to the gods is in abeyance. Everything finally comes down to this obviously (to Lucian) nonexistent relationship, which represents the chaos of reality and the mythos of divine order with which man masks it.

The Dialogues of the Gods are, first, a satire on the anthropomorphic conception of gods and the mythic representation of religion, and so on "the liars," those foolish romancers who create the gods in their own image. But second, it soon becomes evident that although a god-man relation is the tacit ideal behind Lucian's satire, it is not Lucian's own ideal but rather merely the conventional ideal of his fellow men, and that his references to it are not only ironical but part of a satirical mechanism for getting at the follies of men. The gods bear the same ironic relation to men as do the beasts of Aesop's *Fables* or of *Reynard the Fox,* and each little episode is concerned with a specifically *human* folly. A well-known fable is taken—that Zeus obtained his human lovers by assuming the forms of bulls and swans—and interpreted satirically as a comment not on Zeus' cunning but on the foibles of women. The idealization of mythology and religion is thus connected with women's treatment of love as fashion and affectation—they only love the outer appearance, whether bull or swan. Now Zeus must replace his aegis and thunderbolt with the attire of a fop, as in the past he conquered women only by assuming the body of an animal (Dialogue II).

Death. Hades, the exact opposite of Olympus, Lucian uses to stand for reality, things as they actually are. In *The Dialogues of the Dead* death is the dominion of the physical, all that is opposed to the affected, the spiritual, and the pompous. Helen of Troy is only a skull, kings are bones and ashes, and philosophers are reduced to the most physical of considerations—eating or (with Socrates) chasing handsome young men. In the several dialogues concerning Alexander the Great the conqueror is gradually stripped of his pretensions, follies, and affectations down to the nakedness of the dead. In the well-known Dialogue I men on their way to Hades are literally stripped of their affectations, reduced to their real essential being. Death comes to represent

Lucian's ideal. The only real and unchangeable facts, its permanence and finality, are opposed to the greatest evil of the living, the "dash of uncertainty" that always attracts men to false ideals.

Death is also a final stop, the time of solution to all problems, the one moment of time in which all aspects of a situation can be seen clearly. It offers the ultimate perspective for men on their actions. For Lucian the satirist it offers a special situation like the regulated experiment of the scientist in which Alexander can meet Hannibal, or a legacy-hunter can predecease the old man whom he had cajoled into willing him his fortune. Death suddenly puts the legacy-hunter's knavery in its proper perspective of eternity; but the exposure is by means of a *deus ex machina,* death. In Dialogue XI two young men, each of whom has made the other his heir, both die, as it happens, on the same day.

In the legacy-hunter satires death is symbolically justice without detracting from its elaborate functioning as a device of exposition. In the first satire Pluto asks Hermes to let the old men live longer than their legatees; in the second a legatee has indeed died and complains to Pluto of the unfairness of his death; in the third the legatee who has tried to poison his old man has himself been poisoned; in the fourth, the Corbaccio situation of Jonson's *Volpone,* the legatee disinherits his own heirs to make the old man his heir, and then predeceases him; and finally, in the fifth the old man himself appears in Hades to comment on the life of luxury he (Volpone-like) has led on the presents of legatees. The result is an anatomy of legacy-hunting; the situation is approached from all angles and developed from the general statement of the first dialogue to the punishment of the legacy-hunter, of the poisoner, of the man so greedy that he disowns his heirs for the promise of gold, and finally to the other side of the situation, shown to be equally bad, the old man who lives parasitically on the foolish legacy-hunter. The legacy-hunters, who in life appear knaves, have been proved at every step of the way to be mere fools; and at the end they are revealed as the dupes of a fool-knave relation.

Some fools continue to act as they did on earth, persisting in revealing their folly even in death. The moaning and gnashing of teeth in Hades points to the fact that, even in such extremity, the sentimental memories of the past, of gold and power, are still the only things many of the dead think of. Death is finally, then, a test: how one dies tells whether his happiness has been material or spiritual, apparent or real; whether he has only physical superfluities to leave behind him at the shore of the Styx, or spiritual values he can carry across with him. How one behaves in death, among the dead, tells how one lived; and in this sense the *Dialogues of the Dead,* like those of the gods, show the dead as allegorical equivalents of the living.

Love. Two other situations that Lucian employs are the relationship between lovers and the behavior of people on the Saturnalia. If the *Dialogues of the Gods* are based on a hypothetically ideal god-man relation, the *Dialogues of the Heterae* are based on an ideal relation between lovers. But in these dialogues one or both are jealous or unfaithful; one is a parasite, loving for gain, the other is stingy, paying as little as possible for the hetera's love. One invariably loves more than the other, and that person is the fool to the other's knave in the relation. The satire at the same time reflects the relations between heterae, who steal men from each other, and then the betrayed hetera blames it on witchcraft in order to escape the fact that someone else is more attractive than she (myth once again shown to be a way to disguise the unpleasant). Dialogue VIII exposes in quick succession: jealousy (the main theme) as a way to hold or test your lover, misunderstanding which causes jealousy, the stinginess of lovers, the distrust of all other women as possible rivals, and the turning to witchcraft as an explanation for losing a lover.

The Saturnalian satires use a return to the Golden Age for one week as an ideal against which to measure the corruption of the rest of the year. As with death, it is a position from which to view the usual folly and knavery of everyday. This is not so much reality as an extreme position (simplicity) that, like the railing of Diogenes, shows up the evil at the opposite extreme.

The list of fictions employed by Lucian is far from exhausted. For example, the council of the gods or the trial or judgment scene, ranging from the judgment of the dead as in the *Menippus* or the checking of the dead for excess baggage (vanities) to the simple catalog of the types that appear in a group of the dead on Charon's boat: the general, the courtesan, the philosopher, each with his particular superfluity. Another example is the guided tour: the cock who explains things to Micyllus, pointing out the various types of men he has inhabited in his previous transmigrations, and showing him the insides of houses. Still another is an auction *(Sale of Creeds)*, with the various slaves brought to the block, one by one. Any fiction that has a string of events to unfold is useful; and the dialogues of gods, dead, and heterae all break up into the anatomy form, the survey of a subject or of different types.

The immense variation may draw our attention away from the fact that Lucian uses the same characters and basic relationships, with slight variations, over and over. The *Menippus* is a recapitulation of the themes of *The Dialogues of the Dead,* with even the same examples: Mausolus, Tiresias, Socrates, Diogenes (and of course Menippus himself). Repeatedly Lucian gives us Empedocles, always charred or baked from his jump into Etna; Pythagoras, always with reference to his golden thigh, his dislike of beans, his advice to remain silent for five years at a time.

Travesty. Moreover, all Lucian's fictions represent variations of a single technique often associated with his name: travesty, or the exposure of the fishwife under a Didoesque pose. Lucian's general strategy is to reduce romance, ritual, and religion to the concrete particularity of a group of petty, squabbling people. Thus in each of the *Dialogues of the Gods* he clears up a mystery or a deceptive appearance of some kind. Zeus' pretense of outraged justice over Prometheus' theft of fire turns out to be mere self-interest; starting with a tremendous statement of the justice of the sentence passed on Prometheus, it ends by Zeus' quickly releasing him on personal grounds. In another dialogue Hephaestus thinks that Hermes is "such a pretty little thing" and is shown that he is a robber. In the *Dialogues of the Dead* the philosopher's theory is contrasted with the reality of his fear when death comes, and all of the illusions of the living are reduced to skeletons and ashes. In the *Dialogues of the Heterae* Lucian exposes the reality beneath the romance and fine talk of love; to do so he enters the boudoir, overhears the private discussions of the girl with her mother, her older, more experienced friend, another girl, or occasionally with the lover himself. The explicit connection between these scenes and the hero-deflated or liar-exposed situation appears in XIII. A braggart soldier makes up exploits to impress his mistress, but when they only make her sick he has to back down and admit that they are all fabrications. Even the Saturnalian satires, with their norms of irrationality and topsy-turvydom, reduce everything to its simplest, least romanticized form.

When Lucian adapts the situation of an earlier satirist he works the same transformation on his material. *The Feast of Lapithae* follows the *cena* form of Horace's Satire II.8, ending in similar chaos and bloodshed. But the satire is entirely directed against the guests (the host, we are told, cannot even be blamed through his wine for his guests' behavior), and specifically against the philosophers. The ordinary guests merely laugh at what they see, but the philosophers are given a chance to expose "the reality behind the imposing beard and serious countenance"[16] and so end by arguing, getting drunk, and fighting. The dinner for Lucian is an excellent occasion for testing the fleshly inclination of pretenders to philosophy. Again in the *Sale of Creeds* he reduces various philosophies to the bodies of slaves up for sale. Almost every one of his satires involves such a reduction of an abstraction to a physical presence.

The Pseudo-persona. If the mode of travesty is one of Lucian's most significant legacies to later satirists, a second is the rhetoric of black journalism or the pseudo-persona. To a greater extent than any of the other ancient satirists except Petronius, Lucian lets the evil or folly speak for itself. In *The True History* the lying historian, in the *Dialogues of the Gods* the lying mythographer, in *The Liar* the lying superstitious—in each of these we are simply presented with the pseudo-wise exposing his folly.

---

[16] *The Works of Lucian of Samosata*, trans. H. W. and F. G. Fowler (Oxford: Clarendon Press, 1905), IV, 137.

Although, as if to make sure that there are no misunderstandings, he often introduces the satire himself, in general the fiction is left to speak for itself.

Lucian's version of the self-condemning speaker may derive from the rhetorical exercises in which the speaker must make the worse appear the better cause (Seneca the elder offers many examples). In *The Tyrannicide,* for example, one wonders whether the argument is satiric or merely the showing-off of a skillful rhetorician. These exercises, however, lead to the subtle self-condemnation of the philosophers, liars, and gods of the later satires, and represent the embodiment of irony in a fictive speaker. As a rhetorical device, irony emphasizes an attitude or judgment by contrasting a literal, stated sentiment with its implicit, unstated opposite. When a mouthpiece intervenes between ironist and audience, the irony finds cognitive equivalents to the literal and implicit meanings in the speaker. Blame-by-praise irony is thus dramatized in a speaker who is foolishly but sincerely praising obvious follies. It is one of Lucian's two general techniques for deflating illusion, both of which involve the analysis of a custom or convention: in the first he merely presents it and lets the reader draw his own conclusions; in the second he (or a Menippus or Diogenes) asks Socratic questions which bring out its preposterousness.

Lucian is the first satirist with whom we have dealt who is primarily a writer of anti-romance. The basic contrasts that run through his satire—between pride, material things, and illusions and the positive values of independence, plain speaking, indifference, high spirits, and jests—are as vague as Juvenal's, and the method of his satire is related to Juvenal's presentational satire. He is not, like Horace, a codifier of the good life. But while Juvenal juxtaposes the idealized past with the degenerate present (the bust of the ancestor with the wrecked hulk of the descendant), Lucian juxtaposes the misleading appearance with the reality. He contrasts the mythic Zeus with the humanized lecher, the idealized Helen with the eyeless skull, the philosopher Socrates with the pederast, Philip the king with the cobbler in Hades, the heroes of the Trojan War with a pile of ashes, gold as it is esteemed by men with the rock, philosophers with slaves on the auction block.

The difference is clear. Juvenal deals with two realities: a good one in the past and a degenerate one in the present. The good one exposes the evil of the presently accepted one. Lucian works with an appearance or an illusion and a reality, a mask and the face underneath. While in Juvenal the ideal is good and the present reality evil, in Lucian the illusion is evil and the exposed reality not good but—and this is the most important change—real. The presentation of the reality explodes the illusion; and so they are mutually exclusive.

His satire never explores the relation between an ideal and the falling away, or looks into the nature of evil itself. It is far too rhetorical for that; it is always persuading and arguing, revealing and surprising. More than any of the other great ancient satirists, Lucian is the rhetorician first, the moralist second, and his surprises and constant striving for effect sometimes suggest that the effect is achieved for its own sake. He thus depends on the surprise of the exposure, on making the apparently indefensible cause defensible, the apparently guilty innocent, the apparently noble ignoble. Perhaps partly for this reason, Lucian has no strong bias to a particular good as Juvenal does (the past of the true Roman values) nor a desire to map a subtle spiritual course for the auditor as Horace does.

In his apologia, *The Fisher,* Lucian answers the attacks of philosophers whom he has ridiculed by claiming that he is himself in the service of Philosophy, that his life is a search for truth, to which his exposure of false philosophies is incidental. In attempting to invest his attitude with the respectability of a philosophical position, he shows his hand. If true philosophy is his ultimate aim he is different from the other satirists we have discussed. In general satirists have represented the side of tradition and authority, attacking philosophy as a useless search for ultimate reality or truth when the important consideration is the good citizen, neighbor, father or son, husband or wife. Lucian the rhetorician says that he is using his rhetoric for an opposite end.

Lucian's criticism of false philosophies is characteristically based on a reduction of philosophy to the plane of reality, or common sense and usefulness; like other satirists, he would reduce such externals as a solemn face and a beard to conduct. But religion is another false philosophy. The systems of traditional behavior must go too: everything that stands in the way of "naked truth." Horace or Juvenal would perhaps agree as to the myths Lucian travesties, but they would require some pieties as a framework for one's conduct—they would never allow man to wander free of all other men's thought as Lucian seems to do.

But while Lucian's philosophical position, if put into words, would sound something like this, it is not, in fact, a position at all but an attitude. It has as little metaphysical solidity as the symbolic quest of his protagonists; it exists, in fact, only as another satiric device. As his ideals of independence, plain speaking, and jest tell us, his purpose is the very general one of discomfiting his reader, shaking up his cherished values, disrupting his orthodoxy. Lucian is therefore the epitome of the satirist who writes at what he takes to be a time of extreme stodginess and reaction, when values have become standardized and rigid.

We must conclude, on the one hand, that he gives little depth to the object of his satire; with him exposure is all, and the relationships he uses are sleight-of-hand tricks for demonstrating the corrective powers of disruption, not for exploring the fools and knaves who are disrupted. In individual dialogues, although rhetoric is constantly his mode, the genre may be closer to comedy, with the emphasis on the disruption itself, than to satire, with the central image of stasis and stagnation.

On the other hand, a satiric world does emerge, not so much from single dialogues as from the whole range of them; not a world of particular fools or knaves but one of great throngs of useless and parasitic gods, philosophers, and law-givers (religions, philosophies, laws, and customs), all weighing heavily on the ordinary man and totally at odds with his nature and surroundings. The elaborate structures of heaven, earth, and Hades, or of religious cults, symposia, and brothels, act not only as expository forms for the satires but as an obviously artificial and illusory order imposed on the real world. Man, things as they are, and things as they are not make up the elements of Lucian's world; and in this triangle the emphasis clearly falls on the overstructured life and mind materialized in the elaborate structure of things as they are not.

Satura into Prose Fiction

We have said that satire tends to present a subject-object relationship that either combines the reader and fool into a single character, or separates them into an observer, agent, or victim vis-à-vis a fool or knave. These alternatives are splintered into many permutations in formal satires, a single satire perhaps employing all of them in succession. But as persuasion is fictionalized, especially as it becomes prose fiction, a certain general consistency is required, the conventions of narrative forms come into play, and the many permutations are reduced to a manageable few.

Satura, the basic form of Roman (and subsequent) verse satire, descends from various Greek expository but at the same time quasi-dramatic forms, from the *parabasis* of the Aristophanic comedy to the homiletic genres of the philosophers, an example being the Cynic *chria* in which the speaker delivered his social commentary in an ostensibly unplanned, extemporaneous monologue full of personal confession, little stories, beast fables, and the like. The Bionean diatribe, a dialogue with an imaginary interlocutor, was also packed with seemingly improvised anecdotes, jokes, comparisons and contrasts, personal reminiscences, parodies, meditations. All extremely colloquial, they condemn a single vice, expound a single theme, and imply a contrasting virtue.[17] These, and many like them, served as easily-remembered philosophical propaganda. The cynic standing on

[17] See Randolph, "The Structural Design of Formal Verse Satire,"; and her unpublished doctoral dissertation, "The Neo-Classic Theory of the Formal Verse Satire in England, 1700–1750" (Chapel Hill: University of North Carolina, 1939).

the street corner exhorting, attempting to catch the ears of the crowd, halt them in their steps with surprise, and demonstrate the error of their ways: this is the prototype of the basic fiction of Roman *satura*.

This fiction, a simple observer-object juxtaposition, leaves its stamp on the surviving narrative satires of the Roman period in which the satirist has apparently disappeared and his moral is conveyed by a story. The narrative equivalent of *satura* is the journey. A protagonist's wanderings allow for independent satires within a frame, permitting a catalog form and an ironic reference to the more idealized journeys of romances. The accumulation of encounters is a good approximation of the "characters" and anecdotes in *satura,* conveying something of the same claustrophobic feeling of the crowd welling up around the satirist standing on his street corner. A more static narrative equivalent is the dinner party, ship, carriage, or some such gathering in which a group of different types can be analyzed in relation to a general vice. But whenever a narrative action is desired, the protagonist must leave the dinner party and go to different places or meet different people, and the progression of his journey is either unplotted or borrows a plot (e.g., from romance) bearing an ironic relation to the real satiric action, which is only a movement from one kind of folly to another or from bad to worse.[18]

As a structure of exposition, *satura* is like a house of mirrors in which one theme (or vice) is reflected over and over, with distortions and variations but without essential change. In a formal verse satire of Juvenal, every example extends or elaborates the original vice; in one of Horace's, every example offers the reader an alternative of good or (more usually) bad conduct related to a given theme such as riches or love. It is not difficult to detect adaptations of these two possibilities in prose satires. (1) In Petronius' *cena Trimalchionis* all the diners are re-

---

[18] As Alvin Kernan has shown, this movement can also be circular, up and down, etc. Cf. his studies, *The Cankered Muse* (New Haven, Conn.: Yale University Press, 1959), pp. 30–34, and *The Plot of Satire* (New Haven, Conn.: Yale University Press, 1965), *passim.*

flections that contribute to a definition of Trimalchio, or better of Trimalchioism. In the over-all narrative of the *Satyricon, of* which the *cena* is only one episode, the episodes appear (considering their fragmentary state) to represent different aspects of the foolish, roaming protagonist, Encolpius, not immediately evident to (or in) himself. When the narrative protagonist is a villain or a symbol of society's degeneration (Trimalchio) or an observer who is intimately involved in the object of satire (Encolpius), the action tends to be centripetal: the examples all illustrate different facets of the central evil, seeking a definition.

The problem involved in this kind of satiric narrative is overexposure of the evil agent. The reader sees so much of him that he grows to know him too well to condemn him; or the author himself becomes interested in him as a man as well as a villain. In the *cena Trimalchionis* the normative commentator is absent, and the most important device of exposition is the vice's self-exposure. At its simplest, the device calls for Trimalchio to recite a poem attacking conspicuous extravagance and waste in the midst of his famous dinner party; or, with his wizened pathic nearby, to advocate an ideal of chastity. In scope Petronius vastly extends the strategy of Horace's Satire II.3 (where Damasippus is the speaker) and Epode 2 (a usurer speaking on the pleasures of the country life), and he anticipates the unabashed confession of Juvenal's Naevolus (Satire IX) and Lucian's self-condemning speakers. To a great extent, however, Petronius stops with the self-exposure. This is partly the result of the device itself, because there is no one present who can condemn or even admonish. (Encolpius, the first-person narrator, ridicules Trimalchio and his guests in the Horatian manner, but far from admirable himself, he in fact partakes of Trimalchio's own values and exposes himself as a less vigorous and successful Trimalchio.) If Petronius stops short of condemnation, he goes on to complete the representation, and explore the meaning, of Trimalchio.

The conversation of Trimalchio and his guests on the food, on life, and on each other, by the obsessive repetition of subjects and situations, reveals new facets of the Trimalchio character.

The references to death are the most monotonously regular, and the most important. The first fact we learn about Trimalchio is that he keeps a large clock in his dining room and has a servant blow a horn every hour to remind him of the passing time. When his 100-year-old Falernian wine is served he remarks that wine lasts longer than men; this is immediately followed by his servants' carrying in a *memento mori,* a skeleton of silver which is arranged in suggestive positions; and Trimalchio completes the tableau with some verses on mutability. Later, when one of the performing acrobats accidentally falls on him, he launches into another sentimental platitude on mutability. Still later he reads his will and epitaph and discusses the monument he wants on his tomb. As the dinner ends he is again talking about his death, putting on his funerary garments, and asking his guests to imagine that they are at his funeral.

Those other Trimalchios, his guests, are equally concerned about death and extend mutability to a general physical insecurity. During the first course his gossipy neighbor tells Encolpius about Trimalchio and his wife Fortunata—one minute poor and the next fabulously rich; about the guests who have been rich and are now poor; about money quickly gained and quickly lost when everything depends on a turn of the wheel of fortune. Varying responses to this world without stable values are expressed, but they all amount to the same: because these people now have nothing to hold onto, and their own prosperity is insecure, their only interest is ostentation, food, and gladiatorial performances. The themes of mutability, death, and the instability of fortune, together with superstition, join in the series of stories that begins with Trimalchio's of the little unbreakable bottle, whose inventor is rewarded not with gold but with sudden death. In Niceros' story and Trimalchio's second story, a man is turned into a wolf and another, who attacks some witches, is reduced to a bundle of straw. These people who believe in the material instability of man also believe, and are terrified by, stories of transformations into wolves and straw men. The cock's crow (a sign of death), which terrifies Trimalchio and causes him to have the cock caught, cooked, and eaten, points to his superstition. On his doorpost is a diagram of the planets with lucky and unlucky days marked; his guests are required to step across the threshold on the right foot, and his first course is served in the form of a zodiac, which he laboriously explains to his guests.

Yet another response to mutability is embodied in a yearning for the past. The diners, while continuing to talk about funerals and man's fate as a bubble or a fly, also recall the ideal past from which they have fallen away (a theme introduced at the beginning of the dinner in the murals of Odysseus' adventures next to the life story of Trimalchio). But the ideal Ganymedes sees in the past is only his own image, an entirely commercialized ideal—a time when bread was cheaper. No one prays to the gods any longer, and so, he claims, the economy has suffered. Trimalchio also yearns for the past. His story of the sybil of Cumae suggests the degeneration that has taken place since the days of Aeneas: the sybil who directed him to Italy and the founding of Rome now hangs in a bottle and wishes she were dead. Trimalchio's house itself is an old-fashioned one, modeled on the Augustan houses he remembers from his days as a slave. This replica shows his wish to equal his old master, fulfilling the dream of the slave, but it also shows a yearning for those lost days. The curious fact emerges that this parvenu who owes everything to change and the instability of Roman life and economy, yearns for the good old days when, though he was a slave, his life was secure.

A final response to mutability is shown in Trimalchio's exhibitionism and love of appearance. He is constantly liberating slaves or forgiving their blunders, ostentatiously showing his generosity. He is constantly justifying himself, through his murals of his life, his reading of his will, his elaborate apologia with which the dinner ends, even his remarks on his constipation. Encolpius is told that the dinner will be a "show" and Trimalchio first appears at the baths throwing balls to the slave boys and urinating in public, making a show of himself and of his luxury. At the house this theme is connected with the freeing and reprieving or forgiving of slaves. By the door is a sign saying that any slave who leaves the premises will receive 100 lashes. Before long we see that such harshness is part of Trimalchio's method of showing off his generosity and liberality. In order to demonstrate these qualities he must set up strict regulations and punishments which he can then remit. So all through the dinner we have ridiculous shows of authority followed by as ridiculous reprieves, the one set up in order to produce and accentuate the other. As with the careful staging of every course, everything is arranged for effect. First the idea is planted that the guest is being given a nauseous object to eat, then it is revealed to be something else; first the servant thinks he will be beaten (or, rather, the guests think he will), then the reprieve or the truth is revealed. It is as if the fear or disgust adds piquancy to the pleasure of the food or the generosity, as the consciousness of death (the *memento mori*) does to Trimalchio's pleasure in being alive.

The second feature of these "shows" is that Trimalchio has to make everything here and now, including what he considers his virtues, including even his death and the mourning he wishes to accompany it. He produces weights to prove the value of his wife's bracelets, as he later produces his state records and his will. He explains that he is recounting the contents of his will so that his whole household will love him as much while he is alive as after he is dead. He will lose the opportunity of seeing the gratitude of his slaves and friends when they read his will after his death, so he reads it now, when he can see the expressions of grief for himself. Like the pork he serves that is made to seem a goose, he wants to appear dead to accrue the advantages of hearing the weeping of his friends now when he can be sure of them; he wants the advantages of being both alive and dead. If this can be done with meat and poultry, why not with himself? He is trying to be a self-sufficient man who needs no one else, who grows everything he needs on his own estates, who can have geese made from pork, who has power of life, death, and freedom over his slaves. And who tirelessly demonstrates all of these. Reading his will (and later playing his funeral) is one way of exerting more power over death, just as his superstitious behavior is another. Even his tomb is to be a reassurance of this power. In the middle is to be placed a sundial, so that anyone who wants the time of day must read his name. And the worst insult he can think of for his wife Fortunata is to remove her figure from his tomb and not allow her to kiss him on his feigned "death bed."

In general we can say that Petronius has presented a vice and explored all aspects of it. The result, in one sense, is a Horatian satire in which he reveals the unease and discomfort of a foolish man. But he does not say to his reader, as Horace does: Look what this has driven Trimalchio to. Rather, he has shown the *causes* of the ridiculous figure of Trimalchio; the result is not the consequences of folly but rather an explanation of why he is the particular person he is, why he behaves as he does. We feel less a sense of consequences suffered than of an explanation, even a mitigation. In the *Satyricon* we know not only *what* Trimalchio is but *why* he is that way; not only what he appears to be but what he actually is—and here, as in Horace's fool satire, the folly is on the surface, hardly in need of exposure. In Trimalchio's case his folly is the appearance, obvious to all at the outset; what is gradually revealed is his past, the causes of his absurd actions, his insecurity, his fear, his humanity, and finally (as if to explain all the rest) his vigor and stamina. The usual satiric order is reversed; instead of a plausible scoundrel exposed, a patent fool is gradually exposed as a real, suffering, human being.

Because of the gravitation toward representation proper in an extended "character" of the evil agent, the satirist is ordinarily disinclined to write a long narrative devoted solely to the villain; he finds it almost imperative to introduce someone to represent either the author or the reader, an "I" or a "you" to keep the evil figure in perspective. As the gist of the satire tends toward the Juvenalian or the Horatian it will be more concerned respectively with one or the other.

(2) In a second kind of narrative, then, the encounters and stories experienced by the protagonist on his journey offer him

bad examples that he should avoid, and so suggest a narrative adaptation of the Horatian essay form. When the protagonist is the Horatian "you" he still bears a relatively close relationship to the events he witnesses, since they must directly reflect his error or folly. But they do not so much define him as suggest the extremes of his error, its harmful potential, and its consequences to him if he does not mend his ways. Moreover, unlike a Trimalchio, he learns from his experience.

(3) A third kind harks back to Juvenal. When the protagonist is the Juvenalian "I," a hero, martyr, innocent victim, or satirist, there is no need for such a close correlation between him and what he sees, and the direction of the reader's interest is more clearly centrifugal, outward toward the oppressors or objects of the satirist's comments, and the structure can be episodic to excess.

Both of these kinds of narrative, however, carry within themselves the potential of shifting the satire's emphasis away from the satiric object—one toward the initiated or educated hero as he detaches himself from his follies; the other toward the persecuted or passively receptive observer as his emotions become more interesting than the objects that elicit them.

Lucius, the first-person narrator of Apuleius' *Metamorphoses,* will serve to illustrate these distinctions.[19] Through most of his

[19] It is useful to contrast two versions of the same story, Apuleius' *Metamorphoses* (or *The Golden Ass*) and Lucian's *The Ass* (both were probably derived from an earlier lost work). Lucian's work has a short, satiric action: a young Roman of high social standing is made overly curious by talk of magic, particularly of metamorphosis; as a result of his investigation, he is himself transformed into an ass, suffers some harrowing experiences, and at the end is restored to human form. He returns in all his human pride to the lady who had enjoyed his favors as an ass (if she loved him in his bestial form, he reasons, how much more will she love him now!), only to be turned away: she accuses him of having been metamorphosed from a handsome and useful beast into an ape. While Lucian's action is brief and unadorned, a simple satiric fable, Apuleius' is novel-length and has many way stations and diversions; he has inserted innumerable new scenes and stories which often contradict or are irrelevant to the satiric action of Lucian's *Ass*. Second, he has substituted for Lucian's ironic ending a sober religious interlude with Lucius' initiation into a mystery cult which effactually disperses the satiric tone. He has sacrificed the single satiric action for a nonsatiric action that will accommodate a great many

wanderings Lucius is told stories or simply permitted to observe. The only episodes in which he is himself an actor are those concerning Fotis, the Festival of Laughter, and his transformation into an ass; thereafter, another, simpler relationship is set up. Throughout the narrative, until the very last episode of the Isis ceremonies, Apuleius' attention and interest are more obviously on the things seen or heard than on the observer who ties them together. And yet each one of these semi-independent episodes is made to reflect in some way Lucius' progress, which Apuleius has made his over-all action. He has to show a change in Lucius in accordance with the romance action, and so he sketches in something similar to a spiritual pilgrimage, the story of a fallible man's blunders, punishment, education, and rehabilitation.[20]

Lucius' development is shown largely in terms of the people he meets, the stories he hears. Up to his transformation the events he observes illustrate his own flaw and point in directions that he does not wish to, but should, follow. Apuleius' adaptation of the journey or pilgrimage is a narrative equivalent of Horace's *sermo*. The last section, Lucius' initiation into the mysteries of the Isis cult, roughly corresponds to the presentation of the ideal at the end of a Horatian satire. The mysteries of Isis are the golden mean between the opposing tendencies against which Lucius has been warned.

The *Metamorphoses* begins with the story Aristomenes tells Lucius of the consequences he suffered for his morbid curiosity and officiousness, and goes on to the encounter with Lucius' classmate Pythias, who, outraged at the price Lucius has paid for a fish, scolds the vendor and grinds the fish into the pavement with his heel. Pythias' officiousness comes from his extravagant pride in the authority newly vested in him as an inspector of

different satiric (and some nonsatiric) actions. Cf. Ben Edwin Perry's argument that the *Metamorphoses* is merely a story teller's holiday which sacrifices the demands of formal literature to popular entertainment ("An Interpretation of Apuleius' *Metamorphoses*," *Transactions of the American Philological Association,* XLVII [1926], 238–60).

[20] Robert Graves calls it a spiritual pilgrimage, not unlike that recounted in St. Augustine's *Confessions* (Introduction, *The Golden Ass* [Penguin Books, 1950], pp. 15, 19–20).

markets, and so a slight infringement of the law causes him to destroy poor Lucius' supper and impose his authority on the vendor. Lucius is the one who pays, and this behavior in a friend should be like Aristomenes' story a warning to him of such excesses. Yet a further and more explicit warning comes in the sculpture Byrrhaena shows him of Acteon's punishment at the hands of Diana. Acteon spied on Diana bathing and was turned into a stag and killed by his own hounds, just as Lucius for spying on the magic of a witch is shortly turned into an ass. Byrrhaena points up the moral by warning of the witches in the neighborhood, in particular of his host's wife, Pamphile. But far from dampening his spirits, this only kindles Lucius' curiosity the more.

Next Lucius approaches Pamphile's maid, Fotis. In terms of the plot she is, of course, a means to the end of viewing the witch at work, since she helps her mistress with her incantations. But the way Lucius goes about gaining her services suggests the close connection between sexual lust and his lust for forbidden knowledge that is pursued in many images of sexual violation and adultery later in the book. In effect, his spiritual lust is externalized in this passionate affair. His overeagerness to find out about magic is as destructive as his classmate Pythias' officious destruction of the fish, and exactly analogous to Pythias' mistaking the power for the responsibility of his office. It is also, we see, as pointless as his passion for Fotis. And yet, as the next episode proves, the other extreme—skepticism—is as wrong as Lucius' eager acceptance. The skepticism of the miserly cuckold Milo is contrasted with the credulity and curiosity of Lucius as well as the riotous sensuality of his lovemaking.

Thelyphron (in a story told at Byrrhaena's banquet) is as credulous as Lucius of the existence of witches, and he is equally overconfident of his own ability to handle them. He believes that he can successfully defy the witches who want to mutilate corpses, and so he takes the job of guarding the body of a recently dead man. He learns his lesson at the cost of nose and ears. Again the punishment of such folly does not deter Lucius, who goes straight home from the banquet to encounter an example of the witch Pamphile's magic. The wineskins merely turn from their pounding on Pamphile's door and he begins jabbing them with his sword, continuing even after they are down. Obviously they did not, as he later claims in court, attack him. The episode is connected with his passion for Fotis by the military metaphor Lucius uses to describe his relations with her, and by his collapsing exhausted in bed after both experiences. First sexual lust, then lust for violence: both are aspects of his animal nature. Each suggests a quality similar to his curiosity about religious mystery, and contributes to the rightness of his transformation in the next chapter.

The events so far cluster about the central character, Lucius, commenting upon his situation and the general problem he illustrates. Once he is transformed into an ass the theme of his lust for false gods is carried on by the various characters he meets: they are part of his experience now, and with his growing awareness their meaning becomes clearer in reference to his own case. Very shortly after his transformation he hears the story of the three robbers who died in pursuit of their profession. Each, like Lucius, went too far. The first (Lamachus) put his arm into a stranger's house through the keyhole, and his hand was nailed to the inside of the door; the second (Alcimus) was gulled by his victim who, playing upon his greed, got him to lean out a window so as to view a richer neighbor's house and pushed him to his death; the third (Thrasyleon) assumed the form of a bear in order to penetrate a victim's house, and was killed by dogs.

The essential difference between these stories and the ones concerning Lucius is that a criminal element has been introduced. Lucius was foolish, and his folly earned him the consequences he deserved. But now he is dropped into a lower, cruder world in which the various characters who aspire too high are robbers and murderers; the robbers deserve their punishment for other reasons than their pride. Lucius' sexual abandon with Fotis becomes adultery and various perversions; Psyche is persuaded to attempt to murder her husband;[21] and other wives succeed in murdering theirs.

Each of the events produces a small independent satiric fiction, secondarily illuminating the central matter of Lucius' progress and education. They are all instructive in that they offer examples and point fingers for Lucius' benefit. The reader—an alter-Lucius—catches the hints as he watches Lucius blunder into the ass's hide; and then with Lucius he gradually learns about the rest of the world. Lucius can either pass along his road learning from the suffering of the exemplary people he meets, or he can himself suffer punishments that chasten, educate, and initiate him. Up to the transformation the satire is Horatian in direction if not always in tone, with Lucius illustrating errors in conduct. After the transformation the satire becomes Juvenalian in tone and subject matter: like Juvenal, Lucius becomes a passive witness to evil of the most depraved sorts.

As an animal, once he realizes that this is not going to be a short interlude, his first feelings are of despair, an extension of the excessive passion of his human state. As a human he was becoming increasingly animal-like, and now that the transformation has been made, and he has been given his appropriate shape, he continues for a short time in character. He plots revenge on Fotis and is only restrained by his knowledge that she can return him to his normal shape. His first reactions as ass are extremely ass-like, including the plan to feign exhaustion in order to escape the robbers, and even his attempt to mount some mares, a plan which is thwarted by observant stallions.

The danger of his sinking into the animal role he has adopted is pointed up by the story of the robber Thrasyleon. Thrasyleon

---

[21] The largest and most obvious of the parallel actions that make up the middle is the non-satiric story of Cupid and Psyche. Here Lucius' progress is pointed up by the progress of Psyche (the soul), whose naïveté and curiosity cause her downfall and separation from Cupid (love). Like Lucius', her first reaction after her fall is to attempt suicide. She goes through a period of wandering, tutored by nature's servants, ants and streams, and finally after her bondage to Venus which serves as the equivalent of Lucius' initiation into the mysteries of Isis, she is reunited with Cupid. The shorter episodes and stories function in the same way.

assumes a bear hide much as Lucius does an ass's hide, both taking the animal role and suffering appropriate consequences. But Thrasyleon puts on the bear hide of his own volition in order to rob a house, and he slips completely into the role, never once admitting his humanity. By the time he dies, torn by dogs, he is all bear. Lucius does not, finally, allow the change in his shape to dehumanize him: inside his ass hide he grows morally, and so humanly. The human-beast contrast is an important one in the *Metamorphoses:* as Lucius becomes increasingly humanized (more so than when he was actually a human), the people around him grow increasingly bestial; the stories he hears or the vices he witnesses become worse and worse.

In his first adventures as an ass Lucius is only concerned with saving himself: he seeks roses, runs away from the bandits, fights the evil boy for survival. But starting with his service to the eunuchs, his own moral sense as an observer begins to be in evidence. When the eunuchs attack the hefty laborer, he cries (as best he can) rape, and saves him; by treading on a hidden adulterer's fingers he exposes the adultery of the baker's wife. If he begins as simply a victim trying to survive, he becomes a moral observer, almost a satirist. His "old curiosity" in fact is transformed into something finer. It is now the motive force for his observing "the life at that detestable mill with fascinated horror." His "only consolation" now is "the unique opportunity ... of observing all that was said and done around me; because nobody showed any reserve in my presence. . . . Though I had never forgiven Fotis for her frightful blunder of transforming me into an ass instead of a bird, I had one compensation at least: that my long ears could pick up conversations at a great distance."[22] Lucius becomes a satirist through his fall and is redeemed at the end when he has learned all that is necessary for his redemption. He changes, beginning as the revengeful satirist, becoming the detached one who castigates only because what he sees is evil; throughout he carries with him the intelligence of

---

[22] Graves trans., pp. 213–15; Loeb Library edition (Cambridge, Mass.: Harvard University Press; London: Heinemann, 1947), pp. 423–25.

the patrician, but the body and situation of the lowest of beasts. Finally, as a beast his commentary says implicitly that the humans he criticizes are more beastly than the beasts.

The beast-human relationship reaches its climax when Lucius' moral progress is interrupted by another kind of perversion: given the chance by the eunuchs, he spends a night on a human's bed again, and later when he is owned by cooks he sneaks human's food from the kitchen. This superficial return to human actions gives us the image of a beast performing human functions and pointing up their significance. Such dubious human adjustment leads to his employment by Thyasus and a complacency which reaches its peak in Lucius' sexual intercourse with a woman, the human beast and the bestial human joining. The logical end is his public copulation with the condemned murderess in the arena, which is only avoided by his escape and the intervention of Isis in his dream.

The parallel with the trial in the court of the Festival of Laughter is underlined by Lucius' own helplessness in the matter of his salvation. Isis has to intervene, as the judge did in the Festival of Laughter; Lucius is, in a sense, being initiated in both cases. He has survived the winter, and with the spring and the blooming of roses his release must inevitably come.

From the start an oppressive, nightmare world is conveyed in Apuleius' narrative by the repetitions of incidents, the obsessive references to certain kinds of experience. He repeatedly presents the situation of an innocent man's apparent guilt: Aristomenes, left with the incriminating corpse of his companion, imagines that he is blamed for the murder and is on trial; Lucius is tried for an imaginary murder, and later is blamed for the robbery of Milo's house (from which he was himself stolen), and as an ass he is blamed for the killing of the boy by the bear; an innocent traveler is accused of murder, and a boy is falsely accused, tried, and nearly convicted of the murder of his brother.

One scholar has shown Apuleius embroidering Lucian's simple tale, *The Ass,* with all the stories that came into his head as he wrote (the repetition demonstrating Apuleius' obsessions); and the rough edges are easily demonstrated—the inconsistencies in motivation and the illogicalities produced by grafting on a story that does not quite fit.[23] A porter, for example, is able to sleep through the noise made while the witch Meroë breaks down the door to Aristomenes' room (overturning his bed), harangues him, and kills his friend Socrates; but later the sound of Aristomenes falling to the floor (when the rotten rope with which he tries to hang himself breaks) brings him running at once. Thelyphron, and the reader, discover at the very end of his story that the name of the corpse he guarded is the same as his own. And he is punched in the face and severely mauled by the servants of the grieving widow he has insulted, but a few minutes later, at the slightest touch, his false nose and ears fall off. Like the obsessive repetitions, these "errors" contribute to the nightmare world in which one suddenly discovers what he should have known all along, in which he hears only what the witches want him to hear while they perform in profound silence.

As the reader identifies himself with the story-teller—with Aristomenes, Thelyphron, or Lucius himself—he is drawn into the oppressive, monstrous, hallucinatory world of guilt and consequences. Apuleius' rhetorical aim in the first part of his narrative is to make his reader become so involved that he will suffer revulsion at the consequences he and Lucius are suffering and mend his ways; and in the second to work from his own guilt outward to a detached regard of evil.

The result is also, however, the representation of a world: not a pretty one, characterized by irrationality and surprise, by the suspicion of injustice, by the presence and permanence of evil. The *Metamorphoses* shows that in a narrative satire fictions operate through the interrelatedness of characters: not only the relationship between two people, a fool and a knave, but between rich and poor fools, poetic and business-like fools, and so on. They are held close to a theme or a vice, but they also project a visualizable world of total interrelatedness, like a cheese completely infiltrated by maggots, which is common to most prose

---

[23] See Ben Edwin Perry, "On Apuleius' Metamorphoses i. 14–17," *Classical Philology*, XXIV (1929), 394–400 (on Aristomenes and Socrates); and "The Story of Thelyphron in Apuleius," in *ibid.*, 231–38.

fiction satires. As it is unrolled, this world is monotonously similar in all its details, and finally static; but a world nevertheless in which Lucius is himself deeply implicated, in ways that sometimes appear with surprise, in the genus maggot. To see this world clearly he must be completely detached from it, separated by the appearance of an animal, and even then he has difficulty shaking off his vicious human propensities.

Nobody, I think, would claim that the *Metmorphoses,* or perhaps any narrative satire, is pure satire in the sense (formal as well as intentional) of *satura.* The general structure concerning Lucius' education and conversion is too emphatic; and there are stories included (as of Cupid and Psyche) that are *märchen* without any but the most general satiric applicability. The *Metamorphoses* is an example of a prose narrative that contains satiric devices of exposition, satiric symbols, and satiric objects, but much else as well. In the literal meaning of *satura,* it is a medley or ragout that contains a great deal of coarse, highly-seasoned fare. This other material can be considered as impurity in the satire, or evidence of a mixed form, or as part of the disguise often employed by the satirist to get across his vision of evil by tricking his readers into compliance.

As a technician, Apuleius offers one important solution to the satirist's problem of structure. The satirist, by definition concerned with the middle of an action, when conditions are at their worst, rather than with the beginning and the end, has to come to some compromise as to his containing action. Apuleius employs a double action, presenting a series of parallel actions, each one relatively static, usually involving either the contrast of an ideal and its degeneration in a man or an act and its consequences. He connects them with a token over-all action involving a protagonist's error, his punishment and/or education, and ends with his redemption. A satiric character, unable to change organically, must suffer some kind of a conversion: he is transformed into an ass and then back into a man; or he is made mad and then—by a blow on the head or on the psyche—returned to sanity; or he is overcome by a humor (envy or revulsion) and at the end dehumored and returned to normal. The main emphasis falls on the inset episodes of the middle, which are often Juvenalian, but the frame action is almost invariably Horatian in tone and intention, frequently taking the form of opposed excesses and ending with the Horatian solution of the golden mean, the educated man, and the happy life. Thus the middle becomes the plunge into ugly everyday life and the containing action becomes the more generous acceptance of all this, literally *containing* it within a greater truth.

Picaresque Narrative: The Servant-Master Relation

As a satirist, the picaro substantiates Apuleius' opinion that if you look beneath the surface, take an ass's-eye view, you will see the way things really are. The satiric picaresque presents such a rogue who lives by his wits, usually writing in the first person, and the satire's distinctive tone is largely determined by this point of view.[24] *Lazarillo de Tormes* (1554), the first and in many ways the epitome of picaresque novels, gives us one version of the characteristic tone, mingling naïveté and awareness, simplicity and cunning. In a sense the picaro represents, like one of Lucian's self-exposing speakers, an ironic structure embodied in a character: a prudential awareness is joined to a moral obtuseness. Lazaro does not see the truth, but his peasant cunning makes him see something close to it, and so his observations betray himself and his surroundings simultaneously.

---

[24] E. M. W. Tillyard believes that the picaresque "had to do with the underdog, the little man, the fellow a bit worse off than the average, who has his adventures and troubles and somehow just survives" (*The Epic Strain in the English Novel* [Fair Lawn, N.J.: Essential Books, 1958], p. 14). For a useful interpretation of the picaresque along this line, though with greater application for later picaresque narratives, see Robert B. Heilman, "Variations on Picaresque (Felix Krull)," *Sewanee Review*, LXVI (1958), 547–77; and more recently, Robert Alter, *Rogue's Progress* (Cambridge, Mass.: Harvard University Press, 1964). See also Edwin Muir, *The Structure of the Novel* (London: Hogarth Press, 1928), p. 32; Ian Watt, *The Rise of the Novel* (Berkeley: University of California Press, 1957), p. 94; and D. J. Dooley, "Some Uses and Mutations of the Picaresque," *Dalhousie Review*, XXXVII (1957–58), 363–77.

For example, he dislikes the blackamoor who takes to visiting his mother: "But when I saw that our eating improved with his visits, I began to like him right well." When the inevitable happens he simply observes that "my mother presented me with a very cute and dark little brother." Then, as matter-of-factly, he recounts an incident when his little brother noticed the difference in color and ran to his mother, pointing to the blackamoor and crying, "Bogieman!" Lazaro concludes: "I, even though just a boy, caught my brother's expression, 'bogieman,' and said to myself, 'How many people there must be in the world who run away from others because they can't see themselves!' "[25] He has apparently taken in the situation of his mother and the blackamoor, which has for him no moral significance, only a prudential one concerned with finding enough food to eat. But when he sees somebody who is black pointing in terror at somebody else who is black, his sense of fitness makes him draw a conclusion. His awareness directs the reader to one aspect of the larger picture which, we can be certain, his awareness does not completely illuminate.

The discrepancy between prudential and moral knowledge becomes greater in the story of the blind beggar who, Lazaro says, "second only to God, ... gave me life; and although he was blind, he guided me and lighted the way in my passage through life," which we can read as the primrose path (pp. 8–9). In the subsequent episodes the relationship between the prudential and moral becomes somewhat more complex, but the gist of Lazaro's ironic role remains the same. There is no exaggeration of word or scene, just the relating of appalling incidents as if they were commonplace. A secondary effect occurs in *Lazarillo de Tormes* and at least some of the other picaresque novels: the reader tends to associate himself with the confidential, likable first-person speaker—or rather he is tricked into doing so—but becomes increasingly aware of the protagonist's (and therefore his own) shortcomings.

[25] *Lazarillo de Tormes,* trans. J. Gerald Markley (New York: Liberal Arts Press, 1954), p. 6. Subsequent citations are from this translation.

There is a great deal of possible variety within this straightforward, reportorial tone: the picaro may vary from a true innocent to a knave, from a trickster to a satiric observer, from a victim of his encounters to an oppressor of the innocent. But the fiction adopted is almost invariably that of a man recalling his misspent life, and the action begins with his family background, early childhood, and homelife before his connection with his first master. The middle is the series of relationships with masters as he moves up or down, backward or forward, in the world, and the picaresque usually stops with the middle, as the protagonist sails for a new life in South America or departs for a stint in the galleys. When there *is* an ending it is ironic like that of *Lazarillo de Tormes,* where the picaro has at last found the security he has persistently sought—in a life as husband of the local priest's whore.

What appears to be a man's life, however, is in fact a series of discrete relationships. The basic fiction of picaresque satire involves, as in Juvenal's satire, the relationship between a fool and a knave or an innocent and a knave. The helpless, naïve, innocent picaro travels the road and meets men whose knavery is exposed for the reader by their brutal treatment of him. Or he meets men whose folly he can himself exploit, thereby demonstrating both his own knavery and their folly. Or he is corruptible, a willing pupil for the scoundrel he meets, and so a fool to the other's knave. The result is a spectrum of satiric subject matter.

The relationships Juvenal employed were based on the subordination of one party and the benevolence and authority of the other. The most significant people the picaro encounters on his journey are his masters. With them he engages in a sort of compact which involves a reciprocal responsibility that is lacking in his more casual encounters along the road. The master is responsible for his servant's education and welfare, and the servant owes loyalty and duty to his master. Every such relationship in the picaresque begins with the assumption of this norm and then deviates from it in various ways. One or both of the parties fail to live up to the contract (and the ideal).

The earliest form of the picaresque, in sixteenth-century Spain, focuses its attention on the master's obligations to his servant—on the servant's wages, so to speak. *Lazarillo de Tormes* presents a violent clash of personalities in which the master oppresses his servant until he is forced to rebel. The source of the conflict is partly mere cruelty, as in the blind beggar's brutal treatment of Lazaro. More often, however, the conflict arises out of the master's unwillingness to feed his servant enough to keep body and soul together, so that the satire centers around a desperate battle for survival.

The blind beggar is appropriate as Lazaro's first master because he embodies the world Lazaro is going to have to cope with: he is avaricious, cunning, and mean, but vulnerable to a nimble thief. The beggar is a cruel exploiter but he is also blind. He has the advantage of strength and experience over Lazaro, but the boy has the advantage of his eyes. And so they go through a series of skirmishes that demonstrate the impossibility of the servant's surviving without cheating and eventually almost killing his master.

The satiric effect of the relationship with the blind beggar comes from the changes we observe in the servant Lazaro, who reacts like a chameleon, or better, a thermometer, to his environment. It is significant that, unlike Juvenal's dependents, the servant cannot withdraw from the relationship in which he finds himself. If he flees one master, the next is invariably worse. He must either assume the role of fool to his master's knave or die. In this sense the picaro is anything but a rebel; he is, in fact, aspiring to become part of the social order with its security, comfort, and privileges.[26] But this is not enough: in the conflict over food he must, if he is to survive, become himself the aggressor, thus exchanging roles with his master. He must use against his master the very techniques of cheating and bullying that this same master has taught him. Lazaro finally repays his

[26] Cf. Sherman Eoff, "The Picaresque Psychology of *Guzman de Alfarache*," *Hispanic Review*, XII (1953), 107–19. Eoff shows that Guzman's attacks on the established and entrenched are merely made to forward his own ambitions or to express his contempt for what is beyond his reach.

master for his stinginess by sending him flying into a stone post. He has learned his lesson, that in order to live he must become a knave. Because the picaro makes common cause with his corrupt master, the ideal that is often physically present in Juvenal's outcast protagonist is only glimpsed here in the picaro's innocence as he enters into the relationship; once he is entangled with a master the ideal recedes into the past with the ideal master-servant relation itself.

If the blind beggar represents the predatory aspect of life to which Lazaro must adjust, the canon, his second master (and predictably worse than the first), represents the Church that tries to feed men's stomachs on purely spiritual food while hoarding all the material wealth for itself. An element of hypocrisy, lacking in the blind beggar, is added in the canon: the master now claims that by feeding Lazaro with good words he is nourishing him. In order to keep from starving, Lazaro has to steal communion bread from the miserly priest's locked chest. He unconsciously reveals the ineffectuality of the Church in his confusion between religion and reality: "God and my wits," he says, are all that can save him from starvation; he calls the tinker who gives him a key to the food chest an angel sent by God; and he eats a loaf of filched bread "in less time than it takes to say a couple of credos" (p. 25). The relationship keeps pointing up how, in order to survive in a world where the Church does not let flesh and spirit mingle, Lazaro must cheat priests, violate religious precepts, and even wish sick men dead.

Lazaro's third master, the indigent hidalgo, introduces yet another relationship, one in which there is no conflict between master and servant. But with the hidalgo the master-servant relation has completely collapsed, and the servant is forced to take all duties and responsibilities, including the payment of wages, upon himself. The hidalgo represents the gentleman class which through false pride refuses to lift a finger to work. Lazaro was never fooled by the canon's hypocritical talk, but now he is overcome by his master's gentility, his kind manner, his "misfortune," and, never saying a word against him, earns food for both of them. The hidalgo's character is gradually exposed through Lazaro's growing awareness of his pecuniary limitations and through the irony of his respect and willingness to serve kind gentility. Only through the eyes of Lazaro, with his awareness of hunger, can we see the real arrogance, the preposterous pride, and the sadness of the hidalgo.

The object satirized is a folly rather than a vice, a foolish class that has cut itself off from reality; but the hidalgo's exploitation of Lazaro is no less real because the master is passive and allows the glamor of class to replace the canon's and beggar's physical coercion. Although Lazaro is not unhappy with the hidalgo, the reader sees that in a sense he has allowed himself to become the same fool he was with the blind beggar. He has accepted the hidalgo's values, though of his own volition this time, and so has allowed himself to be exploited. If the beggar and the canon are obvious social evils, the hidalgo, because of his fair appearance, his capacity for self-deception, and his ability to make others deceive themselves, is perhaps more subtly dangerous than Lazaro's earlier masters.

The last episode of the book, in which Lazaro becomes a knavish priest's fool by marrying his whore in return for security, picks up and fulfills the earlier tone: he once again accepts the values of his immediate milieu, and exchanges a wife-husband for a master-servant relation. But in the fifth episode (the fourth, seventh, and eighth are so sketchy as to add little or nothing) we are presented with an altogether different and simpler use of the picaresque.

Lazaro's fifth master is a seller of indulgences, a charlatan going through his routine with Lazaro as his assistant. The servant merely observes his master's behavior (his professional activity) and describes it: "And although I was just a boy, it amused me; I thought, 'I wonder how often these swindlers defraud innocent people with tricks like this'" (p. 64). There is no friction between master and servant (Lazaro adds at the end of the chapter that this master fed him well) and no real interaction: while the servant reports, our attention is wholly on the master's chicanery. He is a bad master not because he beats his servant or does not feed him but because he is a bad example, a corrupting instructor. The emphasis, to the extent that it is on the servant at all, is on his service. Since the picaro is never quite so corrupt as the society he enters, he has to be taught the tricks of the trade, and in the process much that is underhanded is exposed and analyzed for the reader. The degeneration portrayed is not so much in the master-servant relation itself as in the occupation of the master into which the servant is drawn and initiated; far from useful or beneficial it is criminal and perhaps murderous.

Lazarillo de Tormes (in particular the first three episodes) is a remarkable and original performance which created a new fiction for satire based on the conventional Juvenalian relationship between a fool and a knave. Its originality becomes apparent on a comparison with the 1555 continuation. This work (obviously by another writer) is also a satire, but it has returned to fantasy, to animal fable, and in particular to the Apuleian metamorphosis. Lazaro, taking part in Charles V's expedition against the Barbary Turks, goes down with his ship, but, praying hard to the Virgin, he is transformed by a miracle into a tuna fish. Thereupon he becomes involved in the politics of this underwater world, which of course corresponds to the world above water. What sets off the original *Lazarillo* from previous satires is its use of the careful reporting of contemporary life as its satiric method—the making of satiric symbols out of everyday objects and scenes; the ironic neutrality of its tone; and, perhaps most important, the involvement of the protagonist in the scene through an occupation (he must eat), and so the interaction of character, profession, and milieu.[27]

[27] A second continuation, by Juan de Luna (1620), captures the intention of the original although it drops both the relationship between innocence and corruption and that between servant and master (except for Lazaro's enforced service for some fishermen who make money showing him as a "sea monster"). Luna picks up his hero after the last episode of his marriage to the priest's whore and makes this the keystone to his character: his complete self-abasement in order to survive. Although Lazaro's wife marries again while he is off with the fishermen, the relationship between wife and husband, or rather cuckold, informs the whole work, and when he returns Lazaro is still willing to take her back.

Picaresque satire, at least in its early stages, aimed at professional, social, or even domestic, relationships rather than at individuals. These basic relationships had been used in narrative satire by Apuleius in the central part of the *Metamorphoses,* but of course with little sense of professionalism between the master and his servant, and a great additive of fantasy.[28] In *Lazarillo* the interaction is based on the most probable of motives and the most inevitable of situations: the servant's hunger and the master's refusal or inability to feed him. The discursive structure and thematic connectives between episodes and characters have entirely disappeared, and with them the fantasy of presentation. Stylization appears only in the orderly survey of society as Lazaro moves up from the service of beggar to clergyman to impoverished nobleman, from type to type; and the progression is merely one of increasing complexity as he advances from crude to subtle exploitation and from obvious to less obtrusive evil. The pilgrimage of Everyman in the *Metamorphoses* has been replaced by a shifting series of relationships in which (with the exception of the episode of the fifth master) the last signs of the satirist-observer have been lost in the satiric object.

As the servant-master relation is conventionalized in later picaresque novels and broadened to include more and varied areas of experience, the most characteristic relationship becomes that between a person punished and his punisher. Satiric punishment, as earlier examples have shown, can expose the knavery of the punisher or the folly of the punished. The picaresque is at its most characteristic when the two movements appear together.

The satiric punishment examined so far has been formalized and emblematic, producing a "character," but this quality is partly counteracted when a second person is involved to do the

---

[28] Whether Apuleius' *Metamorphoses* had any direct influence on the picaresque novel is an open question, but Michel's French translation was published in 1522 and Adlington's English in 1566, while *Lazarillo* appeared in 1554 and Thomas Nashe's *Jacke Wilton, or the Unfortunate Traveller* appeared in 1594.

punishing. In Alemán's *Guzman de Alfarache* (1599; I refer to Mabbe's somewhat inflated version which emphasizes the emblematic quality), there is an old hostess of an inn who cheats her customers and feeds them spoiled food. She has already made Guzman violently ill by feeding him rotten eggs. Two young fellows receive the same treatment and decide to pay her back. They take note of the eggs and go on to order a fish, which they eat; and then, instead of paying her, one of them throws the rotten eggs in the old woman's face,

> seeling up both her eyes therewith, which looked like an old wall all to bedawbed with rough-cast. Which plaistred eyes of hers, he had made blind and painefull unto her, that not daring to open them, she cryed out, as if she had beene mad, whilest this his other Companion, behaving himself, as if he had rebuked him for it, and that he might be ashamed to use a poore old woman in this uncivil kind of fashion, threw me a handfull of hot ashes in the very face of her, and so they got them out of dores, telling her, as they went away; ah you old rotten Carrion, *Qui en tal haze que tal pague,* you are now payd in your owne money: what you got by your coozening, you may now put it in your eye.
>
> She was toothlesse, chap-falne, hollow-eyed, and wappering withall her haire sluttishly hanging about her eares, unkempt, and as greazie, as it was knotty; a fouler Swine no man ever saw: mealed she was all over like a Mullet dressed with Flowre, or a Flounder that is ready for the frying-pan; with a gesture so graciously scurvie, a looke so pleasantly fierce, and in all the rest so handsomely ill-favoured, that as oft as you shall but thinke either of it or her, you cannot (if your life should depend upon it) but you must needes burst foorth into laughter.[29]

The old woman might almost be one of the damned standing in hell for Dante's inspection. The young man's description of her turns her into an "old rotten Carrion," "a Mullet dressed with Flowre, or a Flounder that is ready for the frying-pan"; and she takes on the appearance of her own wretched food. The passage as a whole conveys a mixed image of pain, defeat, and dangerous defiance. Her suffering, like her punishment, expresses her inner ugliness. It in no way mitigates her crime.

But whenever one person punishes another guilt is diffused. The hostess' suffering, just though it be, does to some extent

[29] Matheo Alemán, *The Rogue, or the Life of Guzman de Alfarache,* trans. James Mabbe (1622: London, 1924), I, 113–14.

shift our attention to the agents of punishment, the young men. The author, Aleman, is particular on this point: the story of the hostess' punishment is followed by a priest's lengthy sermon on the evils of revenge. Thus punishment does not alter the absolute folly of the punished, but it does rub off onto the hands of the punisher. When punishment of the wicked is used as a satiric device the evil remains clear-cut; but when the emphasis is on the relationship of punisher and punished rather than on the punishment as definition, the good becomes qualified and ambiguous.

The youths who punish the hostess are motivated more by revenge than by a feeling for justice, and so we are left with the impression of a larger fish devouring a smaller, not of the defeat of evil by good.[30] The guilt of the punished and the guilt of the punisher are often balanced against each other in the picaresque. Guzman de Alfarache has the foolish notion that by dressing up he can seduce a lady of quality. Only too readily he finds a "lady" and carries an enormous meal to her chamber, where (predictably) he is interrupted by her "brother" who sits down with her to the sumptuous repast. The amorous Guzman is forced to spend the evening hidden, appropriately enough, in an enormous jug "that had no water in it, yet was it not without some droppings, and a kinde of sliminesse hanging about the sides of it, and that none of the cleanest." The emphasis is about equally distributed between Guzman's folly and the lady's exploitation of it.

Picaresque novels are built on this shifting relationship between a central character and the many characters he meets. With each encounter the proportion of innocence and guilt shifts into a new ratio. The appearance of either a purely innocent victim or a completely just chastiser is rare, at least in the Spanish and continental picaresque. When the picaro is punished he usually has been caught cheating or stealing; when he is a punisher of wickedness it is usually to exploit someone's folly. Guz-

[30] The behavior of the second youth plays some part in the impression: he pretends to sympathize with the hostess in order to get close enough to cover her face with hot ashes.

man plays the moral agent only for the purpose of showing off his cunning to his master-of-the-moment, and Lazaro punishes out of desperation and exploits in order to survive.

Lazarillo de Tormes shows how closely the punisher-punished relation is bound up with the master-servant relation. When Lazaro's first master, the blind beggar, smashes his head against the stone bull, he is punishing the innocent and so reflecting his own evil; but he also (as Lazaro himself recognizes) vividly demonstrates his servant's blockheadedness. And when Lazaro smashes the beggar's head against a post at the end of their association he is perhaps unconsciously revealing a connection between his master's physical and moral blindness, but the action also reflects the wickedness of the servant.

The moral the beggar draws from the stone bull (that a beggar's boy must not be gullible) is only too true: in the world of the picaresque, stupidity and weakness have become crimes. Lazaro's revenge on the beggar is not so much a triumph of justice as a sign that Lazaro has learned the lesson of the stone bull. There are always two phases to the picaro's relationship with his master: innocent, he is unjustly punished by his master, and, learning his lesson (which amounts to acquiring guilt), he punishes and exploits his master (or trying to do so is caught and justly punished).

The motive force of this world is violent retribution or punishment. The simplest punishment that exposes an evil man implicates all the surrounding characters in a common guilt. The picara Justina's father cheats his customers by selling too much chaff with his barley, until one day a victimized gentleman "gave him such a Stroke [with a half-peck measure] on the Pole, that his Soul flew out into the Measure, and the Body drop'd down for want of it." But the satirist does not use the death of Justina's father only as a symbol of his character but as a touchstone for other characters, a jumping-off place for other satiric portraits. The family reacts phlegmatically to the father's death; the gentleman who has killed him buys his way out of the situation, and the wife accepts the money and settles down to a dinner with the gentleman, leaving her dead husband in a winding sheet full of holes. The poor dead man is not even safe from his dog, who has been left to guard him while the others feast: "The Devil of a Cur smelling the Roast-Meat [of the dinner], began to Bark and Howl to be let out, and finding no Body answer'd, went to complain to his Master, who taking no Notice, he thought fit to whisper in his Ear, which being Deaf he gnaw'd it off, and lest the other should complain nibbl'd it clear away, and some part of the face with it." Threatening to tell that the wife had thrown her husband to the dogs, the gentleman takes his leave; the wife decides not to go into mourning since it would be unbecoming (she is too fat), and because of the wintry weather they "carry'd the Corps to Church faster than he would have gone himself if alone."[31] The act of punishment does not remain isolated but catches up all the people involved, moving outward in widening circles.

The Spanish picaresque posits a world in which crime is always being punished, but punishment is based on superior cunning or strength or luck, not on virtue. Only when Lazaro has shaken off his clouds of glory can he defeat even the blind beggar. If the old hostess were as sharp as the two youths who smear her with rotten eggs she would probably have punished them. It is a world with no moral agent to bring retribution, but either a revenger, a prankster, a desperate picaro, or somebody who, by the very act of punishing, succumbs to the degenerate values of this world. The characters act almost exclusively by prudential considerations, making no moral judgments on each other (Lazaro is grateful to the beggar for what he has learned from him).

The picaro himself progresses not toward a happy ending or moral wholeness, but toward strictly prudential knowledge. At the end he has learned how to survive: he is just out of the galleys, better equipped for more of the same, or he skips out for South America and another chance. His acquired talents are knowledge of how to beg, how to pick pockets, how to steal from a locked chest—as opposed to how to tell right from

[31] *La Picara Justina,* in *The Spanish Libertines,* pp. 17–20.

wrong, or how to find and wed the right girl. For the ideal we have to look not to the punisher or the punished, but to the ideal relationship of which the punisher-punished is a corruption: such a relationship as that between a man and a woman brought together by mutual love and respect, or a servant and master held together by bonds of duty and responsibility. The result is a world of desperation in which the best one can do is get by without hanging, and the best resolution to a plot is the hero's settling for security without honor. Here, where interlocking relationships prevent anyone from standing out as a norm of behavior, the picaresque can be seen shading off from satire into more purely mimetic forms like the novel.

The picaresque mode varies from country to country—changing its emphasis from the picaro to the master, from the traveler to the people met—but it represents the basis for most narrative satire from *Gargantua* and *Pantagruel* to *Gulliver's Travels,* from Byron's *Don Juan* to the novels of Huxley, Waugh, and Nathanael West. Regarded historically, the picaresque also offers as clear an example as can be found of the conventionalizing of a satiric fiction into a cliché. Literally none of the post-*Lazarillo* narratives, except perhaps *Don Quixote* (and in England Defoe's unsatiric novels), captured the sober verisimilitude, the calm, unemotional relation of fact. They all picked up—or reverted to—some of the fantasy of the 1555 continuation, in which Lazaro became a fish and adventured on the sea-bottom. The transition can be traced from the matter-of-fact smashing of heads against hard objects in *Lazarillo* to the elaborately described and overtly symbolic punishments in *Guzman, Don Pablos,* and the *Roman comique.*

Recognizing the convenience and flexibility of the picaresque form, satirists tended to overemphasize its satiric lines, turning it into a crude approximation of *satura.* The diffusion of guilt as a correlative of the picaresque world became an expository device, a net for catching odd and various fish. Master and servant or punisher and punished no longer represented a relationship but an occasion for an elaborate satiric anatomy which catches up a whole spectrum of fools and knaves. Already by the time of *Justina* (1605), punishment was turning playful and losing its original satiric function, becoming merely revenge or merry pranks indistinguishable from those of the German and English jestbooks. Justina, on one occasion, simply sees some women sleeping and sews together their skirts so that when they awaken and try to get up they tumble about.

The relationship between two people dwindled to the juxta-position of an eye and an object. A decided shift of emphasis took place from the master-servant relation to the master, or rather (since the master as such tended to disappear) to the character, object, scene, or place observed. With his fifth master, Lazaro simply reported what he saw and heard, coming close to assuming the role of observer. With this change, the narrative was no longer an embodiment of satire but a conventional ve-hicle for it, a framework for portraits. As an observer, the picaro could assume any tone from urbane Horatian to savage, sarcastic Juvenalian, from *ingénu* to *vir bonus* and heroic defender of the faith.[32] For variety a traveler, an animal, or even an inani-mate object like a coin, traveling from pocket to pocket, could present a series of more or less vivid satirically perceived scenes. The satirist's skill went undivided into the tableaux that were framed. These works were not, therefore, strictly speaking picaresque novels, although they shared the picaresque form, drew upon its style or point of view and its general subject mat-ter, and often attempted to pass for picaresque.

The important difference between stories employing a picaro and those employing devils, gods, spirits, fleas, or atoms is that the latter focused more exclusively on the manners witnessed or on the perceiving apparatus, one or the other being reduced to complete and uninteresting conventionality. The relation be-tween a coin, for example, and its owner is not unlike that of a picaro and his master, except that there is little chance for the coin's character to unfold or develop. The dividing line would seem to be the interaction of object and eye, as mutually influ-

---

[32] See Mack, "The Muse of Satire," *Yale Review*, XLI, 80–92.

encing and satirized. The transitional figure was the metamorphosed character who was changed in each new life to accord with his behavior in the preceding life, and so was both involved in the object of satire and affected by it.[33] The picaresque proper required some kind of interaction between eye and object and some diffusion of guilt that reached the picaro-eye.

An equivocal animal, a dog or an ass, could be used as protagonist not because of its helplessness or the ease with which it is exploited but because of an interesting point of view. A dog will detect doggish parallels with the humans he meets, or he will bring out certain cruel or sentimental traits in his masters or casual acquaintances. Only when the dog himself begins to play tricks on his master or to take on human ways, has he become a picaro in a picaresque situation. The pure object-eye relation, then, is less closely connected to the picaresque, or narrative satire, than to a formal satire on the one hand and to journalistic reporting on the other. Once satire is outside the safe purlieus of *satura,* among the complicated forces of realistic fiction, the conventions of either one or the other are liable to take precedence. The tendency is for rhetoric to separate from representation, producing a narrative whose only function is the exposition of follies, or one in which the satiric interest has been reduced to a general sharpness or pessimism of tone.

I have mentioned convention as one of the intractable materials with which the satirist who would embody his satire in a prose narrative must deal—the convention of a beginning and an end, for example, or of the success or marriage of the hero. Although satire often mixes the conventions of other genres, and at its most sophisticated conveys part of its meaning through these juxtapositions, it has also distinctive conventions of its own. We might say that the bipartite form, the static plot, the crowded scene, the climate of defeat, and—for that matter—the parody-

---

[33] The literary progenitor of the device was Antonio Enriques Gomez, who, in his *Siglo Pitagorico* (1644) "replaced the passage of a servant from master to master by the transmigrations of a soul from body to body" (Frank W. Chandler, *The Literature of Roguery* [Boston, New York: Houghton Mifflin, 1907], I, 13).

ing of other genres are all satiric conventions. They were of course originally fictions shaped to meet the particular generic aims of satire, which then hardened into stereotypes. In general, the conventional in satire naturally gravitates toward the static and discursive and is always trying to reduce relationship to a static pair of characters, the satirist looking (or railing) at a second man, but without any sense of their conjunction or reciprocity. All the satirist's attention goes into the perception of the satiric observer or the emblematic qualities of the object; the great advantages offered by fictional representation, story, and plot are lost. Only in a few periods—it is difficult to say with what combination of omens or forces—have the full potential of both rhetoric and representation been brought together by a few satirists with maximum effect.

II. FROM PANURGE TO ACHITOPHEL

The Satirist and the Satirist-Satirized

The oldest, most intractable yet richly fictive convention of satire is the figure of the satirist—partly so because of his derivation from the vatic figure of the primitive satirist. As Robert C. Elliott has shown in his pioneering study, *The Power of Satire*, primitive societies believed the curse and the satirist who uttered it to possess preternatural powers. The satirist could drive his enemies to hang themselves, rhyme rats dead, cause rivers to dry up or overflow, cause crops to wither or flourish. When satire became an art (the ritual explanation is that art results when form is separated from belief or practical function), the curse remained a part of it only by being domesticated, absorbed into a larger structure. The raw power of the curse is incompatible with the control of art, and in order to survive must suffer compromise.[1]

The original fiction, not radically modified even in Roman *satura,* must have had a satirist flailing out at the wicked people he saw around him, and it has persisted as a basic convention down to the present. But from the start the curse carried within its ritual origin a radical ambiguity that was transmitted to later satire. Both good and bad, healthy and diseased, it returns fertility to the wasteland but leaves the satirist himself suspect. In

---

[1] *The Power of Satire* (Princeton: Princeton University Press, 1960), *passim.*

75

this pristine state, the satirist is purifier and savior while at the same time scapegoat. What he does is good—what he asserts is true; but the fact that he does it (the sort of motive or the sort of man required if he is to be effective in this nasty work) makes him a figure to be feared and driven out of decent society. This primitive ambiguity is a two-edged weapon that most satirists still have to cope with, and it has been reflected in some of the characteristics and peculiarities of the conventional satirist-persona who directs the satires of Horace and Pope, Juvenal and Marston.

The satirist is primarily a means to an end, merely a norm against which to judge the satiric object. Nevertheless, satirists from the earliest times have been inclined to think at least as much about their own sensibilities as about the horrid objects that violate them; the convention of the satirist-persona has often concealed nonsatiric, if not positively romantic, proclivities. More single-minded satirists have also been drawn to place undue emphasis on the satirist-persona; in any context in which the satirist wishes to draw upon some sense of realism—and verisimilitude is also one of the conventions basic to satire—the satirist *within the satire* must be accepted as a real man in relation to other real men.

One solution to the dual problem of his seductiveness and peculiarities is the conventional satiric *apologia,* which every satirist at some point writes in order to defend his ethos as satirist. Another solution—and the main subject of Elliott's book—is the fiction of the satirist-satirized, in which the sinister qualities of the satirist and the curse are counteracted by the author's absorbing them, in the form of a misanthrope's utterances, into a larger structure, and ridiculing them *as well as* the object of his attack. The satirist's curses are powerful and to a great extent true, but the satirist is merely one character within a larger structure of meaning, in terms of which we see his curses as bewildered and excessive, the cries of an idealist who has lost control of himself. The fierce invective is distanced and, indeed, the satirist himself is satirized. The satirist-satirized fiction therefore controls the overtones and ambiguity of the satirist, tries to explain his behavior in realistic if not moral terms, and produces a characteristic satiric device which catches more than one party.

Elliott's argument is that certain satires are clearly "powerful," and that the power derives from the satirist's ambiguity referred to above. His analysis leads him to offer an explanation for the notorious discrepancy in many satires between the actual prose sense of the satire and its emotional impact. He would say that the satiric frame can mitigate the powerful vituperation but not quite conceal it: that the old Adam shows through. And so arise the disagreements and misunderstandings concerning works such as *Timon of Athens, Le Misanthrope,* and *Gulliver's Travels,* about which Elliott concludes:

> Their invective develops all the force of the primitive; we, the readers, feel the magic and show it by becoming obsessed with their incantatory denunciations. One result is that we partially misread; we forget that these are works of art, not magic; that the superb invective is incorporated in artistic structures. The most common misreading takes the form of a facile identification of the fictive railer (the 'primitive satirist') with the actual author. . . . (p. 220).

Then, switching to a genetic explanation, Elliott goes on to make this identification. Swift, he suggests, expresses one side of himself in Gulliver's misanthropic railing; Gulliver indicates the abyss which Swift, in moments of despair, looked into. But Swift the artist seeks to control the excess by ridicule, subordinating it to a more conventional conclusion.

Swift and his use of such fictions as the satirist-satirized is the point toward which our study is moving. But this ungainly fiction is only one of the many ways by which the satirist maintains the tone of the primal curse without giving way to it. Less radical solutions are utilized by Horace and Pope, who avoid the objectionable qualities of the satirist by reducing him to a small part of a rounded man, a fragment which, when given sufficient provocation, speaks out and is then brought under control again; or, in a tea table version of *Timon,* Horace gently undercuts the satirist by occasionally allowing an adversarius to turn the tables on him. Ben Jonson's triumphant solution to the problem, arrived at after some unsuccessful experiments, was to use the railing satirist as both symbol of duplicity and the agent for exposing worse villains. As villains, Volpone-Mosca (or Wycherley's Horner) are more disinterested than the men they expose; Volpone's real pleasure comes from revealing the ordinarily hidden avarice of the Corbaccios, Voltores, and Corvinos. (At one point Mosca is even allowed to rail unpleasant truths at Volpone without breaking the frame.) With these polished examples of accommodation in mind, we may suspect that the power of Elliott's examples arises in part at least from a *failure* of accommodation. The whole meaning, or effect, of the satire has to include the outrageous intensity of the speeches as well as the realization that they are excessive, uttered by a fool. The resulting uncertainty of tone is presumably a source of power: the sort of power engendered by broken columns and ragged mountains.

I mean to suggest that the convention in these cases may not have been totally absorbed into the fiction; the satirist was fictionalized but his invective remained a convention; or something remained beyond the satirist's awareness. Elliott's examples are, in fact, on the outskirts of satire, where the misanthropic satirist, by a slight shift of tone or emphasis, can become the tragic hero: a progression that leads from Thersites to Timon to Coriolanus to King Lear. The satirist-satirized is a convention that can be used in either satire or tragedy; in a work like Shakespeare's *Timon,* whose ends are tragic, much of the peculiarity of effect is due to the jostling of different conventions from different genres.

If we think of satire as having two poles of interest, the satirist and the satiric object, the satirist-satirized could theoretically be drawn toward either pole. In the examples I have given from Horace and Ben Jonson, he has been dragged over to the side of the evil. In Elliott's examples he has dragged the evil over to his side and subordinated it to a concern with his own sensibilities. As the overlap with tragedy indicates, a period which produces satirist-satirized fictions of the sort Elliott describes is more interested in the satirist and his state of mind than in the satiric object, and this may be a partial cause of the ambiguity. The satire has been diverted from the evil, with the satirist as merely a device for getting at it, to a study of the good man (or the tragic hero) who goes wrong through an excess of good qualities or sensibility.

Elliott's bent is toward the doctrine that by the employment of archetypes the artist reaches down to the wellsprings of our preconscious being; and this is essentially his explanation of satire's "power." He comes close to the conclusion that satire is powerful *because* it was magical in origin, and not the reverse. Then we must conclude that the terror felt by a primitive Celt is still in our blood today and is automatically summoned up by satire. My own opinion is that there are no magical overtones in satire per se. It is not Gulliver's curses, his satire, that throw the Fourth Voyage off balance—if it is in fact off balance; it is rather, as we shall see, that with disillusionment Gulliver changes from a persona with the puppet's strings in sight to a particular individual in whom the public role of cursing is not completely reconciled with the private one of husband-father-friend. What all of this amounts to is the suspicion that one must not look for intensity in the magical reverberations of satire to the exclusion of humble literary artifice. The power of satire is reached by the poet through his manipulation of words and associations, or sometimes even by his mishandling of them; the curse carries with it little power of its own. Elliott is right, however, that the satirist himself, by whatever origins and confused history, remains a wonderfully ambiguous figure—part hero, part villain, part public censor, part private man.

The following sections will trace the evolution of some of his different shapes and effects as he relates to the satiric object; and through this evolution, I believe, we can arrive at a clear picture of how the the evil agent of the English Augustan satirists operated and evolved vis-à-vis their satiric observer.

The Satirist as Knave and as Hero: Panurge and Pantagruel

Lucian's satiric observer was outside society, far above it, or beyond life itself. He was very different from the Horatian observer, who was within society and a part of it, and the Juvenalian, a fragment of the true society but isolated within or without the false society. Diogenes, whom Lucian elsewhere attacks as merely another false philosopher, in the *Dialogues of the Dead* is used as a disruptive agent whose questing, probing, and railing serve a useful function. This character is not only an example of Lucian's own approach to his subject; he is an important type in the line of satire that extends to Erasmus and Rabelais, who represent the early, insurgent phase of the humanist revival. Their purpose was to throw open windows, destroy shibboleths, expose the rigidities and stupidities of the Scholastic categories, and so return to an apostolic simplicity. The aim of this satire gives rise to a peculiar protagonist, very different from Juvenal's defeated idealist or Horace's inside man. Following directly from Diogenes or Menippus is such an ambiguous figure as Reynard the Fox or Rabelais' Panurge.

The double-edged quality of the satire of the Reynard stories is most striking. Through many of them one has the impression that Reynard is simply a Scourge of God, like Attila the Hun— a knave who is necessary to expose the follies of mankind. He encounters a large number of different types, to each of whom he poses the possibility of knavery. Each, given the opportunity, bites, and so exposes his own particular folly and is appropriately punished for it. Bruin the Bear, much too proud of himself to begin with, goes to fetch Reynard to court to answer the charges that have been made against him. At the mention of honey Bruin forgets his mission and follows Reynard eagerly to the trap, from whence he emerges earless, clawless, and battered. The cat succumbs in the same way to its lust for mice; and when Reynard finally reaches the court, he readily catches the King Lion himself with a story of great treasure in a ditch. The king releases Reynard and punishes his accusers, including the poor bear.

Enough crimes are committed by Reynard to establish his vicious character: innocent chickens, hares, pigeons, and the like are killed. But every crime that is presented in some detail relies at least as much on the victim's folly as on the fox's knavery. Moreover, Reynard's challengers are almost always bigger and stronger than he is, and, as in his climactic fight with Isegrim the Wolf, the flexibility and cunning of the fox are contrasted to the brute strength and mechanical rigidity of the wolf. It takes the wicked pliability of Reynard to expose the stereotyped behavior of the other, larger, more respectable animals; and it takes a knave to bring out the knavery or folly of these exemplary citizens. When he is not killing the innocent, he almost captures our sympathy: he is one against all those fools, and yet succeeds on sheer intelligence, albeit an intelligence that does not hesitate to stoop to hypocrisy, lies, and subterfuge.

From Reynard follows a branch of the picaresque novel that flourished more noticeably among the northern Protestant nations than among the southern Catholic: the wickedness or folly in which the picaro engages becomes the jokes of a *Tyll Eulenspiegel* (1515) which invariably discomfit the pompous. But the most important example of the knavish character as a satiric device is Rabelais' Panurge, whose abundant coat contains

above six and twenty little fobs and pockets always full, one with some lead-water, and a little knife as sharp as a glover's needle, wherewith he used to cut purses: another with some kind of bitter stuff, which he threw into the eyes of those he met: another with clotburs, penned with little geese or capons feathers, which he cast upon the gowns and caps of honest people; and often made them fair horns, which they wore about all the city, sometimes all their life. Very often also upon the women's hoods would he stick, in the hind-part, somewhat made in the shape of a man's member. In another he had a great many little horns full of fleas and lice, which he borrowed from the beggars of St. Innocent, and cast them with small canes or quills to write with, into the necks of the daintiest gentlewomen that he could find, yea even in the church . . . [etc., etc.] [2]

---

[2] *The Works of Rabelais,* Bk. II, chap. 16, Urquhart translation (New York: Bibliophilist Society, n.d.), pp. 169–70.

Why, one may ask, is the irreverent Panurge, as well as Pantagruel, needed in Rabelais' satire? Pantagruel is the ideal of the Rabelaisian world view. The opening chapters of the *Pantagruel* (1532) connect the book itself with the *Bible* and Pantagruel with a Christ-like genealogy, emphasizing the parchedness of the earth before his birth and the omens surrounding his nativity; the implication is that he is going to be another Savior and his birth a Second Coming to present a new way of life that will ameliorate the stupid rigidity of present ways. His cry for drink and his philosophy of wine-bibbery are answers to the dryness of the earth, as his gigantic size suggests the unbounded potential of the human being. But the characteristic associated with his name (and later utilized in his war with the Dipsodes), is thirst-provoking, imbuing men with an unquenchable "thirst for knowledge" or a "thirst for learning." Stimulation, wine, imagination, and the irrational are the progressive correctives Pantagruel offers to a stifling scholasticism.

The direction of Rabelais' satire is established almost at once by the problem of Gargantua's reaction to the simultaneous birth of a son and death of a wife; his alternate laughing and weeping argue that human experience is too complex and unformulable to be fitted into the standard reaction of either laughter or tears. Do not oversimplify, Rabelais says; be like Gargantua who recognizes both sides. And in the next chapter the baby Pantagruel carries on the theme with his refusal to remain confined in his cradle. Once unchained, "he took his cradle, and broke it into more than five hundred thousand pieces, with one blow of his fist that he struck in the midst of it, swearing that he would never come into it again" (Bk. II, chap. 4).

What then of Panurge? Significantly, he comes upon the scene immediately after Gargantua's famous letter to his son (Bk. II, chap. 8), the manifesto of humanism and the positive statement of the values for which Pantagruel stands. Following this statement of freedom, comes the human-sized Panurge into the story of the giants, ragged and hungry yet showing off his knowledge of a dozen languages before he will get around to saying in plain, comprehensible French that he is starving. Here is "mental freedom for its own sake," as Leo Spitzer has said, "the mind that frees itself from outward reality by building up a world of fancy for its own pleasure . . . [and] self-enjoyment of resourcefulness in the abstract, detached from reality."[3] It is more important, however, to see Panurge as the Pantagruelian qualities carried beyond the ideal of Pantagruel to their utmost extreme. In Pantagruel they are projected into a vague inference about potentialities and the future; in the insurgent Panurge, they are rather a tool for disrupting the comfortable assumptions of the complacent. That Panurge is not intended simply as a rogue, in spite of the appalling acts he performs, is clear from his explicit associations with the Pantagruelian life-force, as when he brings Epistemon back to life by an application from one of the innumerable vials he carries in his bulging coat.

His function is brought out in his debate with Thaumast (Bk. II, chap. 18), in which the world of logic and reason (so refined that it cannot be put into words) is defeated by the vulgar but real world of Panurge's gestures. But in the story of the married lady of Paris whom he treats so shockingly (chaps. 21, 22), he carries the Pantagruelian assumptions to the extreme statement that life is copulation with anybody at any time. Rabelais hardly intends to offer this as his ideal; rather, the extreme is necessary to make people like the lady of Paris stop and revaluate their most commonly accepted assumptions such as the inviolability of marriage. The lady is herself guilty in that, presented with the phenomenon of Panurge and his disgraceful proposition, she cannot react with a flexibility to match his. The scene reveals the lady's conventionality and her inability to cope with any experience that is not codified. The ideal is the complexity of life, and Panurge, with his sinuous and wicked vitality, is its agent. However morally wrong Panurge's action, it forces the reader to stop and question his values; his knavery exposes

[3] See Leo Spitzer, "The Works of Rabelais," in *Literary Masterpieces of the Western World,* ed. Francis H. Horn (Baltimore, Md.: The Johns Hopkins Press, 1953), p. 137. As he points out, Panurge is essentially Pantagruel's Falstaff (p. 129). See also Erich Auerbach, *Mimesis* (Princeton, N.J.: Princeton University Press, 1953), pp. 262–74.

a folly which, in terms of Rabelais' humanistic assumptions, is worse than knavery.

Panurge's relation to Pantagruel can be seen in his indecent suggestion for making safe the walls of Paris (chap. 15). The point of the scene is that walls only cramp and confine. The ideal, as stated by Pantagruel, is the city that does not need any, its men being its walls. In Paris, however, Panurge reminds him, men are not to be had so easily. The cheapest commodity, even cheaper than bricks, is the female pudendum. From a criticism of the quality of Parisian men and soldiers, he turns to the looseness of morals of Parisian women. His elaborate project for securing the walls is simply a more outrageous statement of Pantagruel's ideal, one which takes into account human realities. As an extension of Pantagruel, Panurge's function can reach from the verbal witticism concerning the walls of Paris to the physical discomfort of the lady of Paris, and ultimately to the literal destruction of Dindinault and all his sheep (Bk. IV, chaps. 7, 8). Each sheep dumbly following the leader and plunging to his death, followed by Dindinault (Dingdong in Urquhart's translation) and his shepherds, is the perfect symbol of the rigidity of behavior which Rabelais attacks. But a Panurge is also necessary to cast overboard the first ram that starts the procession and to stand "on the gunnel of the ship, with an oar in his hand, not to help them, you may swear, but to keep them from swimming to the ship, and saving themselves from drowning."

The violence of Panurge subsides when Rabelais goes back to the story of Gargantua (Bk. I, composed in 1534, after Bk. II). Here he creates a plot concerning the tiny man Picrochole, heading sheeplike to his destruction by declaring and pressing war on the benevolent giant, "the good old man," Grandgousier, who, "after supper, warmeth his ballocks by a good, clear, great fire, and whilst his chestnuts are a roasting, is very serious in drawing scratches on the hearth with a stick burned at one end, wherewith they did stir up the fire, telling to his wife and the rest of the family, pleasant old stories and tales of former times" (chap. 28). Rabelais does not mean to suggest that he is opposing the *new* to the *old;* to the charge of revolutionary satirist he would answer that the truth promulgated by Pantagruel, like that of Christ, was not a new truth but as old as the hills. Old Grandgousier by the fire sums up this side of Rabelais' argument. Like Nature itself, Grandgousier has set up Picrochole as a ruler and he bends over backwards to prevent war, the giant humbling himself to the mite. But when Picrochole continues on his single-minded way, Grandgousier and his son Gargantua dispense with him by a single slap. The action is epitomized in all the flexible, fantastic characters who are on Grandgousier's side against the rigid, mechanical men on Picrochole's: for example, Gymnast who vaults about, on and off and around his horse, and then slays the stupefied soldiers of Picrochole who are unable to cope with such a phenomenon.

If one method Rabelais uses is to introduce a disruptive agent who will search out the conventional and give it battle, another is to oppose the two values and, letting the forces of reaction act as the aggressor, show their inevitable and ludicrous destruction. In either case the central aim of Rabelais' satire is to shake up accepted values, to surprise and shock. The constantly shifting scale of size, with Pantagruel one moment so large that cities can be contained in the crevices of his teeth and the next small enough for conversation with normal-sized men, contributes to the effect. If Lucian establishes a point of view from such a height that the distance itself is more important than the pattern detected (indeed, he is too far up to detect any pattern and accordingly attacks the pattern man imposes on his own experience), Rabelais uses the other extreme and, like Juvenal, buries his reader in the minutiae of experience, but with the opposite aim from Juvenal's (or Apuleius'). Even the narrator's style expresses the aim: by his endless lists he implies the similarity between all things, by their heterogeneity the messiness and complexity of things that cannot, as the scholastic believed, be categorized and separated and differentiated in an orderly manner. By his enormous vocabulary, his invented words, and the extreme particularity and thinginess of his descriptions he asserts that the real—the corrective—is disorder.

It is appropriate that Rabelais has adapted to his purposes

the action of the chivalric romance. His first two books, *Gargantua* and *Pantagruel,* break down into the same series of events: the hero's genealogy, birth, and education, leading up to his quest (a war). The general movement toward education and the knightly quest is even carried on in Pantagruel's voyage to fight the Dipsodes, which serves to link the geographical discoveries of the time with the Pantagruelian opening up of new vistas and Pantagruel's own expansion in experience and knowledge and wisdom. The climax of *Pantagruel* is the discovery by a normal-sized man of a new world inside Pantagruel's mouth—a suggestion of all the other worlds like his own, and with as much claim to precedence.

While Lucian's satire remains largely a mechanism of ingenious exposition, Rabelais' expresses a world view. The "world in Pantagruel's mouth" (cf. Lucian's *True History*) is *both* a way of forcing upon the reader a new perspective *and* a picture of the new complexity of the world that was being revealed by explorers, scientists, and philosophers. Rabelais is furthest from Lucian when his emphasis falls on the disruption itself—on Panurge's bulging coat and his crushing pleasantries. At times he gives specific statement to these values, vague as they may be, in the projected Abbey of Thélème or Gargantua's letter to his son. But there is always a tendency in his satire for Panurge's folly-exposing technique to become central. The satire of Rabelais is accordingly very different from the Juvenalian satire in which the vice holds and hogs the center of the stage. Here the Aristophanic explosion of energy as corrective is close to the center; in Rabelais, if not in Lucian, it loses its function as expository device and becomes at times an active symbol of the good.

Rabelais can be taken to represent one phase of the humanist revival—the clearing away of the old, useless, and dangerous. Dryden, Swift, and Pope, coming nearly two hundred years later, represent a later phase that reacted against the excessive freedom and individualism that had replaced the excessive order. While Swift, for example, admired Rabelais' satire, he was opposed to the freedom Rabelais advocated, which for him was equally manifested in the radical Protestant's search for a private salvation and in his search for wealth and property. The focus of religion and morality, Swift argued in his satires, had narrowed from man's awareness of his subordinate position in a structure of duties and responsibilities to other men, to a single concern with himself, with his entertainment, his personality, and his thoughts. Man's freedom and the complexity of his experience are fine as correctives, but pernicious when called the ideal and honored.[4]

These satirists came after a period of upheaval and civil war that seemed to sum up all the dangers of uninhibited human freedom. When Charles I's head fell it was not simply a matter of replacing a king but one of questioning the very concept of kingship, of denying its divinity, and therefore the sanctity of the social structure itself. The Treaty of Westphalia, a year before Charles' execution, sanctioned a divided world, part Protestant and part Catholic; and the idea of one single truth, one answer, was seriously questioned. The more radical Protestant sects that had been let loose in England by the Civil War ultimately advocated a private truth for each man, or, as Milton put it, every man his own church. Faced with these facts, the Augustan satirists were led to reverse the Rabelaisian fiction, making a Panurge figure an evil force and the imitation of chaotic reality the evil he is trying to bring about.

At the same time, they learned many of their techniques from the humanists while reacting against them ideologically. The imitative method of Ulrich von Hutton, the ironic impersonations of Erasmus, and the Rabelaisian transformation of Lucianic devices, all contributed to their satire and supported their central concern in the image of evil. Most important for our purposes, however, is the change from the emphatic hero figure like Pantagruel to an even more emphatic villain figure in the great Augustan satires, and finally the furtive return to a satirist as hero. The ambiguity of Pantagruel's friend Panurge as a

[4] For an interesting statement of the relationship between these two phases of satire, see Jeffrey Hart, "The Ideologue as Artist," *Criticism*, II (1960), 133.

moral agent, still largely rhetorical in Rabelais, prepares us for the metaphysical ambiguity of his reverse, the Augustan villain.

The Satyr-Satirist and Augustan Realism

The Elizabethan was an age of expanding individualism, with the forces of the new and the old engaging in skirmishes on a more equal footing than in the time of Rabelais. Ancients and moderns fought each other with each other's weapons, and though Thomas Nashe was on the side of the ancients his Jacke Wilton (*The Unfortunate Traveller,* 1594) was almost as expansively modern as Panurge. Jacke's attitude toward life is, like Lazaro's, realistic: he accepts the sluttish Diamante and her love for what they are; he has no false illusions about glory and honor. But unlike Lazaro, he sees through his hidalgo master (the Earl of Surrey) and ridicules the absurdities of his courtly behavior with words and occasionally with deeds. While Surrey romanticizes Diamante Jacke makes her his mistress, explaining: "My master beate the bush and kept a coyle and a pratling, but I caught the birde."[5] Even here Nashe relies more heavily on the Rabelaisian verbal violence than on the violence of situation. The cruel pranks Jacke plays on the greedy victualler and the cowardly captain are punctuated by word play and by words simply tumbling over words ("This great Lord," he says, referring to the victualler's pretensions, "this worthie Lord, this noble Lord . . . Lord haue mercie vpon vs" [p. 210]). The satire, as the book progresses, is almost wholly verbal, and in general the behavior and action of characters are subordinated to the old *satura* fiction of an observer's description and contemplation.

In an age like the Elizabethan it is reasonable to expect a central interest in the satirist as a personality—an interest reflected in the predominance of tragedy as a genre (as opposed to the Augustan Age's interest in the epic as genre and in satire as a study of deviation, not of a hero). To the Elizabethans, as

[5] *The Works of Thomas Nashe,* ed. R. B. McKerrow (London: Sidgwick & Wackson, 1910), II, 263.

Alvin Kernan has said, satire meant essentially the satirist, the creating of "the correct personality to deliver the attack."[6] They were interested in the satirist as a man, a consciousness, an individualist posed against stock types (often in the sense of the Rabelaisian rigidity). The object of attack was indeed so conventional that some of its stock types were totally unrelated to Elizabethan realities; and its satire was naturally regarded by the Augustans as an academic exercise rather than a practical tool for reform. The only part that bears much analysis or makes much sense is the satirist and his way of seeing.

In some periods the satirist is utilized in only his most general, normative, and publicly accepted aspects, and the scene he is describing receives the emphasis. When the scene loses its importance, and the satirist steps forward, the convention is seen in close-up and his private life, questions of his excessive rage, and his obsession with vice, become matters of primary interest. In the *satura* of Joseph Hall, John Marston, and their imitators, by far the most important components were the vituperative style and the "satyr-satirist" who served as mouthpiece. The figure of the satirist was a version of the Juvenalian idealist who represents an older and now overthrown order; but for the Elizabethans he became a disillusioned down-and-outer who could recognize the most private vices in others because he knew them in himself, who ranted at his equally vicious but more successful (and he believed less worthy) contemporaries.

The Elizabethan satirists, following the Renaissance etymology, believed that satire came from the Greek *satyra* and the satyr play (one of Dryden's aims in his *Discourse Concerning the Original and Progress of Satire* was to correct this notion). Since satire was thought of as uttered by a crude satyr, half man and half goat, it followed that the style and subject matter should be appropriate to him. The savage indignation of Juvenal and

---

[6] Kernan, *The Cankered Muse,* p. 141. I am indebted to Kernan's study of the satyr-satirist in this section; see also O. J. Campbell, *Comical Satyre and Shakespeare's Troilus and Cressida* (San Marino, Cal.: Huntington Library, 1938); and Eugene Waith, *The Pattern of Tragicomedy in Beaumont and Fletcher* (New Haven, Conn.: Yale University Press, 1952).

the obscurity of Persius—Silver Age satirists—seemed the most appropriate models. But in their use of harsh meters, coarse and slangy language, their concentration on the scatalogical and obscene, the Elizabethans went beyond their models. If the satyr-satirist is, in a sense, an extension of the ass's-eye view of Lucius and Lazarillo de Tormes, the stressing of his Juvenalian heritage produces purple passages and vague and romantic images of evil, often borrowed directly from the Silver Age and hardly applicable to Elizabethan London. Luscus, the satyr-satirist tells us,

> hath his Ganymede,
> His perfumed she-goat, smooth-kemb'd and high fed.
> At Hogson now his monstrous love he feasts,
> For there he keeps a bawdy-house of beasts.

A portrait of a dandy, possibly homosexual, ends with the non sequitur: "Is this a man? Nay, an incarnate devil, / That struts in vice and glorieth in evil." And another is said to be

> a maggot that doth swarm
> In tainted flesh, whose foul corruption
> Is his fair food: whose generation
> Another's ruin.[7]

The satirist's pose was made especially clear by his transference to the stage. The induction to *Every Man Out of his Humour* (1598) is simply echoing many formal verse satires of the time when it exclaims:

> Ile strip the ragged follies of the time,
> Naked, as at their birth . . .
> . . . and with a whip of steele,
> Print wounding lashes in their yron ribs
>
> > (ll. 17–18, 19–20).

And later Asper cries, "Well I will scourge those apes" (l. 117). The literal-mindedness of the transferers forced them to make

---

[7] *The Works of John Marston*, ed. A. H. Bullen (Boston, Mass.: 1887), III, 319, 345, 346.

the satirist a physical chastiser who went about beating or playing pranks upon his enemies.

The Elizabethan satirists' rationale for this cruel, lecherous, envious, melancholic figure can be seen by comparison with the Puritan Robert Crowley's view of satire: "I bark at your fauts, but loth I am to byt, / If by this barkyng ought myght be won."[8] The biting satirist like Hall or Marston argued that things *are* so bad now that one can only bite, can only be sure some good is done when he displeases. As Hall says, "Go to then ye my sacred *Sermones,* / And please me more, the more ye do displease." The corollary is that only a relatively corrupt man can point out this immitigable corruption. Marston claims that it requires "such squint-eyed sight" as his satirist's to "strike the world's deformities so right." The personal motives educed to explain his peculiar behavior are accordingly not pleasant; they run from sadism ("Vexe all the world, so that thy selfe be pleas'd") to the most emphasized motive, envy: "Envie belike incites his pining heart, / And bids it sate itself with others smart."[9]

We must always be wary when dealing with a convention. It may be a meaningful part of a fictive structure, but it also may be only a reflex on the poet's part which has lost any real meaning (the tendency to fall into conventions when he grows tired); or it can be a smoke screen to conceal the poet's personal motives or idiosyncrasies. A reading of Marston's satire shows that (whatever his theory) the effect of an overemphasis on the satirist is to make him more important than his satire. While his diction grows more striking, his personality more curious, the scene he describes becomes blurred, and without any clear norm of behavior indicated, the reader flounders. The satirist becomes an end in himself. One can understand the Augustans'

---

[8] *The Select Works of Robert Crowley,* ed. J. M. Cowper (Early English Text Society, 1872), p. 55.

[9] *The Collected Poems of Joseph Hall,* ed. A. Davenport (Liverpool, England: Liverpool University Press, 1949), p. 51; Marston, *Works,* III, 343; and Hall, *Poems,* p. 60.

doubt as to whether the intention and effect of Marston's work is really satiric at all, or whether he merely uses satire as a device for entertaining. This is a fine point since all satire contains elements of both instruction and entertainment; but it is a very special kind of satire in which entertainment values predominate.

The satiric protagonist, judging by the examples so far observed, can be said to fall somewhere along a spectrum: (1) a hero-satirist, (2) not a hero but in some sense normative, (3) an excess, even bad, but a necessary corrective (and so in some periods registered as a good), (4) a fool or knave, but used as a device for catching worse (at this point he has become unquestionably involved in the image of evil), (5) *the* fool or knave. Panurge is thus more a corrective agent than a satirist, but he falls within the positive pole of the satire, and is perpetuated in satirists like Nashe's Jacke Wilton, and perhaps even Marston's Kinsayder, who are Rabelaisian in their verbal pyrotechnics, their insulting and injuring, but not in function (if indeed Kinsayder has a function). From Rabelais to the Augustans is essentially a movement from (1) (Pantagruel) to (5) on the satiric spectrum.

The self-styled hero-satirist of Marston led only by a kind of ironic inversion to the Augustans; he led directly to the tragic satirist-heroes of Webster, Marston himself, and Shakespeare. In the hands of Jonson, however, he became a villain-satirist (4), a Volpone or Mosca, a Subtle or Face, who resembles Reynard the Fox more closely than Panurge, but nevertheless retains something of the Elizabethan tragic hero. Volpone's fall is made to appear a parody of a tragic fall, but it also draws attention to his closer resemblance to Marlowe's Tamburlaine and Barrabas than to Dryden's Achitophel and Swift's Grub Street Hack. He is still within the general ambiance of Panurge and the Renaissance hero. By the time of the Restoration versions of Volpone, Wycherley's Horner and Manly, the emphasis has shifted to the satiric object, and yet both retain enough of the normative (in manners if not in morals) to have caused Jeremy Collier concern. But in Wycherley's case the dramatic conventions may have interfered with satiric effect, and so we must return to the main tradition of seventeenth century satire for a more radical transformation of the Elizabethan satyr-satirist.

First, however, we should note that the convention of the satyr-satirist's vituperation did not disappear, although its Elizabethan excesses went underground (surviving in popular broadsides and the like). To the extent that the practical satirist of the Restoration needed to lift up a stone and express disgust at what he found, the "byting" style survived; and Rochester's use of the diction and form in his *Satyr against Mankind* served as a link between the Elizabethans and the Swift of *The Legion Club*. Writing at the height of the Popish Plot scare, shortly before Dryden wrote (for the opposite side) *Absalom and Achitophel*, John Oldham explains that the old vituperative tone is the only appropriate one to such times as these:

> Tis pointed satire, and the sharps of wit
> For such a prize are th' only weapons fit:
> Nor needs there art, or genius, here to use,
> Where indignation can create a muse.

All the old characteristics are again present in Oldham's *Satyrs upon the Jesuits* (1679): no time for art, ruggedness of versification, irregular rhythm, crabbed syntax, and jangling off-rhymes. The transitions from subject to subject are rapid and more forceful than logical. No one pretends, says Oldham in his preface, "that Juvenal, when he is lashing vice and villainy, should flow as smoothly as Ovid or Tibullus, when they are describing amours and gallantries, and have nothing to disturb the ruffle and evenness of their style." He refers to his pen as a weapon, his ink as gall, wormwood, vinegar, or acid:

> All this urge on my rank envenom'd spleen,
> And with keen satire edge my stabbing pen,
> That its each home-set thrust their blood may draw,
> Each drop of ink like aquafortis gnaw.
> Red hot with vengeance thus, I'll brand disgrace
> So deep, no time shall e'er the marks deface. . . .

Oldham uses this sort of diction as the best equivalent to the indignation felt at seeing ugly truth revealed. Both the convention of the satyr-satirist and the technique of travesty thus persisted in the party of the opposition, but Oldham was part if not parcel òf the Augustan Age, and in other satires—for example, *The Careless Good Fellow*—he demonstrates a sophisticated sense of parody. And in the first and third of the *Satyrs upon the Jesuits,* which show the Jesuit without his mask, he puts the old rant of the satyr-satirist into the mouth of his villain, Garnet, an instigator of the Gunpowder Plot:

> Thrice damn'd be that Apostate Monk [Luther],
>   from whom
> Sprung first these Enemies of Us, and Rome:
> Whose pois'nous Filth, dropt from ingend'ring Brain,
> By monstrous Birth did the vile Insects spawn,
> Which now infest each Country, and defile
> With their o'respreading swarms this goodly Ile.[10]

According to Oldham's fiction (still essentially part of his strategy of travesty) the ghostly or dying Jesuit, with nothing more to fear, exposes his own villainy, passes on to his followers all that he has concealed during a lifetime of deceit; and his language is accordingly as full of envy, vengeance, and hatred as the satyr-satirist's. The language that always sounded excessive in the mouth of a supposedly sane satirist, helps to characterize the Jesuit's insane zeal.

To the Augustan satirist the railing of the satyr-satirist seemed as indecorous as the enthusiasm of a religious fanatic: it clearly told more about the ranter than about the objects against which he ranted. "How easy is it to call rogue and villain, and that wittily!" wrote Dryden, referring to all the overly direct modes of expression in satire. "But how hard to make a man appear a fool, a blockhead, or a knave, without using any of

---

[10] 2d. ed. (1682), pp. 2, 4, 12. Oldham parodies other styles as well; for example, the rant of the Elizabethan hero-villain (Jonson's Catiline or Marlowe's Barrabas) which, coming from Garnet, sounds like this:

> Lug by the ears the doting *Prelates* thence,
> Dash *Heresie* together with their Brains
> Out of their shatter'd heads. (p. 19)

those opprobrious terms!" The Augustan satirist's aim, he said, is "to spare the grossness of the names, and to do the thing yet more severely."[11]

One way was to let the enemy condemn himself. Dryden was influenced in his solution by his friend Oldham; but both drew on the satire of John Cleveland, John Denham, and the other satirists who drew pen on the Royalist side in the Civil War, and who did much to break down the rigid conventions of the academic satire of the Elizabethans with its panoramic catalog form and its excessive and uniform indignation. They were essentially propagandists whose public included every class and who employed whatever means best served the particular occasion. Popular appeal and persuasive effectiveness were of necessity the primary objects in those dangerous times, and so writers were stimulated to produce an amazing variety of new forms. There was obviously no occasion for the elephantine form of *satura,* but rather for short, sharp jabs; the great catalogs of conventional vices were gradually replaced by the short satire of the single point. The characteristic shared by all of these forms was the drift away from the disreputable satyr-satirist and his simple invective toward ever more indirect approaches—parody, travesty, analogy, and various kinds of imitation.

We can take as an example the Metaphysical style that seemed as indecorous to the Augustan poet as did the curse to the Augustan satirist. The comic possibilities of excess were played upon by Cleveland, who may have drawn for his inspiration on his own earlier work. When he tried to explain his reaction to Edward King's death (1638), he had written:

Mine [eyes] weep down pious beads, but why should I
Confine them to the Muse's rosary?
I am no poet here; my pen's the spout
Where the rain-water of mine eyes runs out. . . .[12]

[11] Dryden, *Discourse Concerning the Original and Progress of Satire* (1693), in *The Poetical Works of Dryden,* ed. George R. Noyes (Boston, Mass.: Houghton Mifflin, 1950), p. 313.

[12] *Minor Poets of the Caroline Period,* ed. George Saintsbury (Oxford: Clarendon Press, 1921), III, 26.

The poet presumably means to suggest the artlessness of his elegy: his pen merely relieves the pressure of sorrow and channels it as a downspout does a heavy rain. But the reader cannot help noticing the disvaluing effect that results from speaking of a spiritual matter in grotesquely physical terms, comparing his inspiration to a downspout and his sorrow to rainwater. The relationship established between tears and the beads of a rosary, ink, and rainwater are so tenuous that they cast the gravest doubts upon the poet's feelings about King.

When such ingenuity is attached to a Puritan, made an example of his perverting imagination, it becomes a brilliant satiric symbol of enthusiasm that suggests at the same time the possibility of hypocrisy. The specific object of Cleveland's attack was the Puritan state of mind, which led by its uncompromising logic to revolution and anarchy. And so when possible he took the equation from the enemy's own lips: the "etc." at the end of the oath the Presbyterians were supposed to take concealed, they feared, a host of dangers for them. Starting with the analogy that emerges from the enemy's words, he works outward, multiplying comparisons until he has created the enormous monster grown out of the tiny "etc." that suggests the wild imaginations of the Puritans who have also created a monster out of good King Charles. In the seventeenth and eighteenth centuries satirists saw that the Metaphysical conceit was of the essence of satire. With the tenor and the vehicle just a little further apart than Donne's parted lovers and compasses, economic security becomes the eating of babies. The basic Augustan strategy follows: the violent yoking of disparate objects, with the irony that some fool or knave does (like the Metaphysical poet) see them as a unity. The satirist and the reader see the disparity. The mock-heroic is only the commonest of these metaphors that bring together two violently different orders of value or of society and have a fool or knave say (or think) they are similar.

Parody was the most effective device for attacking a specific enemy (as opposed to the conventionalized villains of Elizabethan satire), and in particular for exposing the Puritan state of mind. The rigid logic that leads where it will, the alleged hypocrisy of the Puritan, made almost inevitable a form in which the speaker unintentionally damns himself by his own words. Only a step removed from Cleveland's satire is the device of the liturgy or hymn, the prayer or sermon, under whose solemn cadences the Puritan "speaker" unconsciously reveals his impiety, avarice, lechery, and sedition. Another alternative was to put the Puritan "saint" into the Biblical context he asked for—perhaps the story of Moses leading the Israelites out of Egypt, in which he claimed to see a type of his own situation—and let the reader observe the discrepancy. Through a whole spectrum of such devices the Puritan's pious protestations were contrasted with his destructive deeds and his questionable motives.

Beginning with the problem of the disreputable satirist, we can see what has happened. The Elizabethans employed a satirist who attacks corruption out of jealousy—one hypocrite attacking another who happens to be more successful. In effect, a reader might conclude that he uses the rationale of the satirist to justify his envy and bitterness, to conceal his own vices (and such a figure may have contributed to the villain of Augustan satire). The Augustan reaction was to sidestep the issue by changing the focus to the culprit—removing the satirist from the fiction except as an ironic, and so detached, uncontaminated observer. Dryden's satiric speaker remains outside the culprit, but taking the culprit's own view of himself and praising him, he raises no questions about his own (the satirist's) motives.

During the Augustan period English practice transformed irony from a strictly rhetorical device to a vehicle of psychological and cognitive meaning. The transition appears in the development from local or incidental irony to a sustained point of view, and from irony operative on an idea to that operative on a character. The Augustan sense of decorum, which included consistency, must have played an important part in curtailing the use of irony as a local effect. One of Norman Knox's conclusions in his valuable study of irony is that "people became increasingly conscious that irony could be the informing principle of a fairly long piece of writing, and in such writing they saw the necessity of sustaining both the ironic point of view and the ironic mask to the end."[13] Consistency leads to a greater sense of probability; and extended through many lines or pages, the irony appears to be less a device for persuasion than a point of view brought to bear on reality. A further convention of Augustan decorum insisted that the proper ironic pose is one of mock gravity. The pose of the incidental ironist was characteristically accompanied by the curled lip, "that laughing sneer" which a correspondent to *The Gentleman's Magazine* uses to prove that Christ was not an ironist, or "the malignant Grin" to which Thomas Gordon refers.[14] Shaftesbury and the Augustans in general associated this sneer with controversial irony, preferring for higher flights the grave irony of Cervantes and Swift, which in practice was usually the high burlesque or mock-heroic—a form of blame by praise which relies heavily on a pose of fairness.

But if the ironic pose, when consistently applied to experience, may earn the reader's confidence and belief, it may also create a kind of psychological verisimilitude when consistently applied to a character. From Dryden onward there is a relentlessly humanizing tendency in irony: simple concession (accepting the opponent's point of view), fallacious argument, and high burlesque (the last two mad extensions of the enemy's own logic) are all moving in the direction of a dramatic imitation of the enemy—allowing him to speak for himself, or take himself at his own evaluation—and so toward the presentation of character rather than abstract idea.

The Quixote Fiction

Cervantes was considered in the eighteenth century to be "father and unrivalled model of the true mock-heroic," and the usual example cited for consistency and the sustaining of irony

[13] *The Word Irony and its Context, 1500–1755* (Durham, N.C.: Duke University Press, 1961), p. 185.

[14] *Gentleman's Magazine*, XX (1751), 456; Gordon, *Humorist* II (1725), 96–105; cited by Knox, pp. 117, 143.

through a whole work.[15] Cervantes' irony in *Don Quixote* (1605) was essentially dramatic, embodied in a character, his speeches being opposed to his actions. The irony lies in accepting the premise of chivalry, that the world is full of giants and forlorn maidens, and playing it out against real windmills and country wenches. And when the irony is embodied in an old scarecrow of a man who thinks he is a knight, the two parts of the irony tend to become his illusion and his real situation—as it is with his Augustan equivalents, Hudibras, Shadwell, Shaftesbury, and the rest.

If we step back, we can see that *Don Quixote* offered the satirist fictional embodiments of both the basic rhetorical techniques of anti-romance, which Boileau summed up as "Didon et Enee parloient comme des harengeres et des crocheteurs" and "une horlogère et un horloger parlent comme Didon et Enee"; later James Beattie labeled these burlesque and mock-heroic, and still later they were called travesty and mock-heroic or low and high burlesque.[16] Fielding in the preface to *Joseph Andrews* (1742) defined them as "appropriating the manners of the highest to the lowest, or *è converso.*"

Cervantes produces the basic situation embodying travesty when he places an idealist in an antithetical, unidealized world; the knight errant acts and speaks in the idiom of the rickety old man on the pathetic mare, suffering from real hunger and exhaustion, among real shepherds and windmills. His idealistic picture of the world is contradicted by the realistic consequences of whippings, broken heads, and scattered flocks of sheep.

But if Quixote himself is a travesty of the romance hero, the situation in which Cervantes places him is mock-heroic—the particular prototype and model for much of the mock-heroic satire of the Augustans. He is an ordinary gentleman of a decayed family who, taking seriously the teaching of the romances

---

[15] Joseph Warton, *Essay on Pope* (1806), I, 242–43; cited by Knox, p. 168. See also Knox, p. 176.

[16] Boileau, *Oeuvres* (1824), II, 165; Beattie, *Essays* (ed. 1778), p. 396; Richmond P. Bond, *English Burlesque Poetry, 1700–1750* (Cambridge, Mass.: Harvard University Press, 1932).

he reads, gets the idea that he, like his ancestors, is a knight errant. The aspiration of the romance code is embodied in his delusion or insanity. The mock-heroic contrast is not between the ideal and the petty reality but between a man's mistaken idea of himself and the real man. Cervantes' mock-heroic embodiment demonstrates forcibly that if a contemporary were seriously to imitate the courtly ideals of the romances he read he would become both ridiculous and dangerous. The romance itself escaped being ridiculous only because its world was synchronized with the idealized code of manners it presented. In that world love *was* the source of all actions and giants *did* lie in wait. The Cervantean anti-romance reproduced the ideal code of conduct, but placed it as a mock-heroic delusion in a real and unsynchronized world.

Don Quixote contained, in fact, the single most important satiric fiction of the seventeenth and eighteenth centuries. It is fruitless to seek close parallels with Rabelais' fiction (Panurge equals Quixote? Panurge equals the real world?), but the intention of questioning outmoded patterns of thought, the technique of confronting romance with realism, and the ambiguous attitude toward the protagonist were the same. In order to attack the Spanish penchant for living in the past—out of romances of chivalry so to speak—Cervantes resorted to the picaresque fiction of punishment, but he made of punishment a normative action, a consequence that demonstrates and defines Quixote's folly. The Don is sent sprawling by the blades of a windmill as a physical reminder that a windmill is not a giant, and the beatings and purgings he suffers along the road are tastes of reality opposed to his delusion of knight-errantry.

But if punishment in the picaresque tends to incriminate the punisher, the effect is yet more disturbing when it is meted out to an elderly gentleman, quite out of his wits, who has the best intentions behind his every act: such factors complicated no earlier satire. It is not to the point to argue here whether *Don Quixote* is indeed satire or comedy, but only to notice that the balancing of illusion against reality, the most important characteristic of the Cervantean anti-romance, was used by later satirists as a means of catching and exposing more than one kind of folly or knavery at the same time. If Quixote is a dangerously deluded fool, the people he meets are as dangerously *un*deluded; his impossibly high, and unfashionable, standards illuminate their purely selfish ones. The opposite of the hungry, prudent picaro, Quixote's motto is that man cannot live on bread alone.

As a satiric paradigm, the Quixote figure is radically ambiguous. He can be used as a sick madman who has become infatuated with some idea, whether by reading too many romances, or (as Swift will use it) reading too many modern authors, or by accepting hook-line-and-sinker some sharper's project. He is not evil, but he reflects evil through his obtuseness—the knaves being either the romance-writers or the exploiters he meets on his journey. This madman can just as easily become the selfish egoist who tries to make over the world in his own image. His madness may even have a tinge of hypocrisy as with Samuel Butler's Hudibras. In both instances, however, the point is the folly and futility of his quest, proved by his accidents and mishaps. He *cannot* turn windmills into giants or an inn into a castle.

But the madman can also become the reverse, a victim, and so illuminate the people who expose him; or he can even become God's fool and an ideal of honor or simplicity against which the real world is measured and found lacking. It is not too much to say that he contains within himself something of the spirit of Erasmus' Folly, whose radical ambiguity is more directly aimed rhetorically at a clearing-away of Scholastic debris.[17] As so many of his eighteenth-century imitators recognized, Quixote can be turned into the satirist as knight-errant, the ruined exemplar of an earlier and better age. These interpretations all appear, and sometimes simultaneously, in *Don Quixote*. Its imitators produce figures as different as Hudibras and Parson Adams, Geoffrey Wildgoose and Walter Shandy, seen from the Augustan and latitudinarian points of view respectively. Here was a figure who,

[17] For a discussion of Erasmus' Folly in his *Praise of Folly,* see my *Theme and Structure in Swift's 'Tale of a Tub'* (New Haven, Conn.: Yale University Press, 1960), pp. 79–80, 249–53.

turned one way, is a wicked madman, a prototype of the Augustan villain; turned the other way, a satrist-hero.

As corollaries to his two-sidedness, three important fictive elements were educed, of which we shall hear more later. (1) A dupe who, without entirely understanding them, has read all the books of romance and sets out to promulgate their doctrine, or at any rate live by their precepts. (2) A mob of people who react blindly and irrationally to this threat, and so expose the sordidness of their own gross reality. (3) The knaves who exploit the Quixotic dupe for their own purposes, understanding something of the nature of his malady—his romanticism, his pride, his folly; they may simply use him for entertainment, or they may exploit him in more actively vicious ways.

In the satires that followed Cervantes' example in the seventeenth century the mitigations of Quixote's behavior were the first elements to disappear with his age, decrepitude, and good intentions. Most of Cervantes' imitators, especially in the France of Louis XIV, did not wish their readers to sympathize with this disruptive agent. Not too remote from Quixote is the dwarf Ragotin in Scarron's *Roman comique* (1651), who, aspiring to the life of an actor and the love of a prima donna is in consequence beaten, humiliated, tortured, and finally drowned. But whereas in *Don Quixote* the beatings point out the supremacy of hard reality over the hero's dream, in the *Roman comique* they represent an externalization of Ragotin's essentially mean and unheroic being.

Toward the end of Part II (1657) of the *Roman comique,* Ragotin has an unfortunate encounter with some gypsies.[18] He promptly gives evidence of "his natural pride" and choler (he "began to be extremely angry, as little men soonest are") ; then, showing off, he drinks too much (a little man presuming to be a big one), and when he is thoroughly muddled he sets off alone on his mule. Presently the drink takes effect: he falls off his mule, vomits, and passes out. A madman strips him of his clothes, the sun scorches and insects sting his body. The madman's rela-

---

[18] Paul Scarron, *Le Roman comique,* chap. xvi, trans. Tom Brown, *et al.* in *The Comical Romance, and Other Tales* (1700; London, 1892), I, 290–99.

tives arrive, mistake Ragotin for their kinsman, and bind him
and haul him away in a wagon. The wagon turns over, dumping
Ragotin in a muddy slough. He manages to get out and run
away "his body all besmeared and bruised, his mouth dry and
gaping like to the parched earth, his head heavy and dull, and
his arms pinioned behind his back." He is again bothered by
flies. He encounters some nuns whose coach has overturned and
whose priest, trying to keep Ragotin at bay, "with a great deal
of gravity and decorum" asks him how he got this way. Ragotin
answers "very saucily" (reasserting his dignity, though this is
hardly the time or place), and adds injury to insult by toppling
the priest, coachman, and a peasant into a river. They pursue
him for revenge, and the coachman gets close enough to give him
a good whipping, to escape which Ragotin runs into a miller's
yard and is "caught by the buttocks by a mastiff dog"; attempting to escape the dog, he overturns some beehives and is stung
fearfully.

So much for "Ragotin's Misfortune," as Scarron calls it. To
begin with, Ragotin is a tiny man who is too proud. He lacks
the heroic quality of a Quixote. While Quixote in his madness
tries to change the world, Ragotin presumes merely to change
his own status. His punishments all follow from the pride mani-
fest in the dwarf's drinking beyond his natural capacity. His
being purged, stripped, and whipped are steps in a return to the
real Ragotin (not, as in Quixote's case, to the real world). But
the punishment is also descriptive in another sense. When Ragotin's punishment is over, "a bear's cub but newly whelpt, and
never licked into form, could not be so shapeless as our Ragotin
was in human figure, after having been stung by these merciless
creatures, being swelled excessively even from head to foot."
The result is a burlesque of his affected shape in that it is formless and swollen, the very image of false pride. His punishment
embodies emblematic images first of the ugly reality beneath his
pretension and then of the pretension itself.

The punisher is Nature reasserting her sway over the small,
proud man who would try to pass himself off as an actor or a
hero or something else that he is not. The Quixote convention

subsequently descends in the works of Molière, Furetière, and Boileau, to the social pretenders who read the wrong books and begin to ape their betters, bringing ruin upon themselves and their relatives; and in England to the fop of Restoration comedy.

In so far as it contrasted a romantic illusion—of goodness, greatness, or wisdom—with a prosaic or gross reality, the typical satire of Augustan England was also anti-romance in the tradition of Lucian, Rabelais, and Cervantes. In theory, applying either "the manners of the highest to the lowest, or *è converso*" could be revolutionary, intended merely to disturb, but in Augustan practice the mock-heroic structure operates conservatively. It questions neither the high nor the low, the ideal nor the real; both are good, though the high-ideal has the edge, and the low-real is somewhat ambiguous, referring in one sense (good) to the status quo and in another sense (the seeds of the evil) to multiplicity and grossness. But the object of attack is the illusory, which is somewhere between and distinct from the real and the ideal. As in the later Quixotes of the French, the evil man is the low aspiring to, or masquerading as, the high, and the satirist judges him by playing off against him *both* the ideal and the real.

Samuel Butler's Hudibras (1663), the Augustan Quixote, only apes the ideal—religion—while in fact his Presbyterianism is a false religion which he uses as a sanction for his secret propensities toward all the known vices (from lechery to greed and gluttony). His spiritual quest is in reality a physical one, and his high-sounding tirades are belied by his real concerns expressed in the bread, cheese, and fat black puddings with which he stuffs his breeches, and such other physical matters as the courting of a rich widow. His confession, in the form of a mock-catechism, conveys the basic strategy of the satire:

> What's orthodox and true believing
> Against a conscience?—A good living.
> What makes rebelling against kings
> A good old cause?—Administ'rings.
> What makes all doctrines plain and clear?—

About two hundred pounds a year.
And that which was prov'd true before,
Prove false again?—Two hundred more.[19]

Thus Butler reveals the self-interest beneath the religious claims of Presbyterianism, and at the same time shows Hudibras trying to pass himself (a materialist if ever there was one) off as a religious quester and his Presbyterianism as true religion.

The new note, which will crop up again in Swift's satiric protagonists, is that, unlike Quixote who really saw giants in herds of sheep (in a way, they may *have been* giants), Hudibras only finds it useful to see, with the eyes of a Presbyterian, Belial in a bear-baiting or Beelzebub in an astrologer. His masquerade appears to be hypocrisy, but it could as well be the mere tendency of a man to bolster his natural lechery or greed with a doctrine. Even under his hypocrisy there remains a strain of self-deception. Dryden's Shadwell, obviously a wretched poet, fatuously claims to have inherited the mantle of Ben Jonson. Absalom actually believes that he is the rightful heir to the throne of David.

Hypocrisy and affectation are vices that are usually attacked from the security of a conservative, order-conscious society. Generally speaking, the Augustans' mock-heroic subject is the man who pretends, appears, or even believes himself to be part of society, to be pious or rich, a doctor or a poet, while actually he is an interloper from beyond the pale. He is the fishwife who talks like Dido.

Travesty is another matter. In practice, from Lucian onward, it attacks the ideal as ideal, seeing through it to the ugly reality; if the greater amount of space in the mock-heroic is taken up with the romantic illusions, in travesty the focus is on the real— not so much as evil or degeneration, but as simply real. The ideal of the mock-heroic is never treated as illusion.

Reacting politically and emotionally against the repressive years of the Commonwealth, many Englishmen—but most of all the Cavaliers—encouraged an attitude that was bent on expos-

[19] *Hudibras,* Part III, Canto i, ll. 1273–80, ed. T. R. Nash (London, 1835), II, 167.

ing old pious frauds and treating serious subjects like love or life with disrespect. *Rump Songs* (published in 1661), which marks this emergence, was a collection of political satires, suppressed during the rule of the Saints, that made its appearance almost immediately upon the accession of Charles II. As these songs suggest, the mode of travesty had reached an advanced stage of development before Charles' return from his travels. Throwing dirt at something so ostensibly serious and saintly as the Puritan led naturally to travesty as a useful satiric strategy. The Puritans presented and regarded themselves as paragons, and so the dirt-throwing, connecting them with secret sexual proclivities and the like (sometimes, indeed, based on fact), was intended to expose the real man under the false appearance of saintliness. The Puritan Saint was a transitional symbol, capable of either mock-heroic or travesty interpretation. Insofar as the satire showed an ordinary man masquerading as a holy man it was mock-heroic (the ideal remained inviolate), but its emphasis on his animality easily turned the attack onto the possibility of holiness or heroism itself. Travesty exposes as illusory the assumptions that are generally accepted by society; it puts the lie to society's cherished beliefs that pious men are chaste, that love is eternal, or war is heroic. The mock-heroic satirist relies on society's general agreement with his view of the ideal of piety or love or heroism as well as the small size of the pretender to these. The importance of *Rump Songs* lies in its demonstration of the Civil War satirists discovering the appropriateness of these and other techniques.

The travesty tradition was continued by Butler's attacks on the Puritans in *Hudibras,* Cotton's irreverence for heroic attitudes in his *Scarronides or Virgil Travestie,* and Rochester's attacks on the court and the morals of his age in his poems. It was an easy transition from debunking the respectable Puritans to debunking the anointed king and his advisers. Travesty was as necessary a device for the anti-court forces as the mock-heroic was for the pro-court forces. The latter began with the fact of the high position of king and court and showed the upstart's presumption in aspiring toward—or usurping—that unassailable position. The aim of the anti-court satire was to show the real hollowness, human weakness, and corruption beneath the apparently rich and respectable, even divine, façade of the court. The obvious corruption of Charles II's court, like the worldliness of the most pious Puritans, made such an approach almost irresistible. Colley Cibber recounts the story of Rochester's taking Charles to a brothel where he was not known and abandoning him there without any money: "in this ridiculous distress stood the British monarch; the prisoner of a bawd, and the life upon which the nation's hopes were fixed, put in the power of a ruffian."[20] The story is probably a fabrication, but it reflects the situation upon which Rochester built such satires as "The Scepter Lampoon" (*ca.* 1673).

Much of the satire of the anti-court party assumed this dependence of public activity upon private: a king's conquering of a country or raising or lowering of taxes is not a matter of policy but can be traced to the king's private life. The "Advice to a Painter" satires of the 1660's showed the behind-the-scenes history corresponding to the gallant poses in the official paintings; the Cabal satires exposed the roots of public policy in the secret scheming of a few men in smoke-filled rooms; and the Popish Plot satires of 1679 turned these schemers into the cabal of conspirators who meet to propose the overthrow of the state. The "Secret History" accurately bespoke a time when public policy *was* directed by private meetings of a small group of favorites—when a public treaty of Dover was accompanied by a private. In the Nacky-Nacky scenes of Otway's *Venice Preserv'd* (which turned this kind of satire back on the anti-court party) and in the various *chroniques scandaleuses* private actions were explicitly connected with sexuality.

The sexual, mixed with the scatalogical, offered the satirist the most expressive symbol he could find for the exposed private world. It is, of course, an area of experience he persistently turns to when he wishes to remind man of his unheroic, animal self. But the Puritan emphasis on sexual violation as the darkest of sins,

---

[20] *Rochesteriana,* ed. Johannes Prinz (Leipzig, 1926), p. 50.

and the court's opposite view, served as authorities for the Restoration satirist's use of this image as a metonymy for certain aspects of human activity.

To return to the Quixote fiction and irony, we can conclude by noting that Cervantes' ambiguous attitude toward his subject is reflected in the objects of Augustan satire. Blame-by-praise irony and the mock-heroic applied with some consistency to a character, or even embodied in a character, implies a factitious complexity of character. Appearance versus reality does not in itself amount to complexity; for the character to be complex there would have to be a second reality, instead of only a pretense. Dryden, nevertheless, goes so far as to suggest that his aim, at least in *Absalom and Achitophel,* is to show evil in all its complexity; and his use of concession as a rhetorical device tends to become, in terms of the metaphysical nature of the evil he describes, a generally good man with a major flaw, or a bad man with some redeeming feature—a relative of the Horatian knave who turns out after all to be only a fool.

This device and/or doctrine is summed up in *An Essay upon Satire* (1680), a verse satire that purports to be, and to some extent is, an essay on satiric theory. It probably resulted from a collaboration between the Earl of Mulgrave and Dryden; but whatever his share in the composition, Dryden's views are expressed here, among preliminary sketches for the portraits of Buckingham and Shaftesbury in *Absalom and Achitophel.* The *Essay*'s argument is that there is no need to attempt correcting Juvenalian knaves—it would be as pointless as "being devout at play, wise at a ball, / Or bringing wit and friendship to Whitehall." It is better

> with sharp eyes those nicer faults to find,
> Which lie obscurely in the wisest mind,
> That little speck which all the rest does spoil,
> To wash off that would be a noble toil. . . .[21]

[21] Lines 31–36, in *Poems on Affairs of State, Augustan Satirical Verse, 1660–1714,* ed. George deF. Lord (New Haven, Conn.: Yale University Press, 1963), I, 402–403.

The combination of criticism and sympathy acts as a satiric device. The "critic" lists in some detail the monsters ("saunt'ring Charles between his beastly brace") whom he is *not* going to satirize; and then, pretending to deal with good people slightly flawed, he produces a group that makes the reader wonder how bad the more drastically flawed must be. The slight emphasis on the good qualities of these less wicked people gives a false impression of fairness. But the emphasis, like Horace's, falls on the consequences to the person himself of his vicious deeds, whose self-exposure is followed by self-torment—their "harmless errors hurt themselves alone." In theory at least the author of the *Essay* presents an evil agent who is not all bad and who hurts himself more than others, and who is therefore something of a complex, or "mixed" character. The result is an image of evil that is more realistic, explicable, plausible, interesting; one that shows a growing interest in character as well as in the idea of the nature of evil; but not one that is in any way mitigated.

When Dryden said that he wished "to spare the grossness of the names, and to do the thing yet more severely," the key to his method was in the last phrase. Jack Ketch, to whom he turned for an analogy, is still a hangman for all the delicacy of his technique. The model against which Shadwell's pretension is measured is not simply the works of Ben Jonson but Virgil's *Aeneid;* as a figure in the London world of letters, he is held up to Ascanius, the son of Aeneas, and to the Son of God.[22] With the analogues of religion and politics brought to bear on literature, the chasm between his pretension and the ideal is frighteningly large. It is significant that in the satire of Dryden Quixote himself plays only a minor part. The figure of villainy drawn upon is not Quixote but Satan, the Father of Evil. In general then, as Addison and Steele were to notice, Augustan satire is more, rather than less, severe than its forebears.

[22] See Arthur W. Hoffman, *John Dryden's Imagery* (Gainesville, Fla.: University of Florida Press, 1962), p. 29; Earl Miner, "Some Characteristics of Dryden's Use of Metaphor," *Studies in English Literature,* II (1962), 309–20.

Turnus and Satan

The Augustan satirist draws upon two areas, the classical and the Christian, for his normative allusion, and also to a large extent for his fictions. If, as R. L. Brett has remarked, "Satire . . . was a substitute for epic in an age when epic could no longer be successfully achieved,"[23] it was because their assumptions about man and society were the same, and only their focus and emphasis and, of course, tone were different. Like Augustan satire, the Virgilian epic deals with the present as it relates to the past. Virgil, writes C. M. Bowra,

> sought to provide a poem on the Roman character by linking his fabulous hero Aeneas to his living patron Augustus, to bracket past and present in a single whole, and to give a metaphysical unity to Rome by displaying the abilities which had made it great in his own day and had existed in it from the beginning. His first aim is to praise the present, but the present is too actual, too complex and too familiar to provide the material of his poem. So he joins it to the past and exalts it as the fulfilment of a long, divinely ordained process. Augustus gains in glory by being associated with Aeneas, Rome by being traced back to its humble origins.[24]

The opposite of course happens to someone like Shadwell, and an effect somewhere between follows from using a small but dangerous man like Shaftesbury. Both satire and the Virgilian epic are concerned with the present but, while the epic regards it as a fulfilment, satire generally sees it as a falling away. Past and present are linked in order to denigrate the present.

The pro-court satire of the Restoration and early eighteenth century was very nearly epic in form as well as in assumptions. *Absalom and Achitophel* shows the present (Charles II) as a glorious fulfilment of the past (David) and places in the present both the still living tradition of classical culture and the perverse elements of present-day conspiratorial London. In a satire-tinctured work like Pope's *Windsor Forest,* the Treaty of

[23] *The Third Earl of Shaftesbury, a Study in Eighteenth-Century Literary Theory* (London: Hutchinson's University Library, 1951), p. 176.
[24] *From Virgil to Milton* (London: Macmillan, 1948), p. 15.

Utrecht is a happy ending in the present that reaffirms order and the Golden Age. An Augustan optimism—which Brett (pp. 176, 180) perhaps too patly connects with Shaftesbury's influence—is necessary for the epic and satire to come into closest conjunction.

The most general connection between satire and epic, however, is their common concern with society. Tragedy may share this concern, keeping at the back of its mind the image of order as a standard of the normal world; but its sympathy is with the heroic exploration of man's highest potential, the flights that would carry him beyond the cautious outposts of his fellow men. At the end these petty people have destroyed the hero and, though we are aware of a flaw of pride, our sympathy is with him. This man is the villain of the epic, and during the Augustan Age, epic and satire do not entirely erase the heroic element in that villain, but they show it perverted almost beyond recognition.

Pius Aeneas, the good man, is constantly being tempted away from his mission of founding a city, of holding together a society —a truly heroic undertaking, by epic definition. In Book ii, as the Greeks overrun Troy (in the Augustan Age a favorite image of social and moral chaos), Aeneas' first reaction of rushing out and killing as many Greeks as he can is clearly the wrong one. In a striking vignette he sees Helen, whose willingness to destroy her marriage contract and home for love of Paris brought about all this destruction, take refuge in, of all places, Vesta's temple. Aeneas is about to revenge Troy upon her when his mother, Venus, "held [his] hand, the destin'd blow to break" (ii. l. 806), reminding him that he has lost control of himself and is spending his "unmanly rage" in a cause already lost instead of protecting his family.

Thus the wrong in Aeneas' daliance in Dido's arms is not in the love-making itself but in the violation of the larger aims of Venus for a new Troy. Dido's tragic and self-consuming love is both a threat and an image of folly. When Aeneas at last reaches his destination, Italy, he comes into conflict with another deterrent, the main antagonist of the epic, Turnus—an obviously heroic and brave warrior, of impressively noble bearing. Turnus is a surrogate for Aeneas' chief foe, the goddess Juno, who, like Turnus, is capable of bravery and generosity but also of "implacable spite, vengeance, treachery, and stubborn pride, the strong temptations of vanity and delusion, a willingness to invoke the baser passions personified in Alecto, the minister of Hell." This is the evil that Virgil opposes to Venus and her surrogate Aeneas, who represent "the qualities of devotion and loyalty (*pietas*)" and "prescribe such duties as are imposed by the larger utility, a sense of the common and permanent good to be achieved through the suppression of wayward and ephemeral impulses and desires."[25]

Every incident in the *Aeneid* is an exemplum, a parable of proper behavior, that points up this contrast. The action of Nisus who, having fallen when almost winning the footrace, trips the second man so that the third man, his friend Euryalus, can win, may seem equivocal at the time; friendship, like love or courage, is a virtue. But when we see the same action paralleled later the judgment is clear: Nisus stops and, instead of carrying through his mission to reach Aeneas, turns back to find his friend Euryalus, and both are killed and the message is not delivered. The action of a single man—even when inspired by a virtue— which sacrifices the good of the whole, is always shown to be wrong. Immediately after the above incident Turnus, the epitome of such behavior, gets inside the walls of the Trojan fort. He kills Trojan after Trojan, accomplishing monumental feats of valor (recalling Aeneas in the streets of Troy), but he has lost the war while winning this private battle, for he has forgotten his men and his larger aim: he fights on alone and never opens the gates to let them in.

The Turnus-Dido role, called for in the dramatis personae of the Virgilian epic, became a stock figure in the satire of the Augustans. Like the epic antagonist, Achitophel is a man with one virtue in excess which cripples the other qualities that would make him a whole, and so a good man. The example of Virgil

---

[25] C. N. Cochrane, *Christianity and Classical Culture* (New York: Oxford University Press, 1957), pp. 69–70.

also taught the Augustans the pathos, the sadness of folly; and, whether sincerely or as a concessive strategy, they repeated the tears Aeneas or Virgil shed over Dido and Turnus.[26] To some extent the Augustan satirists no doubt felt the need to employ the authority of the epic to bolster the relatively narrow and limited authority of satire (further undermined by the activities of the Elizabethan satirists). More important, however, they adapted some of the epic's fictive richness to the service of satire, giving their villains a seriousness seldom granted before to the objects of satire. Their shift of emphasis from epic protagonist to antagonist, of course, marks off their satire from the epic. But here too the Augustans sought epic sanction—in their own English epic, *Paradise Lost*.

The metaphysical and even ontological basis that satire secured in this period to put it on an equal level with the epic was available in the generally Christian-tinged vocabulary of the controversies that began with the Civil War and burst into flame anew with every crisis after the Restoration. From the outset we have noticed the religious content of satire: in overtones of the fertility-sterility opposition and as part of the action of the *Metamorphoses*. The satire of Dryden, Swift, and Pope follows a tradition beginning in Christian humanism and skipping the aberration of English Elizabethan satire; its subject is almost

[26] Of the other elements of Augustan satire, conventions of Roman satire, that derive additional sanction from the *Aeneid,* we might mention the normative vir bonus who at last snaps and is transformed into an activist satirist. Although of an extremely peace-loving nature, *pius* Aeneas is finally goaded (significantly, by the killing of a son and consequent destruction of a family) into a violent attack; he loses control of himself and kills even innocent men, taunting them with the treatment he is going to give their corpses, until he kills another son, Mezentius' son Lausus, and sees that he has come full circle, weeps over the boy, and promises him honorable burial. Another element is the compromise ending of Horatian satire, which indicates the middle ground that saves the best and eliminates the worst of two extremes. The *Aeneid* offered an epic version of the compromise ending in the marriage of the Latins (the heroic ideal) and the Trojans (the peaceful, friendly ideal), which cancels out the self-centeredness of the former and the indecisiveness and comfort-loving qualities of the latter.

always religious, and when, as in Swift's *Tale of a Tub* or Pope's *Dunciad,* it is ostensibly about literary vices, it is actually about moral and religious issues. The twin referents in *The Dunciad* are Aeneas and Christ, as earlier in *Mac Flecknoe* the literary subject was expanded to include John the Baptist and Christ.

The evil agent in this satire assumes the antithetical role of Turnus, Satan, anti-Christ, or the "uncreating Word." The Augustan view of evil is Christian, or, to be more precise, Augustinian: that evil has no reality independent of good and that the devil himself, far from independent of God or able to affect his creation, is evil because of his false claim of independence. The bad will, Augustine explains, is the "will to power" when "the soul, loving its own power, relapses from the desire for a common and universal good to one which is individual and private." This Christian view of evil is analogous to the classical, and Augustine's description of the City of God versus the City of Man (*caritas* versus *avaritia*) is almost a rephrasing of the opposition between Venus and Juno, Aeneas and Turnus.[27] The classical evil of the subordination of the social unit to the individual *cupiditas, superbia,* even *virtus* becomes the Christian evil of the subordination of the spiritual to material aims, in which the individual refuses to acknowledge his dependence upon the principle of his own life and being. The classical ideal of aesthetic as well as social unity versus division carries over into the Christian view that there is one world, one nature, and one destiny for mankind, and division or multiplicity is a perversion of nature.

It is in Augustine, and not in Virgil or Horace, that the Augustans find the manifestation of independence or self-sufficiency in "a passion to explore the secrets of nature (Faustian *curiositas*) or a thirst for domination over one's fellow men (*tumidus fastus*) or, simply, the filthy whirl of sensual pleasure (*coenosus gurges carnalis voluptatis*)." Pride, which for Augustine as well as Tertullian, "is the devil's own sin, peculiarly, the sin of phi-

---

[27] *De Trin.* xii. 9. 14 (cited, Cochrane, p. 448); *De Gen. ad Litt.* xi. 15. 20; cf. *De Cir. Dei,* xiv. 28 (Cochrane, p. 489).

losophers," expresses itself in an effort "to make one's own truth"—that is, to create a false reality that vies with God's but has no body of its own, and so is a sham. The devil is, of course, the prince of liars and imposters.[28]

Although the situations are analogous and the evil similar, this evil is enormously more intense and disturbing than the Horatian bore who tries to push his way into the Maecenas circle. The self-defeating quality in Virgil's Juno or Turnus and Horace's Canidia becomes the Augustinian bad man who is a perversion of good qualities. As his drive for personal power is only a perversion of his natural and proper impulse to preserve himself from danger and destruction, the sin or evil, the result of his failure to recognize his own highest and greatest good, is therefore a kind of self-delusion. His infirmities blind him to the larger, true reality of things, and so make him blunder from folly to folly. If ignorance or blindness (*ignorantia, caecitas*) is one manifestation of bad will, loss of control is another (*difficultas* or *necessitas*) : "the man who, knowing the right, fails to do it, loses the power to know what is right; and the man who, having the power to do right, is unwilling, loses the power to do what he will."[29] The bad man's search for freedom and independence is accordingly self-thwarting and pathetic.

Milton is the dramatizer of this Christian doctrine for the Augustan satirists. His Satan is enough like Turnus to suggest the similarity in their roles. Both, though heroic and not without virtues, suffer from "a sense of injured merit," and sacrifice their countrymen (Turnus the Latins, Satan the angels) to their personal pride. Milton, however, makes his antagonist more central to his plot than is his Virgilian prototype, and by stressing the role of tempter, implicit but unstressed in Dido or Turnus, he deepens his guilt. He also places a much greater emphasis than Virgil upon the villain's self-delusion and failure.

---

[28] Cochrane, pp. 448, 487.

[29] *De Patient.* 14; *De Lib. Arbit.* iii. 19. 53; *De Vera Relig.* 20; *Retract.* i. 15. 3; cited, Cochrane, p. 449.

Satan, blinded by pride to the reality of his situation, carries on a futile, one-sided battle with God that is grotesque and would be comic (even Quixotic) if his plausible appearance did not seduce otherwise good people to his hopeless cause. C. S. Lewis has drawn our attention to the fact that "At that precise point where Satan...meets something real, laughter *must* arise, just as steam must when water meets fire."[30] That his heroic stature is inextricably mixed with his foolish blindness is epitomized in his speech of triumph to his associates which he concludes hissing on his belly among a parliament of reptiles.

Milton moves Satan very close indeed to the satiric equivalent Dryden was to produce, attaching epic similes that compare his approach to Eden to the prowling of a wolf and modernizing the Bible text about thieves in the night:

> Or as a Thief bent to unhoard the cash
> Of some rich Burgher, whose substantial doors,
> Cross-barr'd and bolted fast, fear no assault,
> In at the window climbs, or o'er the tiles:
> So clomb this first grand Thief into God's Fold:

And he cannot refrain from adding: "So since into his Church lewd Hirelings climb."[31] From a denigrating comparison he has moved to a general and then to a specific contemporary allusion. In the same way, in Book I he connected Satan and his city of Pandemonium with the architecture of Restoration London, its pilasters and Doric pillars "overlaid with Golden Architrave," its sewers and filth; he connected the council of devils with English councils on "State affairs," that "In close recess and secret conclave sat," and the courtiers and cavaliers in general with the followers of Belial (I, 497–502). It has even been suggested that Satan the parliamentarian may have been based on the young Anthony Ashley Cooper (later Earl of Shaftesbury). At any rate,

---

[30] *A Preface to Paradise Lost* (Oxford: Oxford University Press, 1942), p. 93.

[31] Bk. IV, ll. 183–87, 188–92, 193, ed. Merritt Y. Hughes (New York: Odyssey Press, 1935). Cf. *Joel* 2:9, *Obad.* 5, *Matt.* 6:19–20.

Paradise Lost draws upon the contemporary tradition, that goes back to the Civil War, of covert allusions to current political and religious problems.[32]

The grim particularity of present-day London is pointed up by the contrasting descriptions of Eden, Adam and Eve, and Raphael. With Satan's journey through the Void from Hell to Eden, the images shift from the contemporary world of Milton to the classical, which has the effect of moving London, "hell on earth," from the present back to the most remote times, which we dimly discern through Greek myths; that is, from the fallen world of the present back toward a Golden Age.

The contrast is emphasized by syntax as well as imagery. Satan's diction is composed of the complex, often garbled syntax and the exaggerated conceits of the Metaphysical style. In this strange mixture of energy and distortion is evidenced Satan's warped intelligence which almost forces meanings to emerge from a tangle of thought. The complicated syntax and diction that fill his speech and the descriptions of his activity vanish abruptly in the unfallen world of Eden or the Council in Heaven. Book IX opens with this simple diction and subdued metaphor, but as it proceeds toward the moment of temptation the style grows in syntactical and imagistic complexity until a climax is reached in the soliloquy of Satan, with a full panoply of rhetoric, self-asked questions ("For what God after better worse would build?"), grandiosity, and play on words. We follow the growth of complexity in the natural description; nature is so simple in Book IV, so organized, as Adam and Eve awaken, and so lush as they approach the Fall. The sentences become longer and more twisted, miming the oblique course of the Serpent, and offer a telling contrast to Adam's simple speeches. And Satan's victory is announced, at last, by a change in style, as Eve's mind

[32] See Morris Freedman, "Satan and Shaftesbury," *PMLA*, LXXIV (1959), 544–47. For political allusions in Dryden's *Epistle to Charleton*, Denham's *Cooper's Hill*, and, from the later period, Pope's *Windsor Forest*, see Earl Wasserman, *The Subtler Language* (Baltimore, Md.: The Johns Hopkins Press, 1959), chaps., 2, 3, 4.

is transformed by awful consciousness; her speech after the Fall is that of Satan:

O Sovran, virtuous, precious of all Trees
In Paradise, of operation blest
To Sapience, hitherto obscur'd, infam'd,
And thy Fruit let hang.... (Bk. IX, ll. 795–98)

From that point the language of Book IX assumes more and more the dislocated quality of Book I, its terrible richness broken only by Adam's last great despairing soliloquy before he too eats of the fruit. It never reverts to the clarity with which it began and which, until the Fall, Adam and Eve still possessed. For if the tragic act is over, with its events known, history has begun, and all its imperfections can be seen in the obscurity of its tongues.

Paradise Lost juxtaposes the purity of the past with the impurity of the present more in the manner of the satirist than of the Virgilian epic poet. It also develops many of the devices that became the stock in trade of the Augustan satirist:

(1) The Turnus-Dido character, in the satire of the Augustans, became the Miltonic Satan, not merely to make the figure more monumental and dangerous but because their idea of evil was the same as Milton's with the religious overtones in the God-Satan struggle. To the Augustan satirist Satan, the tempter, the destroyer of order, the self-deluded man, was the archetype of the villain. (2) In Milton's story of the Fall they found their most all-encompassing satiric symbol: man's present falling away from a past ideal associated with religious purity (or ecclesiastical unity). In the Temptation they found a religious version of the fool- or dupe-knave relation. (3) Milton's way of dramatizing the opposition between the fallen and unfallen worlds may have offered Dryden, for example, an authority for a wider definition of decorum: a style, ordinarily inappropriate for a certain subject, is appropriate if a certain end is desired which requires such a conjunction. For example, the disdained Metaphysical conceit may well be appropriate when applied to a

schemer or a madman who would "make his own truth." *Paradise Lost* showed how the parodic techniques of the Civil War satires could be used in an exalted literary form. Milton played with genres, imitating and juxtaposing their conventions. In Book IV he imposed the form of a pastoral on Satan's entrance into Eden, and in Book IX he presented the story of the Fall in the form of a classical tragedy. Satan speaks the Euripidean prologue, the "Bard" puts in choric statements between the scenes; there are five scenes, the prescribed number, and three characters—appearing only two at a time. A known genre has been imposed on alien material within another form (the epic) to give it an added dimension of meaning.

(4) *Paradise Lost* also tended to dissolve the distinction between the epic's view of the present as fulfilment and satire's as a falling away. Milton wrote his epic with confidence in the victory of Christ, law, and order; but he was at the same time an alien, the last of the "Saints," defeated and alone in a London full of the "sons of Belial." The overtones of savage denunciation from the days of his polemical writings (when he told Joseph Hall there was no such thing as a "toothless" satire) can be heard, particularly in the early books of *Paradise Lost.* Though by no means a satire itself, *Paradise Lost* opened up possibilities for alert contemporaries who were satirically inclined, and it did use satire as one of its materials. More than anyone else Milton offered a sanction for a satiric form concerned with problems of religion and extended the meaning of epic almost to encompass the satire written by Dryden and Pope.

The meaning of satire was extended as well, and the Augustan satirists could either write works called satires (like the Elizabethans), or write satires that were called travel books, projects, epistles, or even epics, but never satires. To some extent, as the rise of the novel and Fielding's new distinctions would show, the old generic demarcations were breaking down. Satire was beginning to place prime emphasis on its mimetic or dramatic structure—its fictionality—and to play down its "satiric" and argumentative qualities. The satiric observer was disappearing from

works that were not called satires, and increasingly we are offered works like *Absalom and Achitophel,* which calls itself a
"poem" and is in one sense an epic.

The Fictions of Tory Satire

Long before Dryden wrote, the particular fiction that dominated Tory satire was a-building. This satiric fiction, or "myth"
as a recent scholar has called it,[33] was put together to meet the
threat of a specific new force in English life: economic, religious,
and political individualism. In *Absalom and Achitophel* Dryden
brought all the elements together in a characteristic fiction, which
consisted of: (1) A civil war or rebellion, deriving from the
memory of the Civil War and the killing of the king, and from
the analogous rebellion of the angels in heaven. (2) A tempter,
from an abundant choice of Cromwells and regicides, and from
the Biblical and Miltonic Satan. (3) A dupe for the tempter to
act upon, an Adam or an Eve, or (in the case of Absalom) a
pseudo-Christ. (4) An apathetic, restless, easily-swayed crowd,
like the London mobs of 1642 and 1679, as well as like the fickle
Jews of the Bible. (5) A plot to catch the crowd. (6) The loyal
few and the king, who finish off the Biblical analogy as the loyal
angels and God.

Dryden uses these elements to construct the fiction of Achitophel's temptation of Absalom (Shaftesbury's temptation of
Monmouth). The single ambitious man is willing to overthrow
the state in order to gain more power for himself; so he seduces
the king's illegitmate son (a pseudo-Christ) into rebelling
against his father and master (God), and by means of a plot
he turns the crowd into his ally. The plot dupes the crowd by
capturing its imagination (by the fantasy of Titus Oates' tales)

[33] See Bernard Schilling, *Dryden and the Conservative Myth: a Reading of
Absalom and Achitophel* (New Haven and London: Yale University Press,
1961), to which I am indebted for the elements of what I call the Tory fiction.
My text for Dryden's poems is *The Poetical Works of Dryden,* ed. George R.
Noyes (Boston: Houghton Mifflin, 1950).

and giving form to its restlessness and discontent. Civil war is about to break out when the king reasserts order, and the evil crumbles like a sandcastle.

At the center of this fiction is the classical-Christian conception of the nature of evil. A deception is clearly crucial: there must be a fool as well as a knave; someone has to be deceived since no one in his right mind would be a party to such a catastrophe as civil war, an event so cruel to the body politic, so inevitably self-defeating for all concerned. Consequently, the evil agent is presented not only as a tempter but as a hypocritical pretender to religion or to public reform: a memory of the fanatic Puritan and the mercenary London merchants who, professing piety, overthrew Charles I.

The historical image of the religious fanatic, the economic individualist, the political opportunist, rebelling against the anointed king, is paralleled by the religious image of Satan rebelling against God. He is the analogy that almost invariably comes to the satirist's mind—and once Dryden starts the trend in *Absalom and Achitophel,* he becomes specifically Milton's Satan from *Paradise Lost.*[34] Like Satan, his essential character-

---

[34] The contemporary reader's reaction to Achitophel may have been complicated by the hero-villain of Restoration comedy, who carries similar echoes of Satan. In *The Man of Mode* (1676) Dorimant is specifically connected with Satan: Mrs. Loveit, his cast-off mistress, says, "I know he is a devil, but he has something of the angel yet undefaced in him" (II, ii), and Lady Woodvill: "Oh, he has a tongue, they say, would tempt the angels to a second fall" (III, iii). And Busy's song, sung to Harriett who is about to succumb to Dorimant's charms and protestations of conjugal love, clearly refers to him and to Satan when she sings:

"None ever had so strange an art,
His passion to convey
Into a list'ning virgin's heart,
And steal her soul away."

Dorimant, like Achitophel, is a mixed case and the audience's reaction, as well as that of his loves, is ambiguous. But he plays the Satanic role of disguising himself as a part of society and luring its members out into his realm and abandoning them, as Satan did Eve; except that here the situation becomes the comic battle between equals, Dorimant and Harriett, which ends in his (at least apparent) capitulation.

istics are false-seeming, hatred of the social body and the established order (revealed in his sinuous, self-exposing speeches), and impotence to do any lasting harm. Like Satan, Achitophel has a great potential for either good or evil; because of his virtue as a judge he becomes something of a pathetic case when he goes so tragically wrong. Also like Satan, the evil agent is inevitably defeated: not only in the sense that God's creation, or Natural Law, is inviolable, but that his schemes will come to naught for himself. It is in the nature of evil to be self-tormenting, self-entangling, and self-deceiving; being individualistic, the band of conspirators (again, a characteristic form for Augustan evil to take) splinters into individuals who betray each other. "By their own arts" they destroy themselves, and "against themselves" they rebel: "Their Belial with their Belzebub will fight" (ll. 1012–16). Evil is itself (as Dryden's imagery emphasizes) a sickness, a disharmony within the body. The evil agent is sick because he puts all his restless energy into his intellect, into his ability to plot and deceive. His reason—a virtue when applied to his duties as a judge—becomes something else when given complete control: while it feeds itself, becoming by its singleness and overfeeding a dangerous, perverted force, it allows the body (the "tenement of clay") to wither with disease and disuse. He is the contrary of the balanced man in whom mind and body (or in religious terms, spirit and flesh) are equally developed. The idea of Achitophel's withered body gives yet another suggestion of the weakness and inevitable failure of evil, while emphasizing its wastefulness.

The deceived party, the dupe, is as important as the deceiver; he differs from the evil agent in the extent of his vision. The inevitable consequence of civil war, which to the satanic figure is only a means to his end, is beyond the dupe's intention and control. His action always has a blindly, hopelessly limited human end, such as immediate power; and it is self-deceiving to a much greater extent than Satan's. He convinces himself (or is convinced by Satan) that he *is* the Son of God, that his actions are in the best interests of the nation, that he is a benefactor of mankind. He never realizes that he is being exploited by another.

Absalom begins with a misfortune—he had the wrong mother—
and he enters into the evil agent's scheme with perhaps a true
feeling of dedication to a worthy cause.

Absalom is in fact the central figure of the fiction as Dryden
presents it; he has the best of intentions, having deluded himself
into thinking that his cause is good (Achitophel knows the
truth), but his human pride makes him confuse himself with
Christ when the temptation is offered. Without his weakness
nothing could have come of Achitophel's scheme. The tone of
the satire follows from the first association that the Absalom
story recalls for an ordinary reader: "O my son Absalom, my
son, my son!" We think: Poor Charles, poor Monmouth. Dryden further implies the pathos of the situation by contrasting
Charles' son (who sinks from folly to the crime of murder and
then to the betrayal of his father) to the Duke of Ormonde's
son,

> . . . snatch'd in manhood's prime
> B' unequal fates, and Providence's crime;
> Yet not before the goal of honor won,
> All parts fulfill'd of subject and of son. (ll. 833–36)

Between the ideal of Ormonde's son and the other extreme,
Achitophel's abortion of a son, stands the poor, foolish Adam.
In his awkward position, above the beasts and just short of the
angels, he is a constant prey to the temptation of pride and the
desire to usurp godhead, and is constantly re-enacting the Fall.[35]

The crowd, the next element of the fiction, is an image of the
wild, irrational forces in the mind and in society. Like Absalom,
the crowd has to be deceived in order for anything to come of
the evil (thus Dryden's emphasis on eloquence and false-
seeming); and because the effect of evil is largely restricted to
the corruption of fools. The crowd is not itself evil, only weak,
foolish, unstable, and easily molded by orators willing to play
upon its illusions and appetites. It is consistently associated with

[35] The minor characters, Zimri, Shimei, and Corah, are also *used* by Achitophel, but they are less complex cases than Absalom because each is a hypocrite
with a vicious end of his own.

energy out of control, fire about to burst forth, the changes of the moon, restless movement, and instability. Unlike Absalom, it does not know what it wants, and can be changed from day to day. It is held in check by law but, like the irrational element in the individual checked by reason, it is always about to break out in credulity, superstition, and violence. The plot simply looses all of the crowd's vague, repressed desires, and gives them a channel through which to flow.

The sheer quantitative force on the side of Satan is staggering; but unity can hardly be a characteristic of something that is opposed to unity. And when the crowd's emotions shift from day to day, the odds are not so hopelessly against the good people as would seem. They are old, weary, outnumbered (significantly, only the last 10 per cent of *Absalom and Achitophel* is devoted to the ideal), but they are solidly one, and their wisdom is unsplintered because it is based on custom, tradition, subordination of the self, and loyalty to the divine structure of the state. The clap of thunder that approves the king's speech represents the reaffirmation of Natural Law, the swat that removes the annoying fly.

The *Absalom and Achitophel* fiction is essentially an inversion of romance conventions: the disinherited hero seeks his patrimony and ends as king; here he is a usurper and defeated. Absalom is a parody of all the dazzling Montezumas and Almanzors who are rash, easily swayed, and excessively proud, but whose popularity carries the army and populace with them. Their personal identity is obscured, and, through injured pride, they go over to the enemy and sometimes war against people who eventually turn out to be their own fathers or mothers. Achitophel, too, is merely a tin-plated version, a poor copy, of the Father of Evil. Or rather (since Dryden does not emphasize the idea of a "copy" as Swift will), he is related to Satan by a mock-heroic parallel, which shows both the comic discrepancy between the two and the danger inherent in little Achitophel despite his size. After all, the reader is supposed to realize that Achitophel is to David as Satan is to God. The doubleness of discrepancy and threat, a characteristic of Dryden's mock-heroic diction, gives us the peculiarly mixed attitude of the Augustan satirist to the evil man: contempt mixed with fear and awe, even fascination.

But *Absalom and Achitophel* is only half of the satiric fiction as the Tory satirists developed it. A year or so before *Absalom and Achitophel,* in *Mac Flecknoe,* Dryden presents the inversion of all that is in the later poem. *Absalom and Achitophel* is like *Don Quixote* in that it presupposes a world that operates according to orderly principles: a Christian universe, in which Satan and Achitophel, when they try to impose their own views, appear ridiculous. But *Mac Flecknoe* presents an absurd universe, one in which the assumptions of Quixote—or Achitophel or Satan—have come true. The crowd, which was formerly only one element, has become the main one, and the impotent villain is now its king. The result is an unholy parody of the *Absalom and Achitophel* fiction, with the king and his lawfully chosen heir the villains; it presents an alternative kingdom in which every element bears the same relation to Charles and England as the black mass does to the true Mass, the Antichrist to Christ. One is reminded once again of *Paradise Lost* and the building by Sin and Death of the causeway from Hell to the Universe, which is presented as a parody of God's creation of the world. The Spirit of God with "His brooding wings" who creates by warmth becomes the "ravenous Fowl" who creates by cold, and the divine Trinity becomes the infernal Trinity, Satan, Sin, and Death.[36]

This is another form of conservative satire, another aspect of the Tory myth, presenting a fallen world, assuming a parody form of the ideal, usurping its name (and perhaps its reality). In *Mac Flecknoe* King Flecknoe makes the same assertions to Shadwell about his being Christ that Achitophel made to Absalom; but here they are acted upon, and Shadwell does become the Messiah—of Nonsense. Both satires start with the same problem of the succession. But in *Mac Flecknoe* there is no Absalom, no Achitophel, no possible pretender or tempter, no hitches, no conflicts or objections: this isolated realm is unified

[36] Bk. X, ll. 272–305. See E. M. W. Tillyard, *Studies in Milton* (London: Chatto and Windus, 1951), pp. 31–35.

and corporate in dullness, an ideal unlike the fissured reality of England. The crowd is docile: "Th' admiring Throng loud acclamations make," and "He paus'd, and all the people cried, 'Amen' " (ll. 132, 144). The ideal has no place here; it can only be hinted at, as in the references to Rome and Christianity and their subversion in Flecknoe's kingdom.

Absalom and Achitophel is in fact a kind of epic, and ends with the epic affirmation of social values; *Mac Flecknoe* only sounds like an epic, just as Flecknoe only sounds like a king, and it ends with "the yet declaiming bard" being sent through a trapdoor in the stage by his impatient heir. *Absalom and Achitophel* presents the fabric of society inviolate, but with fools battering to get in or making holes in it merely out of malice; it is a satire of the insiders pitying and ridiculing the outsiders. *Mac Flecknoe* presents a small, independent society, isolated like a madhouse in a city or a tumor in a body, busily thriving within the larger structure of England. This parody-England, however, is still isolated to be ridiculed by the people of the great world of true poets and true government. A generation later in Pope's *Dunciad* they invade, and the civil war, which is barely threatened in *Mac Flecknoe,* and smothered in *Absalom and Achitophel,* breaks out, and its success is chronicled as it moves toward St. James' Palace. Pope presents society upside down, overrun by fools, with a human or two hiding to remind us that fools are not the ideal.

The allegory of *The Dunciad,* stemming from the coronation in Dryden's *Mac Flecknoe* and the combat in Swift's *Battle of the Books* and its prototypes, deals with a mythical empire of Dulness which worships a goddess of that name, who is now attempting to restore her empire to its former power, encroaching on the very life of the English nation. The time is ripe: a dunce is king, a rogue is prime minister, a fool is city poet (later another becomes poet laureate), and the public is all gape-mouthed for idiot entertainment by actors like Rich, "moralists" like Orator Henley, novelists like Mrs. Haywood, and eunuch opera singers like Senesino. Dulness (like Virgil's Venus) chooses Theobald-Cibber (Aeneas) to lead her people to their new home; and so we follow the pantomimes and farces, the puppet shows and entertainments as they move their seat from their proper locale among the mad in Bedlam and the vulgar in Smithfield westward to the court itself. Before Pope is finished this has become Dulness' attempt (ultimately successful) to restore the complete sway of her empire over the world. No battles are fought, but the crowd of Dulness moves relentlessly, unopposed, through the streets of London.

The Satanic image of evil outlined by Dryden and Pope in its two aspects—omnipresent but transient, or successful—was essentially the one transmitted in every Augustan satire, reaching at least to Fielding and Charles Churchill. Pope's Sporus and Atticus show the evil agent at his least and most sympathetic, and in the images of Dulness in *The Dunciad* and Vice in *The Epilogue to the Satires,* overtones of Antichrist are added to those of Satan. The Temptation, the Fall, even the Creation are evoked, parodied, and degraded in the works of these agents. If Achitophel was a tin-plated version of Satan, his particular brand of evil was nevertheless defined in relation to Satan's, and in this sense represented part of an ancient tradition of evil. In Pope's satire the pedigree is stressed without such a violent sense of discrepancy: present evil in London is linked with the past, given a tradition, raised to a sinister eminence—honors which Swift carefully strips away in his more prosaic satires.

In the satiric tradition that runs from Dryden to Pope, satire is almost always transformed into art. This satire presents not only the Dunces who make ugliness out of beauty, but also the contrary activity in the verse of the satirist. The effect begins with the metaphoric reverberations bestowed on the evil agent, which make him appear dangerous but also endow him with a sort of grandeur if not beauty that is necessary if the work as a whole is to transcend its immediate, businesslike aim of discrediting or ridiculing Hervey and Addison. Swift, on the contrary, presents a total image of evil, completely directed toward the ends of analysis, description, and condemnation; his poems, for example, have never, I believe, been called beautiful. Pope's most determinedly satiric poems are also beautiful as artifacts.

The image of evil is embedded and displayed in poetic amber—
a means toward a theme that is ultimately (as in the *Epistle to
Dr. Arbuthnot*) not about Sporus and Atticus but about the poet
himself and the power of his art.

Swift refuses to allow his satire this luxury or his evil agent
this dignity. Without abandoning the characteristics of Satan,
he drops the allusion to him, cutting evil off from its past, in
effect defining a new, parvenu evil that has abandoned the
negative as well as the positive values of the past. His evil agents
are no longer aspirers to the mantle of either Virgil or Turnus,
Christ or Satan, but replace the classical and Christian with their
own assumptions. They are not the low putting on the ill-fitting
robes of the high but the low decked out in all their own vulgar
reality claiming to outshine the high. The personal assertions of
their writings claim their value *as* personal assertions. In terms
of Swift's fable in *The Battle of the Books* (1704), they make
no faltering attempt to scale the heights of Parnassus but attempt instead to build a hill of their own that is as high (when
this fails they try to prevail on the Parnassians to lower theirs).
Swift himself, however, was part of the Augustan tradition, and
therefore it must be through his use of Augustan fictions and the
Satanic image of evil that his own particular definition of evil is
arrived at. The Tory fiction has so far been traced only into the
formalized, allegorical, almost stage-like world of poetic satire;
its most interesting evolution takes place in the prose satires of
Swift, which are at the same time more realistic in content and
more illusionistic in form.

III. SWIFT: THE MIDDLEMAN
AND THE DEAN

From Rhetoric to Fiction: *The Drapier's Letters*

Swift's satire descends directly from the argumentative, highly rhetorical satire of Lucian. The many studies of Swift's rhetoric attest to the fact that his satire is at least as argumentative as Lucian's. Often, as in the *Examiner* essays or in a pamphlet like *The Public Spirit of the Whigs,* the element of anything we can call fiction is slight and incidental. Even *Gulliver's Travels,* which does transform abstractions into an action, characters, and incidents, has a noticeably discursive quality: the progression is as often argumentative as dramatic. Swift arrives at his distinctive fiction through original and extremely complex devices of persuasion; accordingly, the surest way to approach his strategy is to take one of his most abstract and discursive works, *The Drapier's Letters* (1724), and isolate the fictional elements that appear in it.[1]

These pamphlets in general take their form from the pamphlet

[1] Rosenheim (*Swift and the Satirist's Art,* pp. 168–74) will not even honor *The Drapier's Letters* with the name of satire, arguing that it is literal polemic. There is considerable truth in his view. The only extended treatment of *The Drapier's Letters* as an artistic creation is Carl Woodring's study of its rhetoric: "The Aims, Audience and Structure of the Drapier's 4th Letter," *Modern Language Quarterly,* XVII (1956), 50–59. For discussions of the character of the persona, see Martin Price, *Swift's Rhetorical Art* (New Haven, Conn.: Yale University Press, 1953), pp. 52–55, 66–71; and William Bragg Ewald, Jr., *The Masks of Jonathan Swift* (Cambridge, Mass.: Harvard University Press, 1954), pp. 100–19.

they answer, argument for argument. Consistency is sacrificed to the debator's art of winning points; sometimes the fiction is merely a decorative fringe upon an argumentative progression. In the first two letters, addressed to the common people of Ireland, the story-telling element is naturally strongest; in the third and fourth, addressed to the upper classes, the argument is logical and fairly abstract, the fictional element being saved as dessert till the end: in III the image of David and Goliath (Drapier versus William Wood), and in IV the consequences of Wood's coinage (in the picture of hundreds of Walpole agents coming to Ireland to make the Irish eat his half-pence).

Swift begins with the historical fact that Ireland needed small change but that the patent for producing and importing these coins (the famous Wood's half-pence) was granted by the Whig government of Sir Robert Walpole to an Englishman, William Wood: the point being that the patent was *sold* to the highest— or most adroit—private bidder in England. Before Swift entered the fracas some of the polemical possibilities had already been exploited. James Maculla, writing in mid-August, 1723, seven months before the first Drapier pamphlet appeared, emphasizes the large quantity, with the accompanying unwieldiness, of Wood's coins as a means of exchange, the shoddiness of the workmanship, and the consequent ease with which they could be counterfeited.[2] If, as the vagueness of his patent hinted, Wood could make as many coins as he wanted, he could single-handedly destroy the economy of Ireland. Maculla's conclusion is that "this Nation will be over-run therewith, if the publick are not on their Guard in the Taking such Coin, and also some speedy Remedy had to stop the vast Inundation which is flowing like a great Sea . . ." (pp. xix–xx). Already, with the image of a flood, a fiction is beginning to take shape: this is the chaos that corre-

---

[2] *Ireland's Consternation in the Loosing of Two Hundred Thousand Pound of their Gold and Silver for Brass Money, Set forth by an Artificier in Metals and a Citizen of Dublin* (Dublin, 1723). For the historical background, and the text, I am indebted to Herbert Davis' edition of *The Drapier Letters* (Oxford: Clarendon Press, 1935). All references are to the pages of this edition.

sponds to the civil war which is Dryden's central symbol of evil consequences. It is not to our purpose to explore the question of whether or not these fears were justified, but from such assumptions Swift constructed a subtle and effective edifice which did not by any means rely exclusively on argument. His main purpose was to persuade the business classes of Ireland that they must not accept Wood's coins. And by the same token, he had to persuade the government of England that they should not introduce the coins.

The idea suggested by Maculla is the one Swift develops in the first of the letters: what will happen given the amount and quality of the coins, and Wood's right to import as many as he thinks fit? To answer this question, Swift has his supposed author, the Drapier, begin by describing a scene in an ale house with a soldier bullying the proprietor into taking his half-pence; and the shopkeeper, forced to accept Wood's coin, has to charge ten times the ordinary price for goods. The Drapier summons up a series of such scenes, going down the line from the customer to the proprietor to the distributor to the farmer to the landlord, showing the whole structure of society being destroyed by the debased coinage: "we are all undone" is his refrain (p. 7). He has projected a series of nightmare images, a vision of civil chaos in the near future: squabbling soldiers, enormous loads of money needed to purchase the simplest necessities, tenants evicted and farms turned to grazing pastures; and behind all this the horror of the irrational—the single man who can assign any value he likes to money. "For then," the Drapier says, ". . . we might be bound to take PEBBLE-STONES or *Cockle-shells,* or *Stamped Leather* for *Current Coin,* if ever we should happen to live under an ill PRINCE, who might likewise by the same Power make a *Guinea* pass for Ten Pounds, a *Shilling* for Twenty Shillings, and so on . . ." (p. 10).

The man who loosed this irrationality on the world, rather than the consequences themselves, is Swift's center of attention. The William Wood Swift gives us is a little man ("a mean ordinary Man, a Hard-Ware Dealer") who would set himself against the corporate good of a whole kingdom, both Ireland

and England: "It would be very hard if all *Ireland* should be put into *One Scale, and this sorry Fellow* WOODS *into the other,* that Mr. WOODS should weigh down *this whole Kingdom . . ."* (p. 10). He is constantly (with diminishing adjectives attached to him) contrasted to "Our whole Parliament put together," or "all the *Kingdom"* (p. 6); in Letter II, "one single, diminutive, insignificant, Mechanick" is put up against "a great Kingdom," "the Entire Legislature," and "the Properties of the whole Nation" (p. 24–25).

The implication is double: that Wood is a selfish individualist who would sacrifice a whole realm to his greed, and that he is alone. Swift's aim (carried out primarily in Letter II) is to isolate Wood from the king, at the same time suggesting that behind him there are unscrupulous Whigs for whom he is, in effect, a mere catspaw. By separating him from power and authority, Swift turns Wood into an impotent threat and his project into an illusion. But as a tempter he remains dangerous, and Swift's attack is thus in a sense on the crowd, the apathetic Irish public who are allowing this man to get away with his scheme when they do not have to. Without the king's backing, Swift is careful to emphasize to the crowd, any such scheme can come to nothing. This line of development reaches its climax in the image of Wood as a housebreaker or highwayman (the appropriate image for Swift's shopkeeper audience, as well as a reductive one for Wood): but significantly he is a highwayman without a firearm.

> If an High-way-man meets you on the Road, you give him your Money to save your Life, but, God be thanked, Mr. *Woods* cannot touch a Hair of your Heads. . . . If a Madman should come to my Shop with an Handful of Dirt raked out of the Kennel, and offer it in payment for Ten Yards of Stuff, I would Pity or Laugh at him, or, if his Behaviour deserved it, Kick him out of my Doors (p. 29).

Wood is turned into a subject for contemptuous laughter: he is the puny evil that is *apparently* powerful—and is dangerous only so long as the people think he is powerful. And so Swift's object is to show him as he really is.

Through equations, adjectives, metaphors, scattered references, and addresses to divergent groups of people, Swift gradually isolates and defines, or builds up an image of, a particular "William Wood": it is not an individualized character, but it is a recognizable symbol around which the reader's feelings (of fear, contempt, or even pity) are strongly realized. He is a man both dangerous and pathetic, both terrible and funny: and this mixture of response makes him memorable.

The consequences of Wood's project are equally ambiguous. If they are shown to be terrible in the first letter, they become comic in Letter II, where Wood appears powerless to effect meaningful consequences. Here the social chaos has become merely the comic multiplicity of potential evil—an image of busy bungling:

> Let Mr. *Woods* and his Crew of *Founders* and *Tinkers* Coyn on till there is not an old Kettle left in the Kingdom, let them Coyn old Leather, Tobacco-pipe Clay or the Dirt in the Streets, and call their Trumpery by what Name they please from a Guinea to a Farthing, we are not under any Concern to know how he and his Tribe of Accomplices think fit to employ themselves (p. 22).

And in Letter IV this becomes the preposterous image of Walpole's agents, computed at 50,000, who must come over to Ireland to feed Wood's coins to the Irish. Part of the image of chaotic consequences, then, is the fruitless busywork of the agents of chaos, just as part of the villain is his incompetence.

The fiction Swift creates thus revolves around a villain, William Wood; his project; the consequences of his project, which are made out to be the utter destruction of Ireland; and the people of Ireland, who, if they are not careful, can become Wood's dupes.

The final element in the fiction is a speaker for the people of Ireland, M. B., Drapier, the first-person "author" who draws our attention to the character of the projector Wood and to the consequences of his project. The Drapier is Swift's mouthpiece, the norm of his satire, and an appropriate one in that he is a middle-class Irishman (much more suitable than a Dean of the Church of England) ; he is an honest and respectable tradesman who will himself be affected by Wood's coins. As Martin Price says, he is "prosperous enough to resist temptation . . . enough an Irishman to identify his interests with the kingdom's."[3] His appeal begins as a sort of triumphant scoffing at Wood and shifts to an admission of the hopelessness of his task, of the crowd's having indeed gone over to Wood, and of his own defeat. Even in Letter II, in the midst of the imagery of Wood as the one lone man against the whole world, we learn that the Drapier too is alone; he is doing his best to save the Irish, but they are all cold and indifferent (p. 28), and in Letter III, when the situation for Ireland has worsened, he pictures himself as the only person willing to meet the threat.

Swift's mimetic method follows directly from the old practice of answering the opponent's argument point for point, where half of the pamphlet is quotation. Given the patent issued to Wood, Swift expands upon the implications that appear to him (overlooked by the authorities, though probably not by Walpole and Wood) until he has projected the image of national fiscal chaos.[4] The more typical Swiftean strategy can be seen in the image of Walpole's agents come to feed Wood's coins to the Irish (Letter IV). This apparition arises not as a logically-computed outcome of Wood's project but out of the mouth of Walpole himself. A pro-Irish pamphlet published in Bristol had Wood reporting Walpole's saying that he "will cram this Brass down our Throats" (p. 85); and the *Dublin Intelligence* quotes Walpole as saying that "he could make them [the Irish] swallow it in Fireballs" (p. xli). Swift gives these words a life of their own so that they can redound upon their "maker," who uncon-

---

[3] Price, *Swift's Rhetorical Art*, p. 68.

[4] *The Modest Proposal,* for example, is essentially the dramatization of a cliché that must have been on the lips of many Irishmen: Swift underlines it when he has his "author" say that the landlords "have already devoured most of the Parents" and "seem to have the best Title to the Children," and that the English *"would be glad to eat up our whole Nation."* "The persons of Quality and Fortune," to whom the children are going to be "offered in Sale," are already metaphorically devouring the children and the Irish poor in general; so this is just an ironic regularizing of a state that already exists. See *The Prose Works of Jonathan Swift,* ed. Herbert Davis (Oxford: Blackwell Press, 1939–64), XII, 112, 117. Cited hereafter as *Prose Works.*

sciously exposes his real intentions toward the people of Ireland. The Drapier explores their implications in a story of

> a *Scotch*-man, who receiving Sentence of Death, with all the Circumstances of *Hanging, Beheading, Quartering, Embowelling* and the like, cryed out, *What need all this* COOKERY; And I think we have Reason to ask the same Question; for if we believe *Wood*, here is a *Dinner* getting ready for us, and you see the *Bill of Fare*, and I am sorry the Drink was forgot, which might easily be supply'd with *Melted Lead* and *Flaming Pitch* (p. 85).

This then leads into the image of 50,000 English soldiers landing in Ireland with spoons to force-feed the Irish the coins and fireballs, "which, considering the Squeamishness of some Stomachs and the Peevishness of Young Children, is but reasonable" (p. 86). The resulting image is somewhere between torture and unpleasant doses of medicine; between the terrible and the ludicrous, the dangerous and the merely foolish.

One important level of the reality Swift constructs (and plays with) is this live, swimming, protean world of words becoming things and things generating scenes and actions. It is a short step from the pamphleteer who exaggerates his opponent's arguments into their caricature to the satirist who steps back and allows the opponent to speak for himself, creating his own absurdities. He simply signs his pamphlet with the opponent's name.

In his most audacious satire, *A Tale of a Tub* (1704), Swift attributes the origin of the imagery to the first-person speaker himself (a nameless Grub Street hack) and their elaboration is attributable to his "converting imagination" in the Puritan manner. Nor are his high-aspiring words mere gibberish or noise, as they are for Pope in *The Dunciad:* they reveal the speaker's hidden thoughts, his secret intentions and motives. The fact that the exposition is beyond the intention and awareness of the speaker is also part of Swift's point. Behind Cleveland's conceits there was doubtless a conservative world view that acknowledged the authority of the past and the common response, as opposed to the ephemeral Puritan who pretended to such permanence. Swift is much more specifically Christian in his emphasis, relying on the same assumption seen in *The Drapier's Letters,* that the evil agent attempts to pervert nature while Nature herself smiles unperturbed or quickly puts him in his place. In Swift's mind this leads to the Lucianic first-person speaker who damns himself out of his own mouth. Nothing else is needed in this formulation: nature, or the good, is implicit in his self-condemnation. Moreover, the speaker's inability to see the import of his own words merely emphasizes the fact that evil is, like Satan, ultimately a tool of God, part of a larger plan of which he is unaware.

Swift's first-person speakers are usually approached through his rhetoric, his use of ironic structures; and this is appropriate, because, unlike other examples of irony embodied in character —for example, Lazarillo de Tormes or Don Quixote—Swift's speakers retain something of the superstructure. The degree of dramatization in Swift's first-person satires is a question that has been debated at length and seems to depend on personal preference. The simplest view is that Swift is himself the satirist adopting a series of ironic poses, one minute blaming by praise and the next condemning without irony. The brilliance is entirely in the rhetoric and the effect is of Swift making a speech. Scott was not the last to remark Swift's ability to "assume any character which he chose to personate."[5] This explanation fits many of Swift's satires and points up the particular direction Swift takes toward dramatization. Nevertheless, when the point of view impersonated does not have the characteristics of the satirist, when it is maintained with some consistency, and when it is implemented by intimate details that do not fit the Dean of St. Patrick's, the dramatic implications of the situation begin to take precedence over the rhetorical. The reader may or may not be aware of Swift's presence behind the mask or that he holds the puppet strings. With Ebenezor Elliston or Isaac Bickerstaff, the intention is to trick the reader into thinking that he is reading a true confession and a true almanac. Indeed, Swift gives us more to

[5] Sir Walter Scott, *The Works of Jonathan Swift* (Edinburgh, 1814), I, 263. For a representative statement of the view that only Swift himself, or Swift assuming a momentary pose, is speaking, see Irvin Ehrenpreis, "Personae," in *Restoration and Eighteenth-Century Literature,* ed. C. Camden (Chicago, Ill.: University of Chicago Press, 1963), pp. 25–38.

go on with his "authors" than Defoe does with a narrator like Mrs. Bargrave's neighbor who recounts the *Apparition of Mrs. Veal;* she is only a woman and a point of view, while the writer of the *Tale of a Tub* is a hack writer, lives in a garret, has had domestic troubles, and has spent time in Bedlam; and the Modest Proposer is a bourgeois, has a wife past childbearing, and his youngest child is nine years old. On the other hand, in most cases (the *Bickerstaff Papers* and *Gulliver's Travels* are exceptions), Swift's speaker is presenting an argument, not describing a scene. Our interest is not focused on his description of people but on the way his own mind operates—however clouded it may be by the diction, syntax, and clichés of the project-form in which he writes.

The device of the pseudo-author goes back to the Restoration. Dryden's mock-heroic served to take a man at his own evaluation of himself: Shadwell *thought* he was as good as Ben Jonson or even Virgil. However, we never hear Shadwell saying this, only the satirist who places the real Shadwell in a world of Virgilian echoes. Denham, Butler, and some of the anonymous satirists of *Rump Songs* had followed the device toward its logical end, moving beyond the analogizing satirist toward the method of direct impersonation, but Swift went so far as to publish pamphlets and whole books that pretend to have been written by hacks, projectors, and astrologers.

The unique effect of Swift's satires is partly owing to his preoccupation with what he considered subversive literary forms. He was not the first to sense in new literary trends a threat to old values or to equate literature with religion and government as part of a moral climate; Dryden had made clear the relationship between the moral and the literary in *Mac Flecknoe* when he showed the poetasters King Flecknoe and Prince Shadwell holding court on a stage in a ruinous part of London well known for its brothels. But in *A Tale of a Tub* Swift made literature the vehicle of his metaphor: his fiction, speaker, syntax, form, and general subject are first a reflection of current literary forms, and then—sometimes overtly, sometimes not—a reflection of religious, political, and moral solecisms. In an imitation of the book in which the author's imagination supersedes principles or examples of order (and introductory chapters, indexes, and digressions overwhelm his book), Swift created his own version of the Achitophel who would overthrow the state to gain his private ends.

Swift's Version of the Tory Fiction

As Swift developed his own interpretation of the Augustan Tory assumptions, he constructed his typical fiction out of the following elements:

(1) The "plot" has become the central element. It is a written work, a project, plan, scheme, or panacea, which the Grub Street Hack or Simon Wagstaff, or almost any of Swift's "authors," proposes and outlines in detail. Besides plausibility it gives Swift's satires their form by offering an argument, a catalog of particulars or proofs, and a list of answers or reasons (as in *An Argument against Abolishing Christianity* or *A Modest Proposal*). The astrologer's almanac of the *Bickerstaff Papers* is a similarly ideal vehicle with its long list of entries, and the rules of a conduct book (as in the *Directions to Servants*) is another. The critical and "literary" hack writing of the time offered an extremely flexible form with a place for everything from the chapbook tale to the Royal Society project, from footnotes to digressions.

Dryden expended his mimicry on the Bible, the *Aeneid,* and *Paradise Lost,* giving his villains a dignity which Swift denies his; Swift imitates the popular forms and idioms that have usurped their place, and his mock-heroic level is accordingly lower, more commonplace and contemporary. In his satiric impersonations this level becomes the prosaic projector's talk of "the universal benefit of mankind" or of the "fair, cheap, and easy" proposal that will "deserve so well of the Publick [or be so "Beneficial to the Publick"], as to have [its author's] Statue set up for a Preserver of the Nation."[6] The reality is the speak-

---

[6] *Prose Works*, XII, 25.

er's economic motivation and the horrible plan itself that emerges from his words; the proposal for making the children of Ireland "sound and useful Members of the Commonwealth" is opposed to the reality of cooking them for profit.

The projector's pamphlet therefore expresses Swift's double aim: verisimilitude and a form for conveying the conscious and unconscious operations of a mind—proposals with a false semblance of reason and order, with paragraphs beginning "First," "Therefore," "In answer to," and "It is further objected." The very ordering and formalizing of raw thought expresses a certain kind of mind (still essentially Puritan) that wishes to mask reality with reason and rhetoric.

(2) The purpose of the Swiftean "author's" project is to implicate or catch the mindless crowd. When blame-by-praise irony is dramatized in a speaker, two elements result: a speaker who is foolishly but sincerely praising obvious follies—moderns' large posteriors or the transience of their works; and an audience of people who can be persuaded to admire large posteriors. The pamphlet presupposes the audience to which it is ostensibly addressed and so a single wavelength on which author and audience communicate; it is crowd-oriented, aimed at their lowest, most restless instincts. One of Swift's satiric assumptions is that the crowd, the ostensible audience of his ironic address, will read and accept the level of meaning that involves selling and cooking babies.

(3) The hint of the good appears outside the fiction in the true audience of Swift's ironic structure, those people with ordinary moral and intellectual awareness. And so inside the fiction it appears in the natural rectitude of language and logic. The reader acknowledges this when he accepts the eiron's (Swift's) level of meaning, as opposed to the persona's illogical, extravagantly personal, and often mad meaning. Common sense, logic, ordinary meaning become the law of nature or of God against which the recalcitrant characters are revolting, and which is constantly reasserting itself.

If the ideal is partly an implied common sense, it is also planted concretely here and there in the text. In the *Argument against Abolishing Christianity,* the "author" remarks, "I have heard it affirmed for certain by *some very old People,* that the contrary Opinion [that is, that Christianity is meaningful] was *even in their Memories* as much in vogue as the other is now; and that a Project for the abolishing of Christianity would *then* have appeared as singular, and been thought as absurd, as it would be at this Time to write or discourse in its Defence" (italics mine).[7] "Real Christianity" existed only, we are told, "in primitive Times" (p. 27).

Swift's foil to the image of evil is often complicated by the fact that he implies both an impossible ideal and a humanly possible norm. The original coat in the tale of the brothers (*A Tale of a Tub*), given by the father to his sons, cannot be recovered; the best that can be managed is Martin's attempt to steer a middle course between Peter's piling up of braid and Jack's ripping of the coat's fabric. Inevitably Martin's coat retains the imperfections of some braid and some rents. By adding an ideal above and beyond the middle way, Swift reminds his readers who correspond to the norm that even they have little to be proud of. In the *Argument against Abolishing Christianity* the implicit advice to the reader is to retain or resurrect as much of "Real Christianity" as is consonant with present-day England (more, clearly, than the name).

(4) The civil chaos that results from the plot or project takes two allied forms in Swift's satire. First, it is the image of imminent destruction, which Pope was to enlarge upon in *The Dunciad.* In Swift's early poem, *The Ode to the Athenian Society,* it is the Flood and the descent of the Goths on European civilization; *A Tale of a Tub* specifically invokes the English Civil War and the split in Christendom as the twin corruptions of politics and religion. In the projects, almanacs, and the like, however, this hypothetical scene in the future takes on a quite different form. The facts, reasons, explanations the projector gives us in his argument create a perfect, orderly anti-utopia in which a gentleman, when he wishes to propagate an heir, summons a

---

[7] *Prose Works,* II, 27.

clergyman (the only physically sound male left), and himself repairs with his mistress to the church for an assignation. Or he projects a world in which babies are sold at a year old for butchering, and so national revenues are enormously increased, prosperity reigns, and gourmets have a new delicacy. Poor tenants will have something valuable of their own (since their cattle are confiscated and money is "a Thing unknown"), and poor mothers will have eight shillings profit and no maintenance of children after their first year. Kindness and love settle over the land: seducers are now inclined to press for marriage, and when married they pamper their wives, not daring to kick them during pregnancy for fear of a miscarriage. Even mothers love their children and care for them almost as if they were calves.

This pseudo-utopia is, of course, based on a false order. A wonderful effect—the most orderly society imaginable—follows from the most appalling causes and motives. Rhetorically, however, the hypothetical situation usually takes the form of Horace's Epode XVI, to which Swift alludes in the *Argument against Abolishing Christianity:* an impossible alternative, like sailing to the "blessed isles" with the whole population of Rome, which reveals the impossibility of the situation as it stands in Rome (or England or Ireland). In the *Argument* the nominal Christianity projected by the "author" points up the impossibility of living meaningfully without true Christianity. In *A Modest Proposal* the projected hypothetical situation first serves as a means of defining the speaker, becoming with him a symbol of the evil; second, it becomes a preposterous alternative which shows up the intolerable situation of human selfishness and indolence which makes this monstrous proposal the only feasible one— better, awful as it is, than the present situation. The Proposer suggests that the parents themselves be asked "Whether they would not at this Day think it is a great Happiness to have been sold for Food at a Year old, in the Manner I prescribe."[8]

(5) The evil agent himself, at his simplest, is the Earl of Wharton, the prototypical "liar" who is descended, Swift sug-

[8] *Prose Works,* XII, 117.

gests, from the father of lies, Satan. He is the complete casuist, distributing lies "every Minute he speaks, and [which he] by an unparallelled Generosity forgets, and consequently contradicts the next half Hour."[9] Like Satan's, Wharton's "lies" are not permanent works but, being made for the minute, transient illusions quickly swept away. They are a mad exaltation of the moment at the expense of the substantial and permanent. The Devil can create nothing permanent or do any real damage. Nevertheless, as Swift insists, "if a *lye* be believed only for an hour, it hath done its work," and some corruption of human value is possible.

Like Wharton's lies, modern writings posted one day cannot be found the next, and the very existence of modern writers "to the moment" is in doubt. The tailor and the spider are both immobile, completely alone, though presumably worshipped by moderns, and their only source of knowledge is within themselves. The tailor invents fashions of the moment, superseded as quickly as they appear, and the spider weaves his flimsy web out of his own guts. The spider has contact with no one or thing besides his own dirty surroundings; and the tailor is surrounded with sexual puns and imagery which connect him with sterility and impotence (Swift is playing upon the old saying: "It takes nine tailors to make a man"). The modern is completely alone, having no contact with others, even quarreling with his own kind, and is ultimately like the madman in Bedlam who (like the spider) feeds only on his own excrement.

But instead of accepting his ephemerality, which (as Swift himself recognizes in the *Verses on the Death of Dr. Swift*) is part of the human condition, the tailor, the spider, the Grub Street Hack, Peter, and Jack try to impose their ephemerality on others: each one forcing others to see things according to his own crazy view. The evil man is merely the ordinary man become proud of his very weakness and ephemerality, and anxious to fortify himself by imposing them on others. He is the man with the heavily braided coat who tries to make everyone he

---

[9] *Examiner* No. 14 (Nov. 9, 1710), in *Prose Works,* III, 11.

sees wear heavily braided coats, or the man with the tattered coat who tries to make the rest of the world tear up their coats.

(6) Swift has gone beyond Dryden, focusing on the culprit without the intermediary of a normative satiric commentator. He does, however, reflect Dryden's approach in a curious but significant way. Dryden's satiric speaker (partly as a reaction against the satyr-satirist) was outside the object of attack but raised no questions about his own character because he ironically assumed the culprit's own view, seeing him as he saw himself. But if this speaker of blame-by-praise irony is taken seriously (that is, fictionalized), he becomes a duped adherent of the culprit. Swift's speakers are related to the unfictionalized ironic commentators of *Mac Flecknoe* and *Absalom and Achitophel* in that the satirist is still praising evil, but now his irony is completely embodied in a fiction. He is not the evil himself any more than Dryden's praiser of evil was, but a combination of satirist and satiric object in a single speaker.

Swift seldom shows his evil directly—only its reflection in his first-person "author." As he makes abundantly clear in his "character" of the Earl of Wharton, such monsters are rarely encountered and require careful study when they do appear. Perhaps thinking of Wharton, he wrote in his *Proposal for Correcting the English Language*: "Satire is reckoned the easiest of all wit, but I take it to be otherwise in very bad times: for it is as hard to satirize well a man of distinguished vices, as to praise well a man of distinguished virtues. It is easy enough to do either to people of moderate characters."[10] Even a monster like William Wood in *The Drapier's Letters* has a greater monster behind him, Walpole in England. In *A Tale of a Tub* the evil hovers offstage in the books of the moderns, in the shadowy figures of Bentley, Wotton, and others; it appears in the tale of the brothers in Peter and Jack; and in such symbols as the tailor and the spider. But all of this is *reflected* in the "author," for he is most of the time reporting the moderns' (as opposed to his

[10] *Prose Works*, IV (ed. Davis and Louis Landa), 243.

own) views. He is a bungling adherent of the wicked who exposes himself and his models to the accompaniment of his laboriously unfolding argument.

To get at the peculiar quality of this figure, Swift's dupe, we should look back at one of his classical sources, Horace's Satire II.3.[11] This satire, a remote relative of the satirist-satirized fiction and a source of the "Digression on Madness," presents a stoic sermon on madness which draws attention to the fact that the people we conventionally think of as mad—spendthrifts or visionaries—are no crazier than their opposite extremes, the misers or hardheaded scoundrels we praise. The gist of Swift's "Digression" is much the same: the kings who start wars, the fanatics who invent religions, and the philosophers who create systems are really no more in control of their wits than the inmates of Bedlam.[12]

The use of madness as a satiric touchstone is by no means unusual; but Swift also follows Horace in a more important particular, that of his structure. The stoic sermon in Horace's satire does not stand alone. Horace has a ne'er-do-well named Damasippus recount (in effect, imitate) the words of a stoic named Stertinius. The recounted sermon is framed by a dialogue between Horace and Damasippus which places the sermon in perspective, casting satiric shafts upon both the stoic philosopher and his new disciple, Damasippus. In the frame dialogue we learn that Damasippus has failed in his crazy business ventures,

[11] Horace's works were among the volumes Swift listed as his reading for 1696/7, when he was presumably working on *A Tale of a Tub*. See ed. A. C. Guthkelch and D. Nichol Smith (2nd ed., Oxford: Clarendon Press, 1958), p. lvi. Citations from the *Tale* refer to this edition.

[12] The use Horace and Swift made of madness is quite different from Erasmus' use of madness in *The Praise of Folly* (which is also derived in part from Horace's Satire II.3). Folly delivers a sermon not unlike that of Horace's stoic philosopher; but Erasmus' satire contrasts the "foolish" man who follows his own simple faith with the "wise" man who relies too heavily on his own reason or on complicated church dogmas. The wise man, Erasmus claims, is actually the fool, while the foolish ideal of Christian simplicity (here specifically a return to apostolic tradition) is ultimately wise. Horace, and following him Swift, use madness as a satiric touchstone, pointing out irrationality where we do not ordinarily look for it. The result is a blanketing of madness rather than the sharp paradox of the foolish-wise man presented by Erasmus.

is a laughingstock, and is on the point of committing suicide. Stertinius the stoic has tried to set his mind at rest by demonstrating in considerable detail that if Damasippus is mad (he has subtly shifted folly, or poor business sense, to madness), certainly so is everybody else: "Now learn why all, who have given you the name of madman, are quite as crazy as yourself."[13] As he ticks off the categories, he shows that literally everybody is in some sense mad. Stertinius proves his point; he uses madness as a satiric touchstone that reveals the irrationality in much supposedly normal behavior. He points out to Agamemnon (in an imaginary interview) that Ajax's fury was less insane than Agamemnon's own "reasonable" sacrifice of his daughter Iphigenia, and that the man who accuses another of madness had better pause to question the rationality of his own behavior. On this level the satire operates as a generalized attack on man's pride and his penchant for self-deception.

But as Stertinius' examples accumulate, the initial truth of his commentary gives way to the reader's realization that he is going too far—his demonstration itself becomes a kind of madness. The sermon ultimately embodies a satiric attack on the stoic philosopher who finds everybody mad except himself. However, even more important is the light the sermon throws on Damasippus. For him the stoic's sermon is not so much an attack on man's pride as a license for his own madness: "Such were the weapons which my friend Stertinius, eighth of the wise men, put in my hands, that no one thereafter might call me names with impunity."[14] Now Damasippus has a taunt he can fling back whenever he does something ridiculous. He has a device for reducing all human behavior to the level of his own folly.

Horace expresses three points of view, three kinds of folly, in the sermon. First, Stertinius exposes our common madness. Second, Stertinius' own intention is to show that only the stoic is sane, and he comes close to proving his own madness. And third, we hear his sermon secondhand, delivered by his convert Dama-

[13] Lines 46–48; *Satires, Epistles and Ars Poetics,* trans. H. Rushton Fairclough, Loeb Library edition (London: Heinemann, 1926), pp. 156–57.
[14] *Ibid.,* pp. 176–79.

sippus, who does not quite see through Stertinius' apologia. Damasippus presents it as a defense of his own madness. This is essentially the form that Swift uses throughout *A Tale of a Tub,* where the Grub Street Hack is recounting the opinions of the moderns in an attempt to excuse his own failures and frustrations. He is giving us not original insights but those "of our illustrious *Moderns"* (p. 92), and behind him there always lurks the "modern" he is emulating. In the "Digression on Madness" he gives us a half-truth (or a satiric truth)—that all men are mad—followed by his own gradual self-exposure, and the reader's growing awareness that this half-truth is an evasion and that the madness of mankind is not an adequate excuse for one's own lunacy. The Hack tries to reduce all evil to a mental instability (ultimately to the effect of a vapor) and all people to his own level of erratic behavior. At the end he admits that he has spent some time in Bedlam himself, and all of the pieces fall into place: he has been reducing "the Notions of all Mankind, exactly to the same Length, and Breadth, and Height of his own," gathering the rest of humanity into the fold of his own madness (p. 166).[15]

Filtered through him the evil of "modernism" is less Satanic than Quixotic. As Satan rebels against God, Don Quixote, a somewhat lower, certainly more comic and ineffectual prototype, rebels against the commonplace world of windmills and sheep. The Grub Street Hack, like Quixote, has read all the wrong books and now sallies forth to act upon their assumptions. The actual evil being attacked lies behind him, as it did behind

[15] In the matter of madness, Swift's fiction follows directly from Horace's. Of the many imitators of Horace's Satire II.3 only Swift duplicates the ironic structure of the satirist-satirized that is its distinctive feature. Boileau, for example, in his fourth satire, simply adapts some of the stoic sermon, but without the frame. He reverses the tenor of the stoic's statement: we say *they* are crazy (he says), but let us look at ourselves. "On others Faults we fall, but spare our own," as Boileau's translator puts it (*The Works of Monsieur Boileau...* [London, 1712], p. 178). In this sense Boileau's satire is perhaps more closely connected with Horace's plea for tolerance in Satire I.3. But Swift uses Horace's message as well as his form: that it is subtler, but no juster, to say that all men are fools *like* me than it is to say that all are fools *except* me. Both amount to the same attempt at self-vindication.

Quixote, in the books of modern philosophy and romance. The reader's attention is on the little man who aspires upward and blunders into codes of behavior which he does not completely understand. But the Hack, a less sympathetic Quixote, is using the moderns to sanction his own weaknesses, just as Damasippus used the speech of Stertinius to sanction his folly.

As a Quixote, Swift's dupe is also the madman who would try to change the world to suit his own limited vision, but constantly collides with hard realities which unhorse him. He serves as a *reductio ad absurdum* of Peter and Jack, the moderns and schismatics he imitates; for all of them are tilting against the real meanings of wills, the true nature of words or cloth, the hard sensuous reality of lampposts and cold, high garrets. The very fact that every evil agent is an individualist is expressed in this lone representative who has his own, slightly askew, slightly misunderstood plan (the moderns themselves, he tells us, have repudiated him).

The important points about Swift's protagonist are his lack of originality and his relative sincerity—his obtuseness rather than hypocrisy. He descends from Absalom rather than Achitophel, the fool who wants to be king and, with the help of Achitophel, persuades himself that he is acting for the "benefit of mankind." In this respect he also draws upon Molière's Orgon, the foolish and incompetent *pater familias* who (like Horace's Damasippus) is duped by the religious hypocrite Tartuffe because the doctrines Tartuffe offers give him the sanction he needs to tyrannize over his family. Lady Fidget and Sir Jasper in Wycherley's *The Country Wife* stand in the same relation to Horner, who offers wives an opportunity to have lovers without losing their "honor," and husbands an opportunity to appear free with their wives without any danger to their honor. Of the various dupes of Restoration comedy, the fop is probably the closest to Swift's protagonist. The latter shares the fop's unawareness, his dedication to the externals, and unconcern for the reality. Like the fop he is an outsider who apes the fine talk, clothes, and love-making of the true rake. Swift merely omits mention of the consequences to his dupes, although he implies them. He also omits all of the characters except the dupe and their reflection in his eyes.

Most important, he omits the satirist. In Dryden the satirist accepted the premises of the fools and knaves, becoming, as a satirist, rather dim; in Swift the satirist has disappeared. The satire's subject is an ambiguous figure, a Damasippus who is one part villain and one part satirist—a self-satirist as he unconsciously exposes himself and a Drydenesque satirist of others as he unconsciously exposes his models.

As a symbol, he is an intermediate figure who, by presenting soberly what he only half understands, allows us to distinguish between his own and a larger, more absolute evil of which he is an imitator or disciple. He is a middleman in the sense that he is a hack writer, a popularizer of other men's ideas, and, to Swift's thinking, a relatively new species (literary, political, economic, moral) : the man who accrues his own profit by peddling the products of other people who are more clearly defined in terms of good and evil.

He stands between two extremes: on one side of him is the evil, on the other side the good, and the unsavory task he takes upon himself is to reconcile the two for his own profit. In *An Argument against Abolishing Christianity* he maintains a position between the evil (the abolishing of Christianity altogether) and the good (true Christianity), advocating nominal Christianity. In *A Modest Proposal* the speaker is trying to put a good face on the barbarism of the Irish and English treatment of Ireland. To one side of him is the selfishness of the English and the absentee Irish landowners, the economic motive that has produced the hopeless situation in Ireland; to the other is the idea of a plan for alleviating Ireland's misery. The Proposer takes the savagery of the evil and combines it with the good intentions of the projects to produce a vicious compromise.

It should be noted that this situation is a parody of a structure ordinarily associated with Augustan satire—the Horatian dialectic with two opposite extremes, both evils, bracketing an inferential golden mean. Swift transforms the Horatian pose of fairness into a false dialectic employed by the speaker who tries to establish a middle way, not between the extremes of opposite excesses, but between the extremes of good and evil. His golden mean is at worst to attach the name of the good to the reality of the evil, at best to split the difference. The result is the *Mac Flecknoe* fiction, a parody of order and law.

The absolute evil, Swift implies, no longer speaks our language, and so we can get at it only through an intermediary—or it can only get at *us* in this way; but he would also say that not the real evil—which is rather easily seen—but the plausible appearance of reason and morality or even strength and order is the great danger. On the other hand, the evil we *can* cope with is human and commonplace. Every man is something of a Quixote or a Damasippus; only some men can submit to the controls of church and law and commonsense, as only some men can be outright knaves.

Dryden, like Furetière and other French equivalents, attacked the aspiring mind, but Swift is the first satirist to dramatize the vice at its source. While Dryden still attacks its consequences in civil war, Swift, significantly, makes the consequences hypothetical, part of a plan that is still on paper, suspended between the inventor's brain and execution. He has to a startling extent taken the evil action from the external world, where it was in Dryden and remained in Pope, and located it in the human consciousness. The evil dramatized in *The Modest Proposal* is finally in the mind spinning its plans, or in the project itself, which is only a physical manifestation of the plans; the cooked and eaten babies are not in the objective world but in a projector's hypothesis. The pathetic situation in Ireland is real enough, but the particular evil that Swift presents is the state of mind that allows the situation to exist and even hopes to make it yield a new source of income.

As a result of the new Lockean epistemology, Ernest Tuveson shows, "literature, from the eighteenth century on, has been drifting steadily toward contemplation of the world as seen by the mind rather than on 'truth' per se."[16] Swift was, of course, terribly concerned with this drift, and so he dramatized over and over "the world as seen by the mind," with a scathing irony that made clear its moral error and so his own confidence in the reality of "truth" outside the mind. The very ephemerality of thought seemed to suggest to him the ephemerality of evil. And Locke's picture of the mind supported his view. By producing the picture of a mind that can have no innate ideas, Locke showed that "no philosophy could clothe itself in an imprescriptible authority, for nothing is above the test of experience. The test, moreover, of common experience, and of the common, but alert mind."[17] Though Swift disagreed with the doctrine of the *tabula rasa,* he found in every other way a philosophy of mind suited to his satiric mission of attacking the reason that claimed too much for itself or that deceived itself.

Swiftean Realism: The *Bickerstaff Papers*

As the example of the Damasippus situation showed, Swift's effects are always means to the single end of ridiculing the morally reprehensible. However complex his fictions become, they are first persuasive structures, every detail making its satiric point, and only second (even incidentally, though it is this which sets off Swift from lesser satirists) profound explorations of certain areas of experience. In this section we shall examine some of Swift's techniques and indicate their rhetorical purpose and their effect.

Black journalism, or the use of a pseudo-author, offers not only a satiric symbol but the real possibility that the reader will believe that a Puritan or hack writer is writing and unconsciously

---

[16] *The Imagination as a Means of Grace* (Berkeley and Los Angeles: University of California Press, 1960), p. 26. See also Tuveson's "Locke and Sterne," in *Reason and the Imagination: Studies in the History of Ideas, 1600–1800,* ed. J. A. Mazzeo (New York: Columbia University Press, 1962), pp. 255–77.

[17] Tuveson, "Locke and Sterne," p. 259.

exposing his sinister motives. As his love of practical jokes and hoaxes shows, Swift seems always to have wished to achieve a kind of ambiguous status somewhere between acceptance as real and recognition as satire. In fact, the interplay of life and art that impinges upon a man's actual existence seems to have been a favorite device of Swift and his circle.

In the most famous of these hoaxes an almanac maker, Isaac Bickerstaff, predicted the death of another almanac maker, John Partridge, down to the exact day and hour. When the day came a second pamphlet appeared announcing the fulfilment of the prophecy—Partridge's death. The fact and the fiction almost merged: there was, of course, a John Partridge, and when Swift's second pamphlet was published the account of his death *was* believed, to the extent that his name was struck from the rolls in Stationer's Hall. Even Partridge himself was shaken: after his 1709 almanac he issued no other until 1714, and this did indeed prove to be his last; the following year Bickerstaff's prophecy was fulfilled.[18]

It is interesting as a sign of the times that Swift was joined in the hoax by Rowe, Congreve, and others; the hoax expresses the insider's scorn for the outsider and, conversely, a feeling of group solidarity. At its harshest it isolates the bore from society altogether, attempting to convince society that, like William Wood in *The Drapier's Letters,* he is alone, against everyone and opposed by everyone or, like Partridge, he is dead.

In a broader sense, however, such hoaxes represented a strategy for conveying a sense of the real by destroying the distinction between real and fictional—the opposite of Cervantes' practice of making the real more real by juxtaposing it with the obviously fictional. This was not a new strategy, but one well explored, like so many of the Augustans' techniques, by the early humanist satirists. The *Epistolae Obscurorum Virorum* (1515) was published so as to appear to be the New Learning's reply to Reuchlin's *Clarorum Virorum Epistolae* of the preceding year; each

---

[18] For background of publication, see George P. Mayhew, "Swift's Bickerstaff Hoax as an April Fool's Joke," *Modern Philology,* LXI (1961), 270–80.

correspondent exposed himself, unselfconsciously, in all his "doltishness, pedantry, and, it must be added, immorality."[19] And in the seventeenth century Pascal used the same technique in his *Provincial Letters.* These works, unlike Erasmus' *Praise of Folly,* or the imitations of Denham and Butler, make claims to be taken as the works of real, live people.

Defoe of course produced such works, sometimes with specifically polemical if not satiric intent (*The Shortest Way with the Dissenters* [1702]), and sometimes with no other aim than to convince of the reality of author, book, and story. Steele's misinterpretation of the *Epistolae,* an edition of which had been dedicated to him,[20] though partly due to reading a work out of its historical and polemical context, showed that Defoe, Swift, and Pope were all writing to a pluralistic audience, a large part of which could (or must) be counted upon to accept the literal level. This made for some very curious effects; but also in Defoe, if not in Swift, for the possibility that the rhetorical aim of persuasion will become subordinated to the aim of simply portraying reality convincingly. At any rate, the members of the Scriblerus Club persisted in producing such first-person narratives that were intended to pass for fact in bookstalls where they rubbed shoulders with Defoe's latest authentic criminal memoir. The Scriblerians' use of illusionistic documents—forged projects, confessions, and travel memoirs—suggests the paradox that as satire increases in rhetorical effectiveness it draws less and less attention to itself as satire; ultimately the most effective satire (given its generic aims) would be the one that passed as something else. (The reader's knowledge that he is reading satire makes him more aware of formal matters and less concerned about combating evil.)

[19] E. G. Stokes, ed., *Epistolae Obscurorum Virorum* (New Haven, Conn.: Yale University Press, 1925), pp. xlv–xlvi.

[20] This edition was published in London in 1710. Steele's comments appear in *Tatler* No. 197, 13 July 1710. It is not certain whether Swift knew of the *Epistolae* before its 1710 edition; Pope alludes to it in *The Dunciad* (see Aubrey Williams, *Pope's Dunciad* [London: Methuen, 1955], pp. 61–62).

The ideal hoax is one in which no reader—no one but the satirist and his friends—can with certainty tell fact from fiction. Thus in Swift's Ebenezor Elliston hoax of 1722 the "genuine" "Dying Statement" of the condemned criminal was advertised in Dublin newspapers, and Swift's pseudo-document was put into circulation at exactly the same time as Elliston's own, as he was on his way to the gallows. The public at the execution could have accepted Swift's as the real one, and Elliston himself (who was doubtless indignant hearing a rival "Dying Statement" hawked) was shortly in no condition to prove which was genuine. The Swiftean statement included the fact that Elliston had left a list of his confederates in crime which was to be given to the authorities if they did not give up their robbing and killing. According to Scott, Swift's realism had its desired effect, and the crime rate in Dublin went down.[21]

Swift's friend and confederate, Alexander Pope, also liked to create an event on paper that was meant to have happened in fact, or even to carry out a fact that could then be recorded and embellished on paper. In either case the physical condition of the enemy was worked upon (fictionally or factually) to accord with the satirist's idea of his spiritual state, and the device was essentially one of punishment. In his *Narrative of Dr. Norris* (1713—again a combined effort, with Steele and perhaps others), he has the critic John Dennis go mad. The appropriateness of this hypothetical situation derived from Dennis' attack on Pope's *Essay on Criticism,* an attack whose violence seemed near the borderline of sanity, and whose main contention was that Pope was not writing poetry with the passion that Dennis, a good Miltonian and Longinian, believed was the duty of the younger poets. The satire takes the form of an authentic doctor's report, and at least partly gains its effect by attempting to convince people that Dennis is in fact out of his senses. Dr. Norris, a well-known quack who advertised his ability to cure lunatics, is called to Dennis' house on the report that he has fallen into a

[21] *Prose Works,* IX, 39; Scott, I, 263. See Mayhew, "Jonathan Swift's Hoax of 1722 upon Ebenezor Elliston," *Bulletin of the Rylands Library,* XLIV (1962), 360–80.

fit, and finds him thus (not so different from the real Dennis as to be improbable) :

> His Aspect was furious, his Eyes were rather fiery than lively, which he roll'd about in an uncommon manner. He often open'd his Mouth, as if he wou'd have utter'd some Matter of Importance, but the Sound seem'd lost inwardly. His Beard was grown, which they told me he would not suffer to be shav'd, believing the modern Dramatick Poets had corrupted all the Barbers in the town to take the first Opportunity of cutting his Throat.... His Flannel Night Cap, which was exceedingly begrim'd with Sweat and Dirt, hung upon his Left Ear; the Flap of his Breeches dangled between his Legs, and the Rolls of his Stockings fell down to his Ankles.[22]

Pope also contributed three papers on the sorrows of Edmund Curll. In the first he describes (or imagines) the results of the purge he did in fact administer (concealed in a drink) to the unscrupulous bookseller who had impugned the honor of Lady Mary Wortley Montagu. In the second he combines an imaginary account of Curll's further sufferings from the emetic with a list of his earlier punishments at the hands of an outraged public, such as his being tossed in a blanket by the boys of Westminster School. Finally, he reports as fact an imaginary parable of Curll's insatiable greed, the cause, Pope assumed, of all his immoral actions from the slighting of Lady Mary to the pirating of Pope's works. He describes the unfortunate outcome of Curll's initiation into the Jewish faith, which he thought would gain him more money and instead renders him another in the line of sterile Augustan villains. In all of these satires on Curll the sexual and excretory are made the symbols of his just punishment: his lust for money is cured by emasculation and his repletion by catharsis.

The creation of a false reality that interferes with, or even supersedes, the real—a false Curll that is confused with the real—is the most powerful way of creating an image of consequences. Thus the world of Pope's formal satires, the Horatian imitations and the moral essays, where he also sought to define

[22] *Prose Works of Alexander Pope,* ed. Norman Ault (Oxford: Blackwell, 1936), I, 158.

by consequences, stands in curious contrast to his direct imitations of reality.[23] Characteristically, Pope acknowledged the former, but not the black journalism we have been discussing. As Aubrey Williams has noted, he carries the effect over into the pseudo-realism of his *Dunciad* notes, which has caused literary historians to call him both inaccurate and a liar; the villains with whom he is dealing are made to appear more real by the contrast between their "historical" accounts in the notes and their symbolic appearance in the poem itself.[24] But at the same time that Pope is convincing his readers of the reality of his fiction, he is obscuring, rendering illusory if not nonexistent the reality itself. Their actual poverty and wretchedness are part of Pope's satiric picture of the dunces—badges of their real being under their false titles and pretensions; but turning one (again Curll) into a syphilitic wretch, or a person so obscure that his existence can no longer be proved, also makes the dunce more real and convincing as well as more exemplary. For an image that convinces, that gets across the satirist's point, Pope and Swift seem to have believed, may finally be the most realistic.

But establishing verisimilitude and grounding his satire in the world of fact are only preliminary steps for Swift. As their derivation from classical models suggests, his characters are primarily devices, as are the situations in which he places them: the Drapier is one minute the triumphant scoffer, the next the lone defender. A good Lucianic satire attempts to make as many simultaneous points as possible—the more different aspects of an evil the satiric symbol catches the better; and in this sense Swift's pre-eminence as a satirist is obvious. The *Bickerstaff Papers* (1708), to which we have already alluded, will serve as our example.

[23] In his Horatian imitations Pope uses an almost eschatological approach to folly. Death in the first and third *Moral Essays* is made the epitome of man's life (as it was in the *Picara Justina*): the portrait of Wharton, ending in his unhappy death, is followed by a list of deaths which epitomize the ruling passion of each of the individuals; and in the portraits of Villiers, Cutler, and Balaam, death is shown as a consummation of the consequences that can be expected from such behavior as theirs.

[24] Williams, *Pope's Dunciad,* pp. 61–62.

First there is the satire on Partridge, the almanac-maker, the creator of an alternative reality which will of course come tumbling down in a few months' time when the prophecy is proved untrue, but profitable at the moment: a neat embodiment of the Swiftean image of evil. The point of the satire is to prove "how ignorant these sottish Pretenders to Astrology are in their own Concerns."[25] Partridge the prophet, placed in the unsynchronized world of *Quixote* or *Absalom and Achitophel,* does not even know that he himself is going to die. Bickerstaff, the "true" astrologer, explains that *he* would offer no prophecy "to the world of which I am not as fully satisfied, as that I am now alive" (p. 143). As he demonstrates, Partridge is not very sure of his own existence, let alone of anyone else's. In a very general sense this is the skeptical reduction which begins with the proud man (here the prophet) and strips away all certainty, even of his own existence, leaving him the bare broomstick he in fact is.

But at the same time Swift is projecting a situation in which almanacs *are* correct and the world is full of Partridges—a world set going from his own assumptions (in this case the truth of almanacs). But therefore *any* almanac must tell the truth, and so Partridge is trapped in his own folly. Once the machinery has started it goes against Partridge, defeating and punishing him, plunging him into a nightmare world.

Bickerstaff himself, as a satiric device, is simply Swift pretending to be a better astrologer than Partridge—and in this normative role he was picked up by Steele for *The Tatler.* But Bickerstaff, too, is used in contrary ways. One wonders how much his *Vindication* is to be taken at face value as a comic criticism of Partridge and how much as a self-revelatory speech? At the end of the third letter Partridge is crying, "I shall demonstrate to the Judicious, that *France* and *Rome,* are at the bottom of this horrid Conspiracy against me"; but in his "vindication" we find Bickerstaff answering a man who has claimed that (contrary to his prophecy) the Cardinal de Noailles is still alive by asserting that he is "a *French* Man, a *Papist,* and an *Enemy*" (pp. 161,

[25] *Prose Works,* II, 145.

223). For, if we have gotten rid of one astrolger, we still have the "art of astrology" advocated by Bickerstaff.

And so the satire is also turned on Bickerstaff. His belief that astrologers are imposters but the art of astrology is true allows Swift to speak direct abuse of Partridge through Bickerstaff's mouth, and yet, without breaking the mold of his fiction, he can expose less directly other aspects of astrology in Bickerstaff himself. On one side is Partridge, the false prophet and primary object of attack, and on the other side the truth that astrology lies. In the middle is Isaac Bickerstaff who (as the author of the *Argument* repudiated the idea of abolishing Christianity) proves that Partridge's astrology lies but upholds the great art of astrology, in particular his own practice of it. Bickerstaff's pride declares that he is not "of the Level of common Astrologers" (p. 149) : he sets himself up as the only true artist. We notice the note of pride in his first pamphlet, and in the second the reporter who has come to verify the prophecy concludes, after Partridge's death: "But whether he [Bickerstaff] hath not been the Cause of this poor Man's Death, as well as the Predictor, may be very reasonably disputed" (p. 155). And in the sequel (supposedly by Rowe), Partridge refers to him as "my nameless old Persecutor," who goes to such lengths to prove him dead that he provides Partridge "a Monument at the Stone-Cutter's, and would have it erected in the Parish-Church" (Partridge calls this a "piece of notorious and expensive Villainy" (p. 222).[26]

The modern in *A Tale of a Tub* forced his reader to follow elaborate rules and conventions, and ultimately to set up in a garret to live his own kind of life, in order to understand his book; Peter forced his brothers to accept bread as claret and roast beef; and in the same way Bickerstaff must *bring about* the death of Partridge once he has prophesied it. He is the "freshest Modern" taking over Partridge's territory, destroying him in the process. Short of murdering him, he simply acts as if Partridge *were* dead.

[26] See *Prose Works*, II, xxiv–vi; Davis places this part of the *Bickerstaff Papers* in an appendix of "Additional Bickerstaff Papers not Written by Swift." I personally suspect that Swift had a hand in it himself.

This is, I think, the proper way to look upon the *Bickerstaff Papers*. They were, of course, a splendid practical joke on Partridge. But the practical joke itself is part of a meaningful fiction, which turns back upon Bickerstaff, too. Partridge is the appropriate sufferer because he shares the mad assumption of Bickerstaff: that if his almanac says something, it will be true. Swift's fiction says that the only way a prophecy will be fulfilled is for the astrologer to act as if it has been.

Swift is demonstrating a number of things: (1) He proves that Partridge *is* really dead, in a factual as well as a fictional sense. As Bickerstaff says, "whether he be since revived, I leave the World to judge" (p. 163), and again, "for I think I have clearly proved, by *invincible Demonstration,* that he died at farthest within half an Hour of the Time I foretold" (p. 164). And we feel that it *is* true: in a professional sense Partridge is dead, and also in a moral sense. In no meaningful sense is he alive, any more than are the modern authors the Grub Street Hack tries so desperately to prove exist (he cannot produce their ephemeral works). Everyone else considers Partridge dead (and offers no objections); and so his claiming he is still alive becomes an act of egotism and pretense to self-sufficiency connecting him with the spider, the aeolist, and the tailor. (2) At the same time Swift proves that Bickerstaff's prophecy (like all prophecies) is false: Partridge *is* still alive. And so Swift's satiric fiction accepts both the fictional fact that Partridge is dead and the real fact that he is alive, in order to reflect on both Partridge and Bickerstaff. In the mad world of his fiction—which is essentially controlled by what he would call the logic of almanacs—both Bickerstaff and Partridge are solipsists: Partridge for refusing to agree with the majority that believe he is dead; and Bickerstaff for creating Partridge's death out of his own imagination and trying to impose it on him. (3) At the same time Swift shows the coercion necessary if *any* prophecy is to come true. And perhaps the further implication that a prophecy is dangerous—it may contribute to the fact it merely predicts: thus Partridge's mental anguish which is vividly portrayed in the second pamphlet. Any prophesier has to kill the man he predicts dead in order for his prophecy to come true. (4) The satire is also, of course, on the crowd, the reader who accepted the news of Partridge's death— the tendency of people to take whatever appears in print (whether prophecy or report) as gospel truth. This is what happens and produces Partridge's nightmare: where it is only "carried at last by two Voices, that I am still alive" (p. 222). (5) Incidental satire is accomplished by the juxtapositions in Bickerstaff's almanac entries, the deaths of a buffoon and of the king of France and the Pope, the affairs of Poland and the fall of a booth at Bartholomew Fair. It gives Swift a chance to kill off a great number of troublesome people such as the king of France, and their deaths, like Partridge's, suggest that in some ideal sense they *should* be dead.[27] In the letter supposedly written by Partridge, his death is used as a touchstone by which to judge the undertakers who literally have such a sharp nose for death that they arrive before the fact, and the sexton who accuses Partridge of pretending death to escape church dues.

Finally, (6) in the second letter the satire catches the aristocratic, rather condescending reporter who "in Obedience to" a nobleman's wishes, "as well as to satisfy my own Curiosity" ("partly out of Curiosity," he repeats later), comes to chronicle Partridge's death. He is, after all, one of those fooled enough by the prophecies Partridge is now abjuring; and he is blind to the extent that he sees as the important consideration not Partridge's death but the accuracy of Bickerstaff's prediction.

, Anyone playing with as many levels or kinds of reality as Swift in the *Bickerstaff Papers* should not be too surprised when the fiction erupts into a reality beyond his intention (if it *is* beyond Swift's intention). One critic believes that this happens in the scene of Partridge's death described by the reporter. He sees Partridge, in this situation, having confessed his imposture, as "momentarily pitiful as he says that he carried on this false

[27] Cf. Steele's adoption of the device, announced in Bickerstaff's *Tatler* No. 1 (Apr. 12, 1709) ". . . I shall from time to time print bills of mortality; and I beg the pardon of all such who shall be named therein, if they who are good for nothing, shall find themselves in the number of the deceased."

art only to support a wife, since he had 'no other way to get . . . bread.' "[28] The truth of the matter is that Partridge, for one intense moment, becomes the norm; he has been pushed into a situation in which he changes roles from villain to Swift's spokesman, putting Bickerstaff in proper perspective. And the switch gives pathos to his abjuration of prophecy:

> He replied, I am a poor ignorant Fellow, bred to a mean Trade; yet I have Sense enough to know, that all Pretences of foretelling by Astrology are Deceits; for this manifest Reason, because the Wise and Learned, who can only judge whether there be any Truth in this Science, do all unanimously agree to laugh at and despise it; and none but the poor ignorant Vulgar give it any Credit, and that only upon the Word of such silly Wretches as I and my Fellows, who can hardly write or read.

He confesses and repents his "fooleries . . . from the very Bottom of my heart," explaining that he had

> a Wife to maintain, and no other Way to get my Bread; for mending old Shoes is a poor Livelihood. And (added he, sighing) I wish I may not have done more Mischief by my Physick than my Astrology; although I had some good Receipts from my Grandmother, and my own Compositions were such, as I thought could at least do no Hurt (p. 154).

Though Swift's emphasis is on the danger of false prophets, still the complexity of response is apparent. The reporter is a fool, and Bickerstaff is beginning to appear a knave. If the character's role is suddenly changed, so is the reader's response. From seeing everything through Bickerstaff's eyes, he has suddenly been made to see through Partridge's. His sympathy for the dying man now outweighs his satisfaction at the sort of poetic justice manifested in Partridge's end, and he sees Bickerstaff's knavery.

In his characteristic first-person satire Swift begins with the Lucianic monologue, which allows for the maximum immersion a reader can suffer in a satiric form, but he goes a step further and removes the safe sign posts of the frame action and the sensible adversarius that Lucian often used to give his reader perspective.

[28] Ewald, *The Masks of Jonathan Swift*, p. 66.

By removing these he plunges the reader into a fictional world in which he must with some difficulty find his own bearings. The speciously plausible argument, the numbing effect of logic, draw the reader on until he is trapped. The concrete detail, the particular name, and the complexity of the speaker's thought processes also contribute. The violently sensuous object or action has the same effect on the reader it did in Rabelais. The most violent, uncontrolled actions served to show the violent upsurge of energy, both intellectual and physical, that Rabelais felt was needed to bring new life into the old religious forms. Panurge, with his bulging pockets and ultimate individualism, serves in many details as a prototype for Swift's protagonists. What Rabelais presents as an ideal—or at least a good corrective—Swift takes as a serious threat.

But he is not content with *showing* the reader the extravagance of the Rabelaisian imagination in syntax, form, images, actions, and characters; he also believes that he must, in fact, cast the reader adrift, as Rabelais does, in this sinister world and show him what would happen. It is important that up to a certain point the reader is fooled—made to accept the early assumptions of a projector's mad plan, or the early pages of a travel memoir, or the prophecy of Partridge's death. As Swift lamented in the preface to *The Battle of the Books,* "Satyr is a sort of *Glass,* wherein Beholders do generally discover every body's Face but their Own." Clearly it was his aim to trap his reader into recognizing his own face in the mirror. He exerts his greatest ingenuity to implicate the reader in the folly in order, first, to give a greater effect to the peripeteia and the reader's anagnorisis when it comes; but also, second, to make him see how close he comes himself to being the monster portrayed—or rather a part of the crowd that is being duped by the monster. He proves, in a sense, how universal the folly is. To do this he must suck the reader in, showing him how it feels to be evil or foolish. Then, by the very violence of the shock when it comes, he turns the reader back to seeing the scene in perspective. In this sense, Swift's constant aim is, by whatever means are at his disposal, to make his true audience read the irony at the level of the false audience.[29]

The notorious difficulty with Swift's strategy is that the effect of identification is often so powerful that some readers do not make the transition back to the world of moral choice and objective facts. Or, looked at differently, a character is raised momentarily to a pitch of reality that is inconsistent with the rest of the work.

Nevertheless, a particular image of reality emerges. If Swift's feigned pamphlets produce static "characters" of their authors, these "characters" only make sense in terms of implied relationships with others above and below them on the moral ladder. In a series of pamphlets, like the *Bickerstaff Papers*, where a group of characters collect, the scene, situation, and characters are used in such a way as to bring out shades of guilt in a succession of unexpected areas. All the characters are linked in a common network of guilt, revealing a close interaction, even interdependence; and the densely satiric scene becomes a spectrum of moral responsibility.

Swiftean Picaresque: *Gulliver's Travels*

So far the center of interest in Swift's satire has been a symbol of the perversion of values, turning this way and that to offer exposition of all its various facets. *A Tale of a Tub* comes no closer to a narrative in time and space than the scattered references to the Grub Street Hack's goings and comings and his increasing concern with his book and its purchasers as he nears the end of his writing and publication time approaches. The Horatian dialectic, seen in the story of the brothers, is reflected in the Hack's attempt to reconcile the value terms of morality

[29] A useful discussion of this effect in rhetorical terms can be found in Henry W. Sams' essay, "Satire as Betrayal," *Journal of English Literary History,* 26 (1959), 41: "One of the ancient principles of debate is to induce an opponent to adopt a position which he will later be forced to abandon. In disputation, the moment of victory is the moment at which an adversary is compelled to adjust his premises to the demands of the argument."

and art (such as "universal benefit of mankind") with the assumptions of the moderns; but the relationship set up remains a static one, a sort of constantly reiterated tableau.

When he turned to narrative in *Gulliver's Travels* (1726), Swift utilized the fiction of the picaresque novel. Some of the time Gulliver is simply an observer, traveling and recording, becoming more or less of a gull by the extent to which he accepts what he sees. But these parts are largely limited to a chapter or so in each voyage and to much of the third voyage. More often he is a touchstone: by his enormous size and equal magnanimity he sets off the puzzled, treacherous, belligerent, or presumptuous reactions of the Lilliputians. At the center of Swift's action is the relationship between the traveler and the strange people he meets.

For example, among the Brobdingnagians, where Gulliver is specifically a servant with contrasting "masters," the brutality of the giant farmer is brought out by his treatment of the tiny, helpless Gulliver; and the pettiness and human pride of Gulliver are shown by his posturing before his second master, the kind King. The relationship shifts as Gulliver goes from master to master. The Emperor of Lilliput is very like Lazaro's first master, the blind beggar, and similarly vulnerable, and Gulliver is like Lazaro, the complacent servant, adjusting to his surroundings, revealing his master's villainy by praising or even imitating it. But the relationship is made overwhelmingly ironic by the servant's being a mile high. Like the picaro, who assumes the values of his masters, Gulliver ends by assuming the values of the people he visits. It follows that his complaisance turns him (as it does Lazaro) into a fool who makes possible his master's knavery. In the case of his good masters, Gulliver imitates that aspect which is least appropriate to him; returning from Brobdingnag he acts like a giant, and returning from Houyhnhnmland he acts like a horse. There are other nobler aspects he could imitate—and in this respect his is a more complex situation than the picaro's. By the end of the voyage to Brobdingnag the emphasis has shifted from the master's tyranny to the servant's willingness to be tyrannized, and this situation no doubt explains something of Gulliver's relationship to his Houyhnhnm master. The relationship between master and servant, then, is Swift's central irony, explored in a slightly different way in each voyage.

Swift's cast of characters owes something to the satiric fiction we have traced in his other satires. In all but the third voyage, which reverts to the old and simple form of the satiric anatomy or survey, the protagonist is given a master, various outside threats to his safety, and a friend. The master represents the structure of order, whether good or bad, which protects Gulliver from the forces of enmity and disorder—unruly soldiers, an enemy like Skyresh Bolgolam, rats, dwarves, nasty children, wasps, and Yahoos. These figures, who like Bolgolam are "pleased, without any Provocation, to be my mortal Enemy," are completely negative.[30] In fact, by placing in parallel functions the Bolgolams and the rats and monkeys who attack Gulliver in Brobdingnag, Swift suggests that such obvious threats are probably amoral rather than immoral. The friend is the unnamed man who warns him of the Lilliputians' plans to destroy him, or Glumdalclitch in Brobdingnag, or the Sorrel Nag in Houyhnhnmland. (Sometimes the friendship proves ironic, as in Reldressel, who argues for the kindness of blinding Gulliver instead of killing him.)

While the forces of evil are hardly even supplied with motives for their natural viciousness, the master is guided by an awareness of his own position or advantage—fear that Gulliver will go over to the Blefuscudians, or the desire to make money, or the fear that Gulliver may cause the Yahoos to revolt. So from Gulliver's point of view we have once again the structure of Swift's first-person satires: the undisguisedly evil on one side (Gulliver is never deceived by Bolgolam or the jealous dwarf) and the obviously good on the other. In the middle is the ambiguous figure who puts a good face on his selfish actions: the emperor who uses Gulliver to carry out his policies, and whose cruelty is marked under fine phrases. Even the King of Brobdingnag and the Houyhnhnm master, though not intended as

[30] *Prose Works*, XI, 24.

evil creatures, are masters and follow the pattern. They cannot see others except in relation to themselves; anything beyond their experience baffles them. The King, though wise, is simply so large that he regards Gulliver with an undue detachment, in effect imprisoning him like a bird in a gilded cage and hoping to find a mate so that this curious species can be propagated; and the Houyhnhnm master, though surpassingly wise, cannot see Gulliver as more than a Yahoo of superior intelligence (and so, dangerous). To both of them he remains a *lusus naturae.* When the Houyhnhnm master explains why Gulliver must be sent out to sea to certain death, he sounds very much like the Emperor of Lilliput justifying the proposed murder of Gulliver (pp. 71, 279), just as Gulliver, when he tries to justify his master's decree, demonstrates an irony as cutting as in his earlier attempt to justify the Emperor's sentence (pp. 72–73, 280).

But the Brobdingnagian and Houyhnhnm masters are present less as comments on themselves than as comments on Gulliver. Gulliver's function changes with the second voyage, and he becomes himself the object of satire, assuming the role of the middleman who attempts to rationalize his miserable situation into a state to be proud of. Even in Lilliput he finds on one side of him the ideals of liberty and duty to one's country, on the other enslavement, and, entirely to his own disadvantage, attaches the name of liberty to the fact of his slavery, justifying his degradation by means of the rhetoric of his masters. He is the man who puts a good face on his own unsatisfactory situation by seeing it as his "masters the Moderns" do. He shows his descent from the Grub Street Hack as well as Martinus Scriblerus (as whom he originated) in his automatic reactions as a correct modern—collecting specimens in Lilliput and weighing hailstones, keeping a cabinet of curiosities, and wishing to dissect a louse in Brobdingnag; showing his pride in England as well as in the latest "modern" inventions for improving warfare.

Like any searcher for a Utopia, Gulliver sets out voyaging to escape the restraints of his homeland. The first page gives us this impression through words suggesting confinement: his father's "small Estate," applying himself "close" to his studies, the cost being "too great for a narrow Fortune," his being "bound Apprentice" to a surgeon, and receiving "small Sums of Money." Opposed to these references and the emphasis on specific numbers of years, pounds, and the like, is the indefinite "long Voyages." After his first voyages, he settles in London, but soon sets out again in order to escape the corruptions of business without which one cannot succeed in England: "for my Conscience would not suffer me to imitate the bad practice of too many among my Brethren" (p. 20) ; and a subsequent business has begun to fail. The sea seems to represent release for him; and so it is the first of a series of ironies on this theme when, running into the ultimate in freedom, the violent storm at sea that sets him free even from the confinement of his boat, he wakes up and attempting to rise, is "not able to stir: For as I happened to lie on my Back, I found my Arms and Legs were strongly fastened on each Side to the Ground." Even his hairs are bound to the earth, and he is in a kingdom far more constricting than his homeland.

The allegorical message (emphasized in Hogarth's print, *The Punishment of Lemuel Gulliver,* published in December 1726) is this: England in seeking freedom (the individualistic freedom for which the Whigs stood) has found itself in the most constricting kind of world—one of people six inches high who treat the good old Englishman as a slave in spite of the obvious discrepancy in their sizes. And the foolish, "gullible" Englishman gratefully accepts this slavery: the privilege of turning over on his side to make water, of living chained in the equivalent of a dog's house, and of kissing the hand of a mite.[31] (One need only recall the figure of Arbuthnot's John Bull, and disguise the allegory considerably—since Arbuthnot was on the winning side when he wrote, and Swift was now on the losing side. The character of John Bull was not unlike Gulliver's—both were ordinary bluff Englishmen, somewhat dense, as their names equally imply.)

[31] See John D. Seelye, "Hobbes' *Leviathan* and the Giantism Complex in the First Book of *Gulliver's Travels,*" *Journal of English and Germanic Philology,* LX (1961), 228–39. Seelye sees the first voyage as "expressing a basic tension between the needs of the individual and the demands of the state" (p. 228).

The situation of the majority cowed by a minuscule, single, actually powerless figure is a usual Swiftean image for the enemy, which he employed about the same time in the image of William Wood. Here numbers are on the Lilliputians' side, but obviously the tail is again wagging the dog if they can order Gulliver around. So on the political level, Swift is ridiculing the folly of the great lethargic mass that allows itself ("in the most submissive Manner") to be exploited by fear or custom or something of the sort when there is no reason to do so.

On the level of human action, however, Gulliver is a foolish, subservient man, easily enchained by plausible knaves and apparent authority. The repetition of the word "liberty" (the refrain of the first voyage) points to the relationship: Gulliver's humble petitions for his "liberty," the Emperor's refusal and limited grant, and "the Liberty of walking backwards and forwards in a Semicircle" (p. 28). Once he is physically released, his liberty is even more restricted without the physical fears. Chapter III begins with the humiliating relationship between the Emperor and his advisers, the rope dancers and the stick jumpers; and it goes on to the equally humiliating, though less reasonable, relationship between the Emperor and Gulliver. Gulliver's eager building of a tilt field with his handkerchief is described, as well as his service as the Emperor's arch of triumph and his humble reception of the "charger" which grants him his "liberty."

The unambiguous self-enslavement of Voyage I becomes in Brobdingnag a less obvious but more sinister one; for here the little Gulliver, whose pride grows as he shrinks in size (a kind of compensation for one's littleness, as it was in the *Tale* for one's transcience), fancies himself free when he is obviously kept as a kind of toy or pet locked in a box;[32] whereas in Lilliput, although he was physically free, he allowed himself to be convinced that he was a servant or captive. Here, more than anywhere else in his travels, Gulliver thinks of himself in terms of his "masters," and his progress can be measured by them. One

[32] For my approach to the second voyage I am indebted to Aline Mackenzie Taylor's provocative essay, "Sights and Monsters and Gulliver's Voyage to Brobdingnag," *Tulane Studies in English,* VII (1957), 29–82.

is a tyrant, one is benevolent—and yet Gulliver's behavior is the same with both. Fear of reprisals, as with the farmer's child, causes him to be obsequious among these huge people, as respect for abstract authority did in Voyage I. But once among the royal family, his servility is based on his growing pride; and the ignominy of being shown off by his first master changes to an anxiety to show off before the King. As soon as he is presented to the Queen he slips into courtier's jargon, and he is soon telling how during meals he sits at the King's "left Hand before one of the Salt-sellers" (p. 106). He is only pleased when the Queen is "diverted" by him, as when the dwarf releases flies under his nose (p. 109), or when she is "agreeably entertained with my Skill and Agility" at rowing a boat (p. 120) or with his laborious performance at the piano ("the most violent Exercise I ever underwent"). He is constantly referred to as a "Sight," "Spectacle," "Show," or "Curiosity"; and even Glumdalclitch, "although she loved me to Excess, yet was arch enough to inform the Queen, whenever I committed any Folly that she thought would be diverting to her Majesty" (p. 124). Even his explanation of the "State of Europe" is a performance and a show as he stands on the top of a cabinet "which brought me almost to a Level with his Face" (p. 127). The resemblance between these shows and the involuntary shows on the farmer's table, with admission charged, completely escapes Gulliver.

The prison box he lives in is thus not a reflection on the Brobdinagians but on his own pretensions. He designed it himself, is safe in it and happy, and does not see it as a prison until the King suggests that if he could get a woman of Gulliver's size he would like to see the pigmy race propagated. "But," says Gulliver, more out of pride than self-awareness, "I think I should rather have died than undergone the Disgrace of leaving a Posterity to be kept in Cages like tame Canary Birds" (p. 139). Even when his first cry upon being picked up by a rescue ship is "to be delivered out of the Dungeon I was in" (p. 143), he sees no connection between the dungeon his box has become floating in the water and the one it was in the Brobdingnagian court. He sees no humor in the reference to Phaeton's fall made by Captain Wilcocks, who cannot understand what was the "enormous Crime, for which I was punished at the Command of some Prince, by exposing me in that Chest" (p. 145).

Much the same situation is portrayed in the fourth voyage. Gulliver's eagerness to become a Houyhnhnm and deny any connection with Yahoos follows from his eagerness to become a show for the Brobdingnagian royal family. The Houyhnhnm master persuades his frends to treat Gulliver "with Civility," because "this would put me [Gulliver] into good Humour, and make me more diverting" (p. 238). Whether we regard the Houyhnhnms and Yahoos as opposite extremes of the human and inhuman, or of human attributes—reason and passion—or of good and evil, the point of Gulliver's role as a whole is to become a middleman who attempts to attach the reason of a Houyhnhnm to the pride and body of a Yahoo.

Therefore, if Gulliver derives in a sense from the corruptible picaro he also derives from the Swiftean middleman, the villain of the other satires examined. However, as the derivation from the picaro implies, if this figure is much lower than Houyhnhnm, he is also not so debased as a Yahoo. He is much more normative than Swift's earlier villains, and this has been brought about by the shifting of emphasis from the wickedness of Gulliver's imitation of his masters to the consequences of his imitation: imprisonment, insecurity, betrayal, and even madness. There is also a much greater admixture of truth and well-meaning in Gulliver's imitations, as well as a more idealistic motive that drives him to emulation in all but the second voyage.

Something of his character, particularly in the fourth voyage, can be explained by reference to another classical source for the dupe of which Swift was so fond. The *Nigrinus* of Lucian, though it derives from Horace's Satire II.3 (concerning Damasippus), produces a more ambiguous and disturbing satirist-satirized situation. Like Horace, Lucian presents a man, A, repeating ecstatically what another man, B, has lectured to him. There may be considerable truth in B's words, which are largely satiric, but they are somehow inapplicable to A, or to people in general, and A's enthusiasm is excessive and his understanding incomplete. The listener, C, ironically agrees to A's account, but by his questions brings out the absurdity of A's position.

In Lucian's fiction a friend reproaches "Lucian" for his haughty airs now that he has returned from a journey—he will no longer have anything to do with his old friends. "Lucian" explains that it all came from seeing Nigrinus, the platonic philosopher, who has revealed to him the real ugliness of the apparently pleasant life he has been living. "Lucian" had gone to Rome to see an oculist about his failing eyesight and instead found Nigrinus, who improved his spiritual vision, turning him into a misanthropic satirist. The consequence, he shows, is halfway between drunkenness and frenzy. In the course of "Lucian's" account Nigrinus is compared to an intoxicating drink, a beacon far out in the ocean upon which he fixes his gaze, an archer who impales Lucian's heart, and (his interlocutor finally adds) a mad dog whose bite Lucian is now communicating. It all suggests that we should approach Nigrinus warily. He has unhinged "Lucian": "I was seized with a violent attack of giddiness; I was bathed in perspiration, and when I attempted to speak, I broke down; my voice failed, my tongue stammered, and at last I was reduced to tears."[33] This is the effect of such philosophy on an ordinary man. Nigrinus states an ideal—but a philosophical ideal which, if taken seriously, would make man simply withdraw from life. His attacks on Roman corruption, which closely follow those of Juvenal, are to be accepted as true. But Nigrinus' platonism causes him to withdraw from all human contacts: "From my high seat in this vast theatre," he says, "I look down on the scene beneath me; a scene calculated to afford much entertainment..." (p. 18). Like Horace, Lucian catches three different groups in his satiric net: he uses Nigrinus as a way to castigate the vices in Rome and to present an ideal; but Nigrinus is also a philosopher, and in a human context his solution is an absurd extreme; finally, "Lucian" himself will have to come down to earth again before he will be a better man for his experience. Yet, we are left with the possible interpretation that Lucian *is*

[33] W. H. and F. G. Fowler trans. I, 24.

presenting Nigrinus' view as the ideal, and the joke is in the discrepancy between this ideal and his own, or any human's, ability to follow it.

In Houyhnhnmland Gulliver, like Lucian, encounters someone who shows him a truth he had never before suspected and it virtually unhinges him, turning him into a railing satirist. At first sight this appears to be a new role for Gulliver; the external revelation is a contradiction to his beliefs in the superiority of people who look like him. But, as soon becomes apparent, Gulliver adjusts the new revelation to his own case, pitting himself *and* the Houyhnhnms against humans; he does not change himself, if anything ending a less desirable man. Like Lucian with his nose in the air, Gulliver refuses to live with Yahoos like his wife and children and spends his time in the stable.

Gulliver demonstrates how the Swiftean villain, by some shifts of emphasis, becomes a character who, if not in fact a hero, can be regarded as essentially ordinary, an Everyman. Much of his effect depends upon the fact that Swift has moved from a static portrait showing this figure at his worst to a narrative in which the decent but fallible man finds his way through a world of frightful or deceiving experiences such as extremes of size and of reason and passion. The acts of folly, though climactic, do not completely cancel out the many neutral or even virtuous acts.

Gulliver is not intended as the hero of a *bildungsroman:* he makes no self-discovery, comes to no awareness of himself, except to the parody of awareness he suffers in Houyhnhnmland. He is closer to the Horatian "you," the test figure who guides the reader between polar errors. But the direction of the satire is less toward a proposed (or implied) code of conduct than toward the eighteenth-century preoccupation with the definition of man. *Gulliver's Travels* is less closely related to Pope's Horatian satires than to his *Essay on Man.*

Satiric structures appear at their simplest in the third voyage, in which the Laputans, Struldbrugs, and the rest, like Lazarillo de Tormes' fifth master, are merely observed by Gulliver. The skeleton is not covered, the rhetoric is naked, and the fiction is the relation between an observer and an object: sometimes the observer is normative, sometimes ironically ingenuous, sometimes gulled by appearances. The relationship at its most complex produces simple error followed by disillusion and revaluation wrought by contact with the ghosts of Glubbdubdrib and the Struldbrugs. Book III is the traditional satiric anatomy of misdirected reason, at its most typical in the survey of the Academy of Lagado in which a tour of the Royal Society is equated with one of Bedlam. The trips up to the floating island, down to the ghosts of Glubbdubdrib, and horizontally to other odd places are unvarnished descendants of the Lucianic dialogues, equally concise and brilliant but largely unintegrated. The voyage does make some sense on two levels other than the rhetorical: on the metaphysical it extends Swift's study of man from body to mind, and on the representational it begins to prepare us for Gulliver's breakdown in Houyhnhnmland (developing the disillusionment begun in the King of Brobdingnag's "odious little vermin" speech). But like the rhetoric these are naked, and roughly indicated (almost a sketch) as compared with the full rendering of the other three voyages. (Though parts of the voyage were written as late as 1724, other parts clearly contain vestiges of Martinus Scriblerus' travels and whatever else did not fit in the other voyages.)

The first two and the fourth of Gulliver's voyages also began as Lucianic devices for getting new perspectives on man but embodied them in close-fitting fictions. Lilliput and Brobdingnag are vantage points from which to see man's true situation and humble his pride; through a telescope or a microscope, or from a far higher or lower physical position, man could be seen with more detachment or in more minute detail. Lucian's and Rabelais' aim with the same device was to shake up the reader's accepted values; Swift's is the same, but applied first to his protagonist Gulliver, and second to the reader who identifies with him. While Rabelais (if not Lucian) intended his reader to emerge with a sense of growth, discovery, and confidence in himself, Swift hopes he will emerge humbled and chastened. Pascal, who had also suggested the use of these vantage points, summed up the effect:

> If a man will look at himself as I suggest, the sight will terrify him; and, seeing himself suspended in the material form given him by Nature, between the two abysses of Infinity and Nothingness, he will tremble beholding these marvels, and I think that, as his curiosity turns to awe, he will rather gaze in silence than dare to question them.[34]

This is the general rhetorical aim of the devices in *Gulliver's Travels,* though many variations are rung. The fourth voyage simply substitutes shape and other opposing qualities for size, probably originating, as R. S. Crane has shown, with Swift's inversion of the traditional equations of *homo* with *rationale* and *equus* with *irrationale* (and, for that matter, *hinnibile*) to be found in Latin logic books.[35] Another of Crane's illuminating insights into the fourth voyage is that Gulliver is used there in the same way as the man in Plato's myth of the cave who is forcibly taken out and brought face to face with reality:

> he will suffer sharp pains; the glare will distress him, and he will be unable to see the realities of which in his former state he had seen the shadows; and then conceive some one saying to him, that what he saw before was an illusion, but that now, when he is approaching nearer to being and his eye is turned toward more real existence, he has a clearer vision,—what will be his reply?[36]

These satiric devices have in common the polarization of Gulliver and what he sees—Lilliputian, Brobdingnagian, and Houyhnhnm. In the general sweep of his narrative Swift uses the extremes of size and shape as part of a dynamic structure which advances from one alternative to another, gradually questioning

[34] *Pascal's Pensées,* ed. H. F. Stewart (New York: Pantheon, 1950), p. 21; the references to the viewpoints offered by telescope and microscope are on p. 19. Cf. *Gulliver's Travels,* p. 87.

[35] "The Houyhnhnms, the Yahoos, and the History of Ideas," in *Reason and Imagination,* pp. 231–53. Crane's argument for the *homo-equus* contrast as a direct source for the fourth voyage is convincing. However, judging by what we know of Swift's satiric method and of the creative process in general, there is no reason to conclude, as Crane does, that he went no further—that this explains all of the fourth voyage.

[36] *Republic* vii, Jowett trans., I, 774; see "The Rationale of the Fourth Voyage," in *Gulliver's Travels: An Annotated Text with Critical Essays,* ed. Robert A. Greenberg (New York: W. W. Norton, 1961), pp. 300–7.

and defining the poles of Gulliver and his alter egos. Like the earlier narrative satires we have examined, Swift's is constructed on a series of parallels established through echoes and allusions. For example, when Gulliver expresses nausea at the Queen of Brobdingnag's "craunch[ing] the Wing of a Lark, Bones and all, between her Teeth, although it were nine Times as large as that of a full grown Turkey" (p. 106), the reader recalls his earlier remark that his Lilliputian servants "were astonished to see me eat it [a sirloin] Bones and all, as in our Country we do the Leg of a Lark. Their Geese and Turkeys I usually eat at a Mouthful . . ." (p. 64), or, yet earlier, that the great pieces of meat the Lilliputians prepare for him are "smaller than the Wings of a Lark" (p. 24). Gulliver's drawing his sword and amazing the Lilliputians with the sun glancing off it (p. 36) is echoed in the Brobdingnagian horsemen who do the same, with the same effect on Gulliver (p. 138). The contrast shows how different the little man among the big is from the big among the little. There is, of course, dramatic irony, as in the Brobdingnagian king's desire to find Gulliver a woman his size "by whom I might propagate the Breed" (p. 139) in the light of Gulliver's similar desire when he was preparing to leave Blefuscu (p. 78). Thus the rat who ate some of his Lilliputian sheep on the return voyage becomes the rat who tries to eat Gulliver in Brobdingnag, and the doghouse and chain in Lilliput becomes Gulliver's box in Brobdingnag. The effect of such parallelism and contrast in a satire like *A Tale of a Tub* was to give a thematic unity to a work that represented a radical disunity on the level of action (the speaker's conscious argument). In *Gulliver's Travels* the effect is to create a series of parallel experiences.

If each contrast has an immediate point to make about man, together they serve as alternatives of action that suggest the direction the reader should or should not take—and that test the protagonist and reveal his growth or lack of growth. For instance, Gulliver's fear, when he is at the mercy of a Brobdingnagian field hand, that "human Creatures are . . . more Savage and cruel in Proportion to their Bulk" (p. 87) is contrasted with the reader's memory of his gentle treatment of the Lilliputians.

The reader, feeling apprehension with Gulliver, should still remember and recognize that size limits viewpoint, and that in fact
the *smaller* the man the crueller he is likely to be. But once placed
as part of a temporal and causal continuum between voyages,
the scene makes the reader also aware that Gulliver, as the same
character who visited Lilliput, sees no connection between this
situation and his own gigantic benevolence toward the Lilliputians—he has not learned from his experience.

The parallels run through all four voyages (though less no-
ticeable in the third), beginning with the basic situation of each
voyage: Gulliver arrives in a new country, slips into the assumptions of the natives, is threatened with catastrophe, and escapes
and returns to his own country. From one to the other there is
a progress not so much from good to evil as from safety to
danger, or from experiences that Gulliver can take in his stride to
those with which he cannot finally cope. The progression is reflected in the disasters that place Gulliver in each strange land.
These advance from natural disaster that wrecks his ship to
shipmates that run for their lives and leave Gulliver among the
Brobdingnagians (we can hardly blame the sailors, however, for
leaving him in their fright, particularly since he had no business
going ashore; the sailors went to get water, he to gather scien-
tific specimens); then from the pirates who capture him and the
wicked Dutchman who prevails upon them to cast him adrift to
the final evil of his own crew mutinying and marooning him on
a remote island. While these events trace a downward plunge in
human experience characteristic of the satiric world view, they
also influence Gulliver's changing attitudes as he moves from the
harmless land of pigmies to the dangerous land of giants, from
the mad or evil lands of the third voyage to the shocking experience of the Yahoos.

The system of parallels also sets up expectations of other
parallels that help to clarify some of the more obscure parts of
the fourth voyage. In the first two countries Gulliver is examined by philosophers and concluded to be a *lusus naturae* (pp. 49,
104), and so when the Houyhnhnms cannot decide whether
Gulliver is a Yahoo or a unique creature we tend to accept this

as another case of man's inability to grasp what does not fit his picture of himself, as well as a sign of how difficult it is to define a human being. In each country before Houyhnhnmland (with some exceptions within the third voyage) Gulliver adjusts to the viewpoint and customs of his hosts. In Lilliput he is soon bragging of his title of nardak and, when he hears that the Emperor intends to kill him, he can barely shake himself free of the assumption that he is a loyal subject; so in Brobdingnag he begins "to imagine himself dwindled many Degrees below [his] usual Size" (p. 107), as in Houynhnhnmland he sees himself through the Houyhnhnms' eyes as a Yahoo in a suit. When he returns from Brobdingnag, however, he has come to see himself as a Brobdingnagian, regarding the sailors who rescue him as "the most little contemptible Creatures I had ever beheld" (recalling the king's opinion that Europeans are "little odious vermin"), and when he walks along a road in England he is "afraid of trampling on every Traveller" and calls "loud to have them stand out of the Way" (pp. 147–49). Thus when he sees things from the viewpoint of the Houyhnhnms in the fourth voyage, he also ends by looking upon the sailors who rescue him as the Houyhnhnms look upon Yahoos, and later can get no closer than a table's length from his wife and children, spending his time in the barn with the horses.

It will be noticed, however, that most of the parallels that appear in the fourth voyage go back to the second voyage rather than to the first. The monkey who takes Gulliver for a relative in Brobdingnag (p. 122) becomes the female Yahoo who takes him for a Yahoo of the other sex in Houyhnhnmland (p. 266), and the normative Captain Wilcocks who rescues Gulliver from Brobdingnag certainly suggests that we are to take Captain Mendoza, who rescues him from Houyhnhnmland, as similarly normative. One set of parallels concerning relative sizes connects the first and second voyage, and another, concerning Gulliver's pride, which only begins to emerge in Brobdingnag, ties together the second and fourth.

With the scene in which the King of Brobdingnag and his philosophers with difficulty decide that Gulliver is a *lusus naturae*,

Swift enters upon the theme of human definition that has been latent though implicit in both the contrast of sizes and the centrality of Gulliver-Everyman. Pascal concluded from his beneficial shock of showing man "the two abysses of Infinity and Nothingness": "For, I ask, what is man in Nature? A cypher compared with the Infinite, an All compared with Nothing, a mean between zero and all."[37] Thus Swift asks, is it still a man if it is only six inches high, or six miles high? Or if it has the body of a horse or of an ape?[38] The question of when is a man free is merely a part of this larger question. Gulliver is clearly no *lusus naturae;* but he is, on the one hand, the individual lowering himself to the role of a slave, an animal, a show; on the other hand, by this very process, he demonstrates how unsuitable human pride is to man's real circumstances. Having cast away all liberty and independence, of action and thought, Gulliver increasingly exults in his own integrity, courage, and nobility. His prison box is in fact his reality—or the human reality, like Pascal's image of life as a condemned cell. The vermin speech of the king, though it applies to the people of Europe Gulliver has described to him, acts as a correlative to Gulliver's own unconscious decline. That man can build this prison into a myth of pride is the subject of Swift's satire; but much besides is involved in the image of the helpless Gulliver in his box or on his little show platform.

Regarded as generalized Man, Gulliver in Lilliput is at his best the large heroic spirit who defends his country and holds no grudges even when betrayed by that country, though he escapes from it; at his less than best he is a fool, a gull who accepts the standards of the Lilliputians and allows himself to be exploited, rationalizing his exploitation with terms like liberty and duty; at his worst he is the man who, acquiring a Lilliputian sensibility, exploits his size and desires to take back these little people to European laboratories and museums. At the end of his stay

[37] *Pascal's Pensées,* p. 21.

[38] See Kathleen Williams' chapter on *Gulliver's Travels,* in which she develops this idea (*Swift and the Age of Compromise* [Lawrence, Kans.: University of Kansas Press, 1959], pp. 154–209).

among the pigmies he has become himself a pigmy and a master. Thus he represents the various things that can befall man as a larger-than-life creature: he *can* be good, generous, and heroic; but he can also accept the standards of the mites, or, on the other hand, regard them as less than human.

Then, in his next voyage, Gulliver begins as the scientist he was at the end of his first voyage. He has set out this time because of his "insatiable Desire of seeing foreign Countries" (p. 80), and he insists on going ashore with the party seeking water on Brobdingnag: "that I might see the Country, and make what Discoveries I could" (p. 85). In short, he is off in search of specimens, and instead of another Lilliput (for which he is now presumably prepared, with bottles and pins) he finds a people for whom he is himself a specimen.

But if the sudden reversal from telescope to microscope image uses Gulliver to define a new aspect of man, it also catches the Brobdingnagians, who themselves figure in the over-all human definition. They are part of a natural progression such as Pascal suggests: Gulliver exhibits the Lilliputian cattle, is himself exhibited by the Brobdingnagians, shows himself off to the Brobdingnagian royal family (a way of seeming important), and finally shows the teeth and other Brobdingnagian rarities to Europeans. Even the huge Brobdingnagians, as the ancient book (chap. 7), shows, have no reason for pride.

If we take the famous and climactic scene in which the King utters his condemnation of contemporary Europeans, we can see how Swift's fiction supports, extends, and yet qualifies the satiric and metaphysical strategies to which we have referred. As a rhetorical device the King is of course a satiric perspective—a way of seeing the politics and wars in Europe from a position that will render the Europeans indeed "the most pernicious Race of little odious Vermin that Nature ever suffered to crawl upon the Surface of the Earth" (p. 132). But he is also part of a fiction, which causes the reader to recognize two simultaneous facts about his speech: that people in Europe *are* awful; and that from his point of view, people in Europe are awful. What he says is true, but at the same time he is a mile high and setting straight the mite who has been entertaining him and bragging too much. The first clearly carries the satiric impact; the second, a version of the satirist-satirized fiction, complicates the whole satiric situation but also qualifies the impact of the King's speech. Facing each other in this scene are Gulliver, in his pettiness and pride, and the giant, too detached King. As the King is a telescope for seeing in perspective the wars and follies of Europe that appear in closeup heroic, so Gulliver is a magnifying glass that reveals the ugly reality of the apparent beauty of Brobdingnagian ladies (p. 92).

Satirically—or rhetorically—the King's point of view is a good corrective for shortsighted men, as Gulliver's is in some instances for the farsighted Brobdingnagians. But we have by no means exhausted the fiction, which goes on to place the King himself one chapter later when Gulliver reads the old treatise which describes the Brobdingnagians in very similar terms to those used by the King on the Europeans: "how diminutive, contemptible, and helpless an Animal was Man in his own Nature" (p. 137). This is a treatise, Gulliver learns, that is now "in little esteem, excepting among the Women and the Vulgar." Gulliver, as usual, sees no connection; but the reader sees the King and his point of view as they look to super-Brobdingnagians—those giants of former days to whom the King might appear the same *lusus naturae* Gulliver is to him.

If the King is placed in relation to the nature of man, he is also placed in relation to his immediate environment. His point of view is not only an effect of his stature but must be taken also as a psychological reaction to the appalling praise Gulliver has been bestowing on obviously wicked and foolish behavior; the King is inextricably part of a relationship with the mite who is trying to impress the giant. Nor can Gulliver's speech be disentangled from the traveler's long-repressed chauvinism, the courtier's desire to be useful ("I hoped I might live to do his Majesty some signal Service"; p. 127), the pigmy's need to overcompensate for his size, and Gulliver's particular tendency to find common cause with his masters. Some of these qualities are indicated as he speaks; others come from his placement in relation to his past. Gulliver standing on his platform addressing the King on the state of Europe has to be placed satirically and psychologically in relation to his exhibiting the Lilliputian livestock, his being taken for a specimen himself and exhibited in Brobdingnag, and his later performances for the royal family. In the same way, Gulliver's attempt in Chapter 7 to argue the King into using gunpowder to overcome all his enemies (p. 135) asks to be placed in relation to his earlier magnanimity toward the conquered Blefuscudians against the wishes of the Emperor of Lilliput (p. 53), one of the few instances when he refuses to fall in with the assumptions of a master.

Where the satire and the ramifications of the fiction part is hard to say, but as causes are indicated, and the situation particularized, the traveler's chauvinism may come to be read as homesickness and the pigmy's desire to shine as insecurity—qualities less easily satirized. This juncture of the representational and rhetorical-metaphysical structures, I believe, explains much of the effect of *Gulliver's Travels,* especially in the great scenes like the one just discussed and Gulliver's self-recognition as a Yahoo. The representation at every point extends the satire and complicates the image of evil but not without qualifying in some sense the central condemnation. My own feeling is that Swift understood the effect—up to this point at least—and was willing to sacrifice the absoluteness of the King's powerful speech to the larger realization that the King is only right in one sense about one aspect of man; and that his and Gulliver's speeches themselves represent other aspects.

Swift is trying to suggest, ultimately, what man is, not just what he is not, and the Brobdingnagian-human, Houyhnhnm-Yahoo contrasts are the approximations through which he seeks his definition. Moreover, his metaphoric parallels show man not only what he is, but why he is that way. The reasons for man's slavery to material forces, as opposed to spiritual, are shown to lie in his foolish fear of authority and in his equally foolish pride in himself, depending on the circumstances. In a way, *Gulliver's Travels* is simply a satire of consequences: slavery results from uxoriousness or pride; the simpler third voyage points this up, showing that a misdirection of reason leads to abstraction, loss of wives, impractical inventions, and rundown estates. In the fourth voyage we are shown that filth and squalor result from overreliance on the body and, as a final warning, that withdrawal from the human, even cruelty, result from overreliance on the otherwise good reason. The third voyage, in a reversion to an older type of satire, dwells on consequences; however, the other voyages spend much of their time on *causes,* showing with almost Defoe-like relish *how* and *why* a man becomes an object or a proud slave, a satirist or a misanthrope.

Gulliver's reaction to the Houyhnhnms and Yahoos has been so carefully prepared for that the reader is left with a strong awareness of the causes of his behavior. On the one hand he has been shown succumbing to foreign customs, seeing things through his host's (or master's) eyes in each country; on the other, he has been presented with an increasingly unpleasant and disillusioning set of experiences, climaxing in the revelations of the King of Brobdingnag and the magicians of Glubbdubdrib and, more personally for Gulliver, in the mutiny of his own crew. Everything has led him to think worse and worse of man. A third chain of causes can be traced to his increasing feeling of inferiority and, as compensation, his pride. Perhaps his self-exile from his wife and family also contributes. All of these details are, of course, perfectly consistent with Swift's primary intention, which is satiric. But when the system of parallels is embodied in the man himself instead of in what he observes (in the analogues of himself), they give Gulliver a past—perhaps even more of one than Robinson Crusoe. Crusoe exists in each moment of time as a man in a particular problem and with a particular past, which has been given us in detail. But his past bears on the present only as (if we can believe him) sin leads to consequences, and the reader may not be inclined to accept this interpretation of causality; while Gulliver's past contributes directly to the crucial moment of his confrontation with the Yahoos.

The multiple functioning of a satiric device find its *locus classicus* in Gulliver's fourth voyage, which critics continue to argue about because they think it must be taken in only one way:

either Gulliver is being satirized or he is not, either the Houyhnhnms are the ideal or they are not; whereas, not only does Swift use Gulliver in different ways at different times, he often uses him in two different ways at once. Gulliver is both satirist and satirized, the norm and the object of satire, and however factitiously, he appears to change in time. Each change is a new function; at best it is a kind of conversion, from subservience to princes and ministers to distrust, from fatuous admiration of all things European to skepticism and disillusionment, and from horrified awareness when his crew maroon him to stupid acceptance when the Houyhnhnms cast him adrift. But Gulliver conveys a sense of time, and the satire directed at him is qualified by the impression we have of the causes of his foolish actions and his gradual collapse.

Even the sheer fact of living with a first-person speaker through 300 pages, or 290 pages more than *The Modest Proposal,* contributes to the general effect of the satire. This effect has been commented on by Ian Watt, who believes that Swift has placed "a general representative of man collectively considered" (Gulliver as Everyman) in a situation where he becomes "man individually considered, with a particular wife and a particular problem," in short, a particular John, Peter, or Thomas. As Swift wrote in the famous letter to Pope, when he turns to these particular men from "that animal called man," his hatred changes to love; "and our feelings change," Watt writes, "if not from hate to love, as in Swift's letter, at least from amused detachment to a much closer emotional involvement."[39] While Watt accepts the effect as an accident, I believe,

[39] "The Ironic Tradition in Augustan Prose from Swift to Johnson," in *Restoration and Augustan Prose* (University of California, Los Angeles: William Andrews Clark Memorial Library, 1956), p. 34. The problem, Watt believes, is that "in so far as he is an ironic device, his effectiveness is directly proportional to the completeness of his disciplined subordination to his creator's purpose; while, *qua* individual character, the *persona* can become living and effective only by transcending the role he is allotted as the vehicle of the transparently dual or multiple presentation of reality which irony requires" (p. 31). See also The *Correspondence of Jonathan Swift,* ed. Harold Williams (Oxford: Clarendon Press, 1963), III, 103. Cited hereafter as *Correspondence.*

as I suggested earlier, that in part at least it served the important rhetorical function of submerging and implicating the reader.

When Gulliver realizes in Chapter 2 of the fourth voyage that he himself physically resembles the abominable Yahoo— that his body alone does not make him a human being—Swift obviously intends his reader to feel a powerful shock. This is one of the great moments in satire, and it has produced howls of outrage or thoughtful revaluation from readers. The effect depends on the reader's seeing at that moment through Gulliver's eyes. It is characteristic of Swift's method that he does not stop at this point but proceeds to demonstrate that Gulliver's (and our own) reaction is subject to satiric scrutiny. The satire catches all of us who forget that we are, after all, related to a Yahoo and those of us who, accepting this, try to repudiate the Yahoo in ourselves altogether.

Gulliver is the definitive embodiment of Swift's reader, his true audience, who can tell the difference between humanity and inhumanity, but whose complaisance, whose ability to adjust to the values of knaves, draws it into reading with the false audience. Swift draws the reader into Gulliver's own character (or into sympathy with it) so that he can experience Gulliver's feeling of revulsion in his famous discovery, and his subsequent hatred of humans, before being turned about to see that he (and Gulliver) were seeing life in oversimplified terms.[40] But implicating the reader can have two effects—as Fielding was to recognize fifteen years later when he satirized Richardson's *Pamela*. It can catch the reader in a folly and shake him into moral awareness, or it can turn satiric entanglement into empathy, which is the effect Watt experiences in the fourth voyage.

The effect is also to shift the reader's attention away from an idea and onto a character; he becomes more aware of Gulliver

---

[40] Another well-known example is the "Dressing Room" poems, in which the reader finds himself in Strephon's shoes, enters Chloe's dressing room with him, sees, feels, and smells with him and experiences all of his revulsion; and then he is forced to step back and see the *other* side of the situation—that Strephon's (and also his own) reaction is excessive and based on a false system of values that places all its emphasis on external appearance. See below, p. 202.

talking (of how he speaks and why) than of what he says. The Yahoos and Houyhnhnms are at times less real than the perception of them and the mind that does the perceiving. Swift has used a satirist-satirized fiction in *Gulliver's Travels* which, very different from the version in his earlier satires, draws him in the direction of the satirist-observer, away from the image of evil; it has involved him in problems of definition, and focused his interest in the operations of the perceiving mind on a complex satiric device that represents more hero than villain. Perhaps the crucial point about Gulliver's behavior in Houyhnhnmland is whether the reader focuses on the internal or the external as the subject. That we can do both not only shows Swift as an efficient satirist, less concerned with consistency than with thorough exploitation of his material, but also that he is at the crossroads of the old and new epistemologies. Reality for him is still in the Yahoos and the Houyhnhnms, and in the consequences suffered by Gulliver and his family, but it is also in the interior drama of the observer's mind.

Swift seems to have considered the most effective satire (both as persuasion and as representation) to be one in which the satirist himself is missing or transformed beyond recognition; one that does not draw attention to itself as a satire and is, in fact, a complete rendering of the satiric object. As the satirist disappears, interest in him is displaced to the satiric object, and then, first, to a greater interest in his ethos, in attempts to understand the how and why of him (with Swift, who regards his mind as the center of danger, the operation of his mind becomes a main concern), and, second, to a greater attention to verisimilitude, a desire to make the satiric object (which includes the form in which it expresses itself, its project, and so forth) more convincing.

Given this general trend, Swift's procedure has been to create a middleman as his villain—partly because he expresses Swift's idea of present-day evil; but also because he serves to catch larger and smaller fish as well, often including the reader. In *Gulliver's Travels,* then, Swift uses these characteristics of his middleman but applies them to his voyager, Gulliver. The Grub

Street Hack's isolation and defeat, his gullibility, his use of other's theories to justify his own shortcomings, his pride and feeling of sufficiency—all are transferred to the relatively normative figure, the obtuse but developing protagonist, becoming in many cases sources of sympathy.

In one sense, we shall see in the next section, this transference facilitated a change from the gullible but normative character to the hero-satirist, with many of the same characteristics (thus the villain, William Wood, and the hero, the Drapier, are equally isolated and ignored by their would-be supporters). But it also produced a series of relationships whose complexity is evident from the attention that has been given to them by readers, scholars, and critics to this day. Contemporaries, however, learned little from Swift. It is ironic that the eighteenth century, which brought to perfection the ironic persona, the dramatized satire, should in general have thought (like the Elizabethans) of satire as a tone, usually invective. Swift's influence was doubtless felt more as a creator of satirists, from Bickerstaff to Gulliver in Houyhnhnmland to the "Dean" himself, than as a creator of complexly ironic fictions. The main influence Swift exerted on Fielding, for instance, was through the less inverted of his fictions, and Fielding seems to have been typical in regarding him primarily as a rhetorician, the outraged satirist—or ironist —standing behind every one of his satires. Therefore, when the run-of-the-mill writer attempted satire, he introduced a satirist attacking a satiric object.

Swiftean Romanticism: The Satirist as Hero

We have treated Gulliver as a relative of the pliable picaro, the servant who adjusts to his master's height or shape. But Gulliver is also, when the situation calls for it, something of a hero, at least in Lilliput: he dares to tell the Emperor that he will "never be an Instrument of bringing a free and brave People [the Blefuscudians] into Slavery" (p. 53). While blind to the unimportance of Lilliputian honors, he is nevertheless a good man—a public servant who saves Lilliput and the royal palace and is repaid with treachery. His huge size and corresponding magnanimity, even the way he puts out the palace fire (which recalls Gargantua's drowning half the populace of Paris), suggests an almost Rabelaisian life force that is opposed to the "dexterity" of the Lilliputian courtiers, who survive by delicate and intricate acrobatics.

Gulliver in Lilliput marks the beginning of a change of emphasis in Swift's satire, not only from the evil to the good man, but to the good man as an outsider or even revolutionary. After the 1714 debacle of the Tories Swift becomes increasingly classical republican on the one hand and Christian mystic on the other, leaving behind the authoritarian norms of his earlier work (though not the standard of public good) and turning more exclusively to the unattainable ideal. His hero becomes Brutus or Cato the Younger, (1) the good member of society who is forced, when that society becomes too corrupt, to revert to an older social order, and this involves, in effect, a revolution; or (2) the political martyr, the Socrates or Sir Thomas More, who makes no violent gesture but is isolated and destroyed. Either way the end is physical defeat and spiritual victory.

Marcus Brutus emerges as the greatest of the heroes summoned up by the magicians of Glubbdubdrib for Gulliver. Gulliver is

> struck with a profound Veneration at the Sight of *Brutus;* and could easily discover the most consummate Virtue, the greatest Intrepidity, and Firmness of Mind, the truest Love of his Country, and general Benevolence for Mankind in every Lineament of his Countenance.

Brutus and Caesar are friends in the afterlife, and Caesar tells Gulliver "that the greatest Actions of his own Life were not equal by many Degrees to the Glory of taking it away" (p. 196). When Gulliver has finished with his visions from history, he concludes:

> I hope I may be pardoned if these Discourses inclined me a little to abate of that profound Veneration which I am naturally apt to pay to Persons of high Rank, who ought to be treated with the utmost Respect due to their sublime Dignity, by us their Inferiors (p. 200).

The appearance of Cato, perhaps even more than Brutus, among the heroes in Glubbdubdrib shows how Swift has adopted the Whiggish connotations of Addison's famous play. As Swift put it himself in *A Panegyric on Dean Swift* (1730):

> When *J*[onathan]n was great at *Court*,
> The *Ruin'd Party* made his Sport,
> Despis'd the *Beast* with *many Heads*,
> And damn'd the *Mob*, whom now he leads.
> But Things are strangely chang'd since then,
> And *Kings* are now no more than *Men;*
> From whence 'tis plain, they quite have lost
> God's *Image*, which was once their Boast (ll. 159–66).

Lilliputian authority has been condemned first indirectly by Gulliver's conforming to it, and second by his inability to conform completely because of his greater size and magnanimity. Laputan authority is challenged by the virtuous revolution conducted by the city of Lindalino (Dublin). At the same time that Swift was writing *Gulliver's Travels* he created M. B. (Marcus Brutus?), the Drapier who urges disobedience against the constituted authority in Ireland. And in these years Swift began the long series of Irish poems and pamphlets that operate by reducing the authority of men like Richard Tighe and Lord Allen, indeed the whole Irish parliament, to its lowest fleshly denominator. Swift's satire is changing from mock-heroic to travesty, and his role as satirist becomes literally the stripping away of the deceiving appearance of authority; in *A Vindication of His Excellency John Lord Carteret* (1730), he compares himself to a surgeon who, having

> received some great Injustice from the Earl of *Galloway,* and despairing of Revenge, as well as Relief; declared to all his Friends, that he had set apart one Hundred Guineas, to purchase the Earl's Carcase from the Sexton, whenever *it* should dye; to make a Skeleton of the Bones, stuff the Hide, and shew them for three Pence; and thus get Vengeance for the Injuries he had suffered by its Owner.[41]

[41] *Prose Works,* XII, 157.

He threatens the same to Traulus (Lord Allen) :

> I am afraid lest such a Practitioner, with a Body so *open*, so *foul*, and
> so *full of Sores*, may fall under the Resentment of an incensed political
> *Surgeon*, who is not in much Renown for his Mercy upon great Provo-
> cation: Who, without waiting for his Death, will *flay*, and *dissect* him
> alive; and to the View of Mankind, lay open all the disordered Cells of
> his Brain, the Venom of his Tongue, the Corruption of his Heart, and
> Spots and Flatuses of his Spleen—And all this for *Three-Pence* (pp.
> 157–58).

While Swift reverts in some ways to the conventions of the
satyr-satirist whose chief tool is travesty, he is more emphatic
about this figure's essential isolation and defeat. In his fifth
letter, waiting for some effect to follow from his earlier letters,
the Drapier sees himself as the lone man, now in hiding with a
price on his head, struggling for virtue against the apathy and
hostility of the many, and he regards himself at this point as
defeated. Explaining why he attacked Wood, he writes a typically Juvenalian apologia for the satirist:

> It is a known Story of the Dumb Boy, whose Tongue forced a Passage
> for Speech by the Horrour of seeing a Dagger at his Father's Throat.
> This may lessen the Wonder that a Tradesman hid in Privacy and
> Silence should *cry out* when the Life and Being of his Political *Mother*
> are attempted before his Face, and by so infamous a Hand.
>   But in the mean time, Mr. *Wood* the *Destroyer* of a Kingdom walks
> about in Triumph (unless it be true that he is in Jayl for Debt) while
> he who endeavoured to *assert the Liberty of his Country* is forced to *hide
> his Head* for occasionally dealing in a Matter of *Controversy*.[42]

The Drapier's attack on Wood is a direct consequence of the
evil, a spontaneous reaction like Juvenal's to the evil he feels
around him; and the evil goes his own way, while the lone good
man must hide and suffer.

The satirist disappears in Swift's early and middle satires to
be replaced at one extreme by the Grub Street Hack, at the other
by the satirist-satirized, Gulliver. But the satirist disappears only
to return in separate works that are about him, and often only

---

[42] *The Drapier's Letters*, ed. Herbert Davis (Oxford: Clarendon Press,
1935), p. 111.

secondarily about fools and knaves. The *apologia* becomes a typical form, a main arena of the satirist. Pope, for example, spends much time building up a Horatian picture of a *vir bonus* and then submits this "Pope" to such overwhelming evil—a Sporus, a conquest by Dulness—that he cannot contain himself. He thus accounts for the satirist's motive and uses him as an occasion for his main subject, an attack on vice. Swift in his later poetic satires, however, shows the same interest in his satirist's consciousness—his attitude and perception—that he showed in his villains'.

Persons named "Swift" or "Pope" figured in Swift's early poetry, serving as norms of piety, traditionalism, common sense, Scriblerian solidarity, and sound poetic craftsmanship, opposed to the imbecility being satirized in equally concrete names like "Wood" and "Walpole." But in later poems the portraits of himself and his friends function less as glimpses of the good than as embodiments of a separate theme that grows out of their own situations. In the *Verses on the Death of Dr. Swift* one wonders how Swift relates the motto from Rochefoucauld

> In all Distresses of our Friends
> We first consult our private Ends,
> While Nature kindly bent to ease us,
> Points out some Circumstances to please us. (ll. 7–10) [43]

which informs the first part of the poem, to the eulogy of himself which comprises the last quarter of the poem.

The *Verses* sets out to illustrate Rochefoucauld's maxim, showing that man is so self-centered that he is as pleased by his friend's disaster as chagrined by his success. Almost at once, however, the examples are narrowed down to Swift himself, for whom friends like Pope, Arbuthnot, and Gay are suspect because they excel him in some kinds of writing: "Pox take him,

---

[43] My quotations are from *The Poems of Jonathan Swift*, ed. Harold Williams, 3 vols. (2nd ed., Oxford, 1958). For an interpretation (to me unconvincing) of the eulogy as ironic, see Barry Slepyan, "The Ironic Intention of Swift's Verses on his own Death," *Review of English Studies*, XIV (1963), 249–56.

and his Wit," he says of Pope (l. 52). Then, shifting his role from that of an illustration of self-love to one by which the self-love of others can be tested, Swift imagines the reactions of friends to his death. True to the maxim, they feel a certain relief, whether because it has not happened to them, or because it saves them from repaying obligations; his female friends do not allow his death to interrupt their card game, and even his best friends are only slightly affected: "Poor Pope will grieve a Month; and Gay / A Week; and Arbuthnot a Day" (ll. 207–08). If friends near his age grieve with more genuine intensity it is because Swift has been a screen between them and death, and now it is removed.

A year passes: there is "no further mention of the Dean," he is "no more mist, / Than if he never did exist" (ll. 246–47), and even his writings are now serving pastry cooks. Finally, the scene changes to a coffeehouse, where a stranger delivers a long eulogy of Swift's virtues and accomplishments. How, then, does this idealizing commendation of Swift follow from, or illustrate, Rochefoucauld's maxim and the earlier part of the poem?

One must consider that the eulogy may not have been part of the poem as Swift originally conceived it. In *The Life and Genuine Character of Doctor Swift,* an earlier version,[44] Swift does not use himself as an example of the maxim, but as a test case, and he tests only two men by his death; so, as opposed to the single eulogist of the *Verses,* here a pro-Swift speaker and an anti-Swift speaker discuss the dead Dr. Swift. The former is detached and reasonable, but the latter demonstrates that men's attitudes toward someone like Swift are dictated by their private needs: ". . . since you *dread* no further *Lashes,*" his adversary chides him, "You freely may *forgive his Ashes*" (ll. 201–02). Swift leaves the reader, as in many of his works, to make out for himself the real Swift who is somewhere between.

Taking this as an early version of the *Verses,* we might suppose that Swift lost patience with the vague and unsatisfactory

---

[44] For a discussion of the questions of authorship and dating, see Williams, II, 541–43, 551–53; and Joseph Horrell, ed., *Collected Poems of Jonathan Swift* (London: Routledge and Kegan Paul, 1958), II, 796–97.

approximation of the median and in the later poem while still suggesting a median ("They toss my Name about, / with Favour some, and some without") he substituted the ideal instead. It should not be forgotten that most of Swift's poems concerning the man called Dr. Swift or the Dean were prompted by attacks: like Pope's *Epistle to Dr. Arbuthnot,* they are at least partly apologias, presenting a respectable self-portrait in order to justify his right to compose satire. But it is only necessary to compare the *Verses* with *Arbuthnot* to see why Pope, when preparing Swift's poem for its first printing (in London), abridged the eulogy and inserted parts of the antithetical speeches from the *Life and Genuine Character.*[45] In his various apologias, Pope is always careful to provide a device like an interlocutor to anticipate the hostile reader's questions. Swift's eulogy offers no such device; rather it flaunts ingenuous lines like "By Innocence and Resolution, / He bore continual Persecution" (ll. 399–400).

But if the eulogy is an error of strategy, an overplaying of cards in the traditional apologia, what, in terms of Rochefoucauld's maxim, was Swift's reason for reducing the *pro* and *contra* argument of the *Life and Genuine Character* to a single *pro?* "Friend" is a key word which may lead us to Swift's intention. Rochefoucauld says that even the adversity of our friends pleases us, so great is our self-love;[46] while Swift, shifting the emphasis slightly, says that it is the adversity not of our enemies but of our friends that pleases us. The climax of his first series of examples (his "Proem") is the generalization:

> To all my Foes, dear Fortune, send
> Thy Gifts, but never to my Friend:
> I tamely can endure the first,
> But, this with Envy makes me burst. (ll. 67–70)

---

[45] Pope was afraid Swift's eulogy would prompt the accusation of vanity. See *The Correspondence of Alexander Pope,* ed. George Sherburn (Oxford: Clarendon Press, 1956), IV, 130.

[46] The French text, as Swift gives it with the poem, is "Dans l'adversité de nos meilleurs amis nous trouvons quelque chose, qui ne nous deplaist pas" (Williams, II, 551).

"Friend" is one of those ambiguous, pivotal words we find in Swift's satires. When we arrive at Walpole's reaction to Swift's death, we find him *sorry* that Swift is dead because Swift has been far away in Ireland and relatively harmless; he wishes his "good friend Will [Pulteney]" were dead instead. Here "friend" has come to mean its opposite, enemy. Pope is Swift's friend, but it hurts less to see some unknown poet write well; and Swift is Queen Caroline's friend in that he does her favors, but obligation has led her to hate him. The various ironic meanings-of-the-moment add up to the conclusion that "friend" is a person who in any of several ways is closest to us, most engaged with our passions, about whom we can be least detached and objective.

In this sense of the word, the point of the ending is that when Swift's "friends"—those who have something at stake—are gone, we shall have a truer picture of him. The critique of Swift is distanced by the lapse of a year. Both "those I love" (like Pope) and the ironically designated "friends" (like the Queen) have forgotten him now that he no longer impinges upon their lives. And so the commendation is delivered not by a "friend" but by "one quite indifferent in the Cause," who is "impartial."[47] In terms of Swift's version of the maxim, this man's portrayal is as close to the truth as is possible. Swift has simply split the *contra* and *pro* of the *Life and Genuine Character,* putting one close to the death, where passions are still warm, and the other where it belongs, a year away.

The effect of the separation is to produce a "truer" picture of Swift, and also to tell us something about the permanence of one aspect of Swift that is still alive a year later and the transience of the other that was associated with "friends" and is

---

[47] Swift may have recalled Addison's *Spectator* No. 101 (June 26, 1710/11): a great man "is never regarded with an indifferent Eye [cf. "One quite indifferent in the cause"], but always considered as a Friend or an Enemy. For this Reason Persons in great Stations have seldom their true Characters drawn, till several Years after their Deaths. Their personal Friendships and Enmities must cease, and the Parties they were engaged in be at an end, before their Faults or their Virtues can have Justice done them."

dead. The poem falls into two parts that correspond to the two aspects of its protagonist. In the first part we are shown the realm of material things such as advancement or failure in the world, health or sickness, living or dying. And when death comes and all the physical facts are gone, including the man's presence, his body, his books (which are no longer in fashion), and even the men who actually knew him, then something else remains that Swift is trying to epitomize in the eulogy with which he ends the poem. The man is gone, but a spirit, or a virtue, remains. It is important to notice that this spirit, though opposed to the physical, is not something vague, like the enthusiast's spirit; rather it is materialized in the deeds the eulogist recounts. The compromise ending of the *Life and Genuine Character,* although effective as an apologia, blurred this theme.

While the eulogist praises Swift's deeds, he gives Swift's character and circumstances considerable weight as well. The deeds are contingent upon a man who cares nothing for rank or other material rewards, a public figure above the dictates of self-love; in short, the opposite of the "friends" of the earlier part of the poem, which includes the petty, envious aspect of Swift himself (omitted in the *Life and Genuine Character*). One Swift is the physical man with the same fears and desires as Walpole and the Queen, but the other is the exiled patriot of the eulogy who "boldly stood alone" for liberty (1. 349). The eulogist's account of his withdrawal from the corrupt world of the court to barren Ireland recalls "Swift's" earlier account of the failing of his senses as death approaches, and thus the passing of material considerations leads to both the Irish hero Swift and the spirit that outlasts body, defeat, and corrupt courts. Finally, the ironic "friendship" that is Swift's ostensible subject conspicuously excludes any spiritual element, and this latter, more ordinary sense of friendship remains in the reader's mind as an assumed ideal behind the satire.

Swift is at work on two levels in the *Verses.* On the apologetic level he simply uses himself and his maxim as a vehicle for getting in slurs on the regime in England, praise of his friends, and vindication of himself.[48] On the metaphysical level the poem is a statement about the two aspects of man, the egocentric physical and the disinterested spiritual. The two levels of meaning come together in the figure of Swift himself.

The theme of body and soul can be traced through Swift's other apologetic writings. But to see how he arrived at this conjunction of theme and apologia, it is necessary to go back to his earliest poems, the pindaric odes. Each of the odes is about a man of ideals who stands out as a shining example in the world but is forced by politics and scheming to retire; and in solitude he either, like Sir William Temple, writes down his experience for the guidance of others, or, like Archbishop Sancroft, acts as "some guide from Heav'n to show / The Way." Unlike the great body of Swift's work, but like the *Verses,* these poems put their emphasis on praise of the hero rather than ridicule of the evils that overthrow him. To this extent they represent, as J. M. Murry has suggested, "the brief and neglected 'romantic' period of [Swift's] life."[49]

The odes show, at its least ambiguous, what Swift means by the "good." His ideal is the man of practical affairs, a king, a primate, an ambassador, or a society that promulgates useful information and traditional values. King William's virtue is eminently practical: "A three Hours Scene of empty Pride, / And then the Toys are thrown aside" (*Ode to the King,* ll. 17–18); not the trappings of the king but "Doing Good" proves his

---

[48] Much of the polemical burden of the poem is carried by the explanatory footnotes Swift appended. To take an example of the interaction of levels: by admitting that he envies Pope and Gay he establishes a reputation with the reader for honesty which will later help win the reader's acceptance of the eulogy. But by saying he envies his friends he is subtly praising them. And finally, the point he is building to is that "To all my Foes, dear Fortune, send / Thy Gifts, but never to my Friend"—which implies that his foes *need* luck when they tangle with the Scriblerians. But on the metaphysical level, Swift uses the same fact as an illustration of the perversion of values caused by an exclusive concern with material considerations.

[49] *Jonathan Swift, A Critical Biography* (London: Jonathan Cape, 1954), p. 34.

royalty. But there is also evil in the world, attempting to dethrone William; there are Louis XIV and the Stuarts abroad and the disloyal and the dissident at home, aided by the "Giddy British Populace," the crowd that is always willing to sacrifice heroes. As William carries the banner of an unreliable England, so Temple wins peace for his country and for all Europe by his diplomacy, and both Sancroft and the Athenian Society uphold ideals in a world threatened by new barbarian hordes.

But while William defeats his enemies at home and abroad, Temple and all the others are forced to withdraw finally in the face of defeat to a less concrete and more spiritual victory. As Temple retires before the deceit of a corrupt court, so Sancroft puts down the symbols of worldly power rather than compromise his ideals; and in Sancroft, who is compared to a star and to Christ, the good has become other-worldly. In the *Ode to the Athenian Society* the "Great Unknown" (the oracles who answer the questions) are linked with God: the Hobbist wits believe in the existence of neither. Here, where there is no specific defeat to be recorded, Swift introduces a vision of inevitable defeat in the future, from which only a few "Traces of . . . Wit" will be shored up. Finally, in the poem on Congreve, the hero is surrounded by corruption, his work is distorted by fools, and he has slipped into the background; and now we are in the more familiar mode where the hero is only an occasion for Swift's attack on the ascendant wits and scribblers.

Irvin Ehrenpreis has shown that Swift, as a writer of histories, inherited from his mentor, Sir William Temple, a view of history which saw martyrdom as necessary for the hero, and victory as necessary for the schemer and double-dealer.[50] The idea is given memorable form when Gulliver, who has been witnessing the procession of the great summoned from the dead by the magicians of Glubbdubdrib, learns that they have all been evil; asking for those who were actually virtuous and of benefit to their country, he finds that they have been the defeated, the

---

[50] *The Personality of Jonathan Swift* (London: Methuen, 1958), pp. 68–69.

execrated, the disgraced. This picture is much older than Temple; it is a convention of satire that Swift inherited from Juvenal. Many of Swift's satires assume that in this world the heroes cannot survive. But while the early poetry is focused on heroes like Sancroft and Temple, the more characteristic satires focus on the evil-doers; and, as in Juvenalian satire, the defeated idealist becomes the satirist who laments that chaos has taken over his world. To Ehrenpreis' list of defeated statesmen—Brutus, Cato, Temple, Harley—can be added Swift himself.

The development of the figure of Swift in the apologias falls into two parts: before the fall and after, or before the 1714 retreat to Ireland and after. In the early years he is an amused observer of folly, conspicuously balancing the life of the spirit (Swift the divine) with the life of the flesh (Swift the wit), and is shown playing cards, making rhymes, entertaining the ladies. In the account of himself he wrote in 1713 to explain the reward of a deanery, he uses Horace's Epistle I.vii. to give form and typicality to his experience, making the deanery a huge joke forced upon him by the witty Lord Treasurer. The "Swift" of this portrait is conventional: a well-rounded man, a moderate who agrees with the majority and feels so strongly about the evils of faction that, long before Harley knew him, he had attacked the Whigs.[51]

But when the Tory ministry was tottering the Swiftean persona shifted easily and naturally from the Horatian to the Juvenalian.[52] Much of the "Swift" of the earlier poems remains in *The Author upon Himself,* but there are two notable changes: his influence in the ministry and participation in greatness are emphasized (perhaps overemphasized), and, second, he has

[51] "Part of the Seventh Epistle of the First Book of Horace Imitated," ll. 27–45.

[52] Herbert Davis traces Swift's Juvenalianism back to early verse like the lines in the ode to Congreve in 1693: "My hate, whose lash just heaven has long decreed / Shall on a day make sin and folly bleed" (Williams, p. 47; "Alecto's Whip," *Review of English Literature,* III, No. 3 [July, 1962], 7–17). But these early references are conventional and interspersed with Horatian echoes; they do not bear the conviction that makes the later references so powerful.

now become the "pursued"—"By an old redhair'd, murd'ring Hag pursu'd, / A crazy Prelate, and a Royal Prude" (ll. 1–2). He dwells on the misunderstanding, jealousy, lying, and deceit that attack him, and above all on his duty and his final retirement:

> By Faction tir'd, with Grief he waits a while,
> His great contending Friends to reconcile.
> Performs what Friendship, Justice, Truth require;
> What could he more, but decently retire? (ll. 71–74)

His talent, its use in the service of his country, his great friends, his loyal service, and then retirement in the face of jealousy and faction, followed by exile in Ireland: these form the picture of the great years and the fall that are the facts behind all the later poems in which the Dean appears. In the *Verses on the Death of Dr. Swift* this picture has become:

> Pursu'd by base envenom'd Pens,
> Far to the Land of Slaves and Fens;
>
> . . . .
>
> By Innocence and Resolution,
> He bore continual Persecution;
> While Numbers to Preferment rose;
> Whose Merits were, to be his Foes.
> When, *ev'n his own familiar Friends*
> Intent upon their private Ends;
> Like Renagadoes now he feels,
> *Against him lifting up their Heels*. (ll. 395–396, 399–406)

The other important elements in Swift's final self-portrait are his advanced age, his failing health, his deafness, and his increasing cantankerousness. These elements can appear humorously, as in the poems to the Sheridans, Delanys, and Achesons, or gloomily as in *The Holyhead Journal* and the poems to Stella; but they are behind most of Swift's Irish poems.

Self-pitying reminiscence, however, soon shifts to an exploitation of his situation in satiric terms. A poem like *In Sickness*, a despairing expression of his early days in Dublin, pictures Swift separated from love and friendship:

> But, why obscurely here alone?
> Where I am neither lov'd nor known.
> My State of Health none care to learn;
> My Life is here no Soul's Concern.
> And, those with whom I now converse,
> Without a Tear will tend my Hearse. (ll. 3–8)

In the political satire Swift wrote once he was settled in Ireland, this situation proved to be an ideal one. As he recorded in the *Verses on the Death of Dr. Swift,* involvement or closeness to friends produces self-centered reactions; one has to step back and distance himself to see truly. Failure and exile can be accepted as at least a solid position from which to observe the virtues and follies of others; the satirist now has no reason to speak anything but the bitter truth.[53]

With the affair of Wood's half-pence and the Drapier's victory, Swift emerges as "that vexatious Dean," a rebel and champion of the oppressed; as he puts it in the *Verses*:

> Two Kingdoms, just as Faction led,
> Had set a Price upon his Head;
> But, not a Traytor cou'd be found,
> To sell him for Six Hundred Pound. (ll. 351–54)

By now it has become an advantage to be only a dean: if he were a bishop he would represent wordly office, reward, and

---

[53] The attitudes of the poems can also be documented in letters of the time written back to friends in England. See, e.g., Swift's letter to Bolingbroke (May, 1719; *Correspondence,* II 319, 321): "I forget whether I formerly mentioned to you what I have observed in Cicero; that, in some of his letters, while he was in exile, there is a sort of melancholy pleasure, which is wonderfully affecting. I believe the reason must be, that, in those circumstances of life, there is more leisure for friendship to operate, without any mixture of envy, interest, or ambition." But later in the same letter, he writes: "When I reason thus on the case of some absent friends, it frequently takes away all the quiet of my mind"; and about his health, "at best, I have an ill head and an aching heart." In a letter to Charles Ford (Dec. 8, 1719; *Correspondence,* II, 329–30), he writes: "You live in the midst of the World, I wholly out of it," and later compares himself in Dublin to "a prudent Prisoner."

interest; while he "On Drapier's Hill must lye, / And there without a Mitre dye." He is above worldly rewards, the gross physical perquisites. We can see his attitude toward his lost bishopric in his reply to Smedley's taunt that "were he [Swift] a less *witty Writer,* / He might, as well, have got a *Mitre*":

> And were you not so good a Writer
> I should present you with a *Mitre.*
> Write worse then if you can—be wise—
> Believe me 'tis the Way to Rise.[54]

This half-serious declaration, later developed in *On Poetry* and elsewhere, carries Swift's apologetic conclusions to their furthest extreme: if one writes well and sincerely, he cannot succeed in worldly things:

> Had he but spar'd his Tongue and Pen,
> He might have rose like other Men:
> But, Power was never in his Thought;
> And, Wealth he valu'd not a Groat. (*Verses,* ll. 355–58)

Being merely dean is almost a sign of his talent and worth, and being defeated is almost a sign of his virtue (even the Drapier's victory was ultimately, with the relapse of the Irish into their accustomed apathy, a defeat).

The image of Swift as defeated idealist and indignant satirist plays an important part in his Irish satires, but the idea of the superiority of spirit over body celebrated in the image is subordinated to the satiric point of the moment. When Swift's satiric exploitation of his situation and his serious reflections on it merge we have a poem like the *Verses.* But before that we have the reflections, the preoccupation with mutability, detached in the Stella poems and in the dressing room satires.

---

[54] "A Dialogue between an eminent Lawyer and Dr. Swift . . . ," ll. 55–56; "An Epistle to his Grace the Duke of Grafton, Lord Lieutenant of Ireland," ll. 9–10; "His Grace's Answer to Jonathan," ll. 9–12. For Swift's attacks on the Irish bishops, see Williams, III, 801–09; e.g., of Bishop Hort Swift says, "To the *Court* it was fitter to pay his *Devotion,* / Since *God* had no Hand in his *Promotion*" ("Epigram, on seeing a worthy Prelate . . ." ll. 5–6).

In the poems to Stella the old man Swift ("an House decay'd") joins the aging woman Stella ("An Angel's Face, a little
crack't"). In these poems, however, unlike those we have referred to so far, Swift focuses on Stella; she is the exemplum,
and "Swift" acts as her foil.[55] By the very fact that these are
birthday poems, their emphasis falls on her age and her aging.
In Aristotle's image, there is a stamp that is Stella, but the wax
refuses to retain its shape justly. The discord of body and the
unity of soul are increasingly contrasted as she ages year by year.

In the first of the birthday poems (1718–19), the harmony
of the physical and spiritual in Stella is insisted upon (as it was
in Swift's early apologias) : though she is now thirty-four, her
form is "little . . . declin'd / Made up so largely in [her]
Mind" (ll. 7–8). However, by 1721 Swift is comparing Stella's
body to the signboard on an inn, where "though the Painting
grows decay'd / The House will never loose it's Trade" (ll.
7–8) : the spirit within endures after the exterior begins to decay. To the new inn with its new sign he replies, "No Bloom
of Youth can ever blind / The Cracks and Wrinckles of your
Mind" (ll. 55–56). Already in "To Stella, Visiting Me in My
Sickness" (1720) Stella's "honor" is stressed alongside her
"beauty," and the realization is implicit that her beauty, like the
sick body of Swift, is subject to deterioration, that her "Palace"
will someday be like Swift's "House decay'd"; while honor is
not affected by such accidents. "The World shall in its Atoms
end," we are told, "E'er *Stella* can deceive a Friend" (ll.
57–58). Consistently associating Stella's virtue with permanence,
Swift comes closest to the view of the *Verses* in the last of the
birthday poems (1726–27), where he denies that virtue

[55] Stella, however, bears affinities with the Temple-Sancroft-Swift hero. This
is not to suggest that Swift is making her a projection of himself, but simply
that he values her for the same virtues he sees in all his heroes (he does much
the same with Vanessa, too). For example, cf. the lines on Stella: "What
Indignation in her Mind / Against Enslavers of Mankind! / Base Kings and
Ministers of State, / Eternal Objects of her Hate" ("To Stella, Visiting Me,"
ll. 61–64) ; and those on Swift in the *Verses,* ll. 339–50.

> Should acting, die, nor leave behind
> Some lasting Pleasure in the Mind,
> By which Remembrance will assuage,
> Grief, Sickness, Poverty, and Age. (ll. 29–32)

The view of the body-soul relation in these poems is the one given to Pausanius in Plato's *Symposium:* "Evil," he says, "is the vulgar lover who loves the body rather than the soul, inasmuch as he is not even stable, because he loves a thing which is in itself unstable . . . whereas the love of the noble disposition is life-long, for it becomes one with the everlasting."[56]

While the positive side of the situation is presented in the birthday poems to Stella, the negative is dealt with in the satiric dressing room poems. This series starts with *The Progress of Beauty* (written about the time the Stella poems were begun), and fastens its attention on physical appearance as the basis of man's desires. The question posed by these poems is what would happen if Strephon should see his Celia "from her Pillow rise / All reeking in a cloudy Steam, / Crackt Lips, foul Teeth, and gummy Eyes" (ll. 14–16)? Showing what goes on out of Strephon's sight, Swift traces the decay of Celia's face that parallels the waning of the moon; the wearing away by Time is opposed to the hopeless patching to deceive and defeat Time:

> Two Balls of Glass may serve for Eyes,
> White Lead can plaister up a Cleft,
> But these alas, are poor Supplyes
> If neither Cheeks, nor Lips be left. (ll. 113–16)

Swift concludes that the only solution for the men like Strephon who attach their love to physical appearance is to "Send us new Nymphs with each new Moon" (l. 120). They have reduced value to physical terms; it is taken off or put on like clothes, and the glass eyes and white lead are Swift's symbols of an over-emphasis on physical appearance.

As he points out in the birthday poem for 1724–25, the ears are a more important sense organ than the eyes; eyes only re-

[56] *The Dialogues of Plato*, Jowett trans., I, 311.

cord appearances, while the ears hear the voice that comes from within and reflects the mind:

> Thus you may still be young to me,
> While I can better *hear* than *see;*
> Oh, ne'er may Fortune shew her Spite,
> To make me *deaf,* and mend my *Sight.* (ll. 51–54)

In Stella, body is unimportant because she and her friend focus on her mind, her spirit, her virtue, and so a new nymph with every moon is not required: "his Pursuits are at an End, / Whom *Stella* chuses for a *Friend.*"[57]

Appropriately, in *The Lady's Dressing Room* (roughly contemporary with the *Verses*) Swift tells Strephon to use his eyes —for in this and the poems that follow it he resolves the question of *The Progress of Beauty,* and Strephon does see. He is appalled to learn that Celia performs natural functions; that there are other elements of the physical than beauty. When Strephon finds his idealistic concept of the body flawed in this way he gives up the ghost entirely: he begins to regard women in the same way that Gulliver regards human beings after his return from Houyhnhnmland: "And, if unsav'ry Odours fly, / Conceives a Lady standing by."

The same pattern of disillusionment is recorded in *Cassinus and Peter* and *Strephon and Chloe,* but in the latter, disillusionment is followed by Strephon's acceptance of the filth he has discovered, and his adjustment to a "Society in Stinking" with Chloe. This solution can be traced back to one of Swift's earliest poems, *The Problem: That Sidney E. of R-mn-y St--ks, When He Is in Love* (1699), where our attention is drawn from personal attack on Romney to the general question: "So sweet a Passion, who cou'd think / Jove ever form'd to make a S---k?" Here it is the woman who observes the excretory processes of the man; nor does she feel anything but pleasure. It is, in fact, Romney's "s---k" that draws the women to him. Here, where

---

[57] *To Stella, Who Collected . . . His Poems,* ll. 23–24.

love is synonymous with the act of excreting, Swift offers an extreme metaphor of the passion for body alone.

Thus man's excessive love of external beauty leads either to passion for even the grossest aspects of the loved one, or to disillusionment and misanthropy. The true marriage, Swift tells us, is based on more permanent values, the mind and the heart. As he puts it in *Strephon and Chloe,* echoing the house metaphor that runs through the Stella poems:

> What House, when its Materials crumble,
> Must not inevitably tumble?
> What Ediface can long endure,
> Rais'd on a Basis unsecure?
> Rash Mortals, e'er you take a Wife,
> Contrive your Pile to last for Life;
> Since Beauty scarce endures a Day,
> And Youth so swiftly glides away;
> Why will you make yourself a Bubble
> To build on Sand with Hay and Stubble? (ll. 297–306)

"On Sense and Wit your Passion found," Swift concludes, "By Decency cemented round" (ll. 307–08). They make the body, when it deteriorates, irrelevant. In fact, in the later birthday poems Swift argues that Stella's virtues increase as her body decays with illness and age.

In the little poem for 1723–24 "Written on the day of her Birth, but not on the Subject, when I was sick in bed," we are shown both Swift and Stella in failing health, and their different reactions are contrasted. It begins, "Tormented by incessant pains, / Can I devise poetic strains?" with the rhymes paralleling the uncontrollable body ("pains") and the manifestation of spirit ("poetic strains"); the physical infirmity is hindering the spiritual part of Swift from expressing itself. Illness makes him dumb and ungenerous, revealing his "brutish passions" (he later calls himself "a brute" and refers to his "base actions"). But Stella, who is sicker than Swift, nurses and looks after him; much as Swift's exile and decrepitude lead to his fearless attacks on entrenched evil in the *Verses,* a physical disharmony is necessary in order to reveal the virtue of Stella's spirit—without sickness there would be no way of demonstrating it:

> Her firmness who could e'er have known,
> Had she not evils of her own?
> Her kindness who could ever guess,
> Had not her friends been in distress? (ll. 25–28)

The point of the poem is that body can drag us down if we allow it to, as with Swift, in whom sickness reveals the brute; or it can merely act as a vesture for our soul, a way of revealing our virtues, as with Stella. The parallel with the dressing room poems, in particular *Strephon and Chloe,* is obvious.

The relationship between body and spirit in the Stella and dressing room poems is analogous to that between physical victory and spiritual victory in the poems defending Swift's character. The temporary success of faction and Walpole in England is contrasted with the lasting value of Swift's unconquerable spirit in Ireland, the world of preferment with the world of unselfish public devotion. The *Verses on the Death of Dr. Swift* simply takes the process of physical decay to its logical conclusion—the actual death of Swift's body.[58] We follow its deterioration—his failing memory, his deafness—until it ceases operation completely. His friends and enemies first react, not toward Swift, but toward his body—different only in their orientation from Strephon and Lord Romney's admirers. But the *Verses* differs from the dressing room poems in its conclusion, in its emphasis on the good in the eulogy of Swift's spirit. In the dressing room poems, as in the Irish satires, Swift uses spirit, virtue, and permanence merely as satiric ideals by which to judge the evils that are the subject of the poems. In the *Verses* he gives the ideal equal space with the evil, and the result is closer to the Stella poems or to the early pindaric odes of praise than to satire.

---

[58] The relevance of the Struldbrug episode in *Gulliver's Travels* is at least partly to point up by the Struldbrugs' meaningless death-in-life the meaningful deaths of the great patriots shown in the visions of Glubbdubdrib, who were not afraid of death and were willing to choose dying for love of their countries in preference to living a life of tyranny.

To put the platonism of the Stella poems into perspective it is necessary to look at a poem to Vanessa, who was unable to accept a role like the one Stella played in Swift's life. In *Cadenus and Vanessa* Swift intended to show Vanessa their situation, as well as Stella's situation, in the larger context of the whole world.

The concerns we have noticed in the Stella poems are here. But as Martin Price has pointed out, Swift combines both reason and passion, the spiritual and the physical, in Vanessa.[59] It is not altogether clear whether he wants her to appear an ultimate ideal for human beings (like the Houyhnhnms) or the defeated ideal (like Temple or Sancroft). In the first part of the poem he hints at both interpretations; but the general conclusion we must draw from the poem is that she is that rare thing, a complete person; and her completeness is contrasted to the exclusive fleshliness of the foppish lovers and the fleshlessness of Cadenus (Swift). Swift opposes Vanessa to Cadenus much as Plato opposes Socrates and his tale of Diotima of Mantineia to Pausanius in the *Symposium*: "Do not then insist," says Diotima, "that what is not fair is of necessity foul, or what is not good evil; or infer that because love is not fair and good he is therefore foul and evil; for he is in a mean between them."[60] Cadenus is the man of reason who has allowed his passion to die with his aging body. His explanation to Vanessa of his position turns out to be the same espoused in the later Stella poems. Love, he complains, is a chaotic experience, made up of "hot and cold . . . sharp and sweet" passions,

> But Friendship in its greatest Height,
> A constant, rational Delight,
> On Virtue's Basis fix'd to last
> When Love's Allurements long are past. (ll. 780–83)

But here the view is ironically distanced and qualified—spoken ("in exalted Strains") by an old man withheld from love by "his Dignity and Age," who is trying "to justify his Pride." Here

---

[59] Price, *Swift's Rhetorical Art*, p. 109.
[60] *Dialogues of Plato*, Jowett trans., I, 327.

Swift shows the whole picture, whereas in the Stella poems he shows only a part of it.

In the latter he is, by the very form and tone of the poems, limiting himself to the picture of an old man talking to a younger (but aging and ailing) woman; and this suggests something of the poems' unique quality. Swift is not, as in his more public utterances, speaking in terms of a norm or an ideal for all men —just for these two people. What he says is complimentary; it is intended only for Stella, and only in terms of Stella. He is explaining her situation to her, adjusting the world to her (and, for that matter, his) circumstances. By contrast *Cadenus and Vanessa,* though supposedly written only for Vanessa's eyes, is a much more public and official utterance.

The Stella poems are dramatic structures in which the speaker and listener are characters, and the words are only part of a complex that includes the motives and emotions that condition them. The *Verses on the Death of Dr. Swift,* however, joins the reflections of the Stella poems with the public utterance of a satiric apologia. I suppose the greatest discrepancy in this merger appears between the "impartial" eulogist and his passionately committed eulogy. We hear Swift talking to himself as he talked to Stella a few years earlier. But, perhaps because of this lack of dramatic distance, the eulogy combines with the physical frustration and decay expressed in the "Proem" to create an image that conveys, as memorably as anything in the Stella poems, the agony of man's predicament in a physical world he cannot control.

The personal image begins in Swift's poetry as a typically Augustan persona and, with a sort of inevitability, moves toward the autonomy of symbol. The persona itself presupposes a generalizing or conventionalizing of the individual, and in time the satirist sees his situation as symbolic. As Swift's case shows, the Juvenalian persona offers subtle temptations. The Horatian persona is like everyone else except that he sees more realistically and can point out consequences that someone else may not foresee. He has no illusions or suspicions that he is morally better than others; only his manners are better, and he is better off because of his commonsense and his position in Maecenas' circle. Juvenal, on the other hand, is an ethical hero—the man who has a definite moral superiority over the people he describes; he lashes them from his superior position. As Juvenal presents him, he knows the truth and they do not. The opposite of Horace, his authority comes from deprivation—from not being one of the socially acceptable. The paradox of Christianity is implicit in the Juvenalian speaker: the least shall be the greatest; and it is not difficult to see why the Church Fathers adopted a more or less Juvenalian pose for their tirades against the heretics. God, and not the state, was usually on their side.

When the satirist can construe the direction of his own life as corresponding to the convention, he leaves satire behind as his interest shifts from the evil to the peripheral "good man" who suffers from it—himself. This progression may even suggest an unwillingness on Swift's part to be satisfied with a persona; a tendency toward self-dramatization that connects him with the Romantic poets. Nor is Swift alone an example of this progression. G. K. Hunter has noted a similar tendency toward romanticizing in Pope, who tends to turn his Horatian satirist, without losing the Horatian connotations, into a Juvenalian. The Popean persona of the *Epistle to Dr. Arbuthnot* indeed has much in common with the Dean, including sickness and misunderstanding.[61] In the 1743 *Dunciad* he becomes a lone representative of order that is being overwhelmed by the onrush of Chaos, whom he invokes as the only muse that is left:

> Ye Pow'rs! whose Mysteries restor'd I sing,
> To whom Time bears me on his rapid wing,
> Suspend a while your Force inertly strong,
> Then take at once the Poet and the Song. (Bk. IV, ll. 5–8)

The Augustan Age was a satiric period in which interest was almost wholly focused on the object of attack—on the ethos of evil, and its complexity. This could only happen in a period when

---

[61] "The 'Romanticism' of Pope's Horace," *Essays in Criticism*, X (1960), 390–404. See also Elias F. Mengel, Jr., "Patterns of Imagery in Pope's Arbuthnot," *Publication of the Modern Language Association*, 69 (1954), 189–97.

the satirist felt he had a firm position from which to regard the deviant evil unflinchingly and objectively, without losing himself in fear or loathing. *Absalom and Achitophel* represents this moment, and the whole remainder of the so-called Augustan period, at least as far as the Tories were concerned, tried to keep up the pose—first from conviction, then as a rhetorical stance, and finally as a whistle in the dark, before abandoning it. With loss of security and order, defeat brings more concern in the satirist and his own suffering (or nobility) than in the enemy. The satirist emerges, we can conclude, in times of great confidence or of despair. Emphasis on the satirist can imply either no great concern with a specific threat, or such a hopeless time that there is nothing left to do but congratulate or commiserate with oneself on being the last honest man.

The assumptions of the later Augustan satirists, Swift and Pope, were necessarily somewhat more Miltonic, mystical and pessimistic, than Dryden's. Except for four years (1710–14) the Tories were out of power, watching their society being swept toward what they thought to be destruction, as Juvenal watched Rome becoming non-Rome. For them the mock-epic showed the heroic echoes not as "the fulfilment of a long, divinely ordained process" but as a nearly dead ideal against which to measure the perversion of such values in the Walpoles, Cibbers, Haywoods, and Riches of the present. At this point, when the social and civil ideals of classical Rome seemed no longer possible, the satirists turned increasingly away from the external world for their ideal—inward to their own sacred flames and upward to the final judge, God. Juvenal expresses this point of view in satire: the reign of Domitian is the equivalent of the Georges' except that the latter still pose as Augustus. So the mock-heroic overlay only exposes the discrepancy. From Juvenal the satirists took their persona and their image of aggressive evil; but from the Augustans they continued to take their allusions and the ironic context of their satires. So that the Horatian satire, when applied to George I, George II, Hervey, or Cibber, is almost as much a mock-heroic ideal as the Virgilian epic is in *The Dunciad*.

Dryden moves steadily away from his satires toward the religious poems, mixed with satire, of the late 1680's. Swift abandons the classical orientation of the Augustan Age for the more Biblical-prophetic tone of the tradition that runs from Juvenal to Jerome, Tertullian, and other Church Fathers. Pope, in a work like the *Epistle to Bathurst,* shows that the classical ideal (in Bathurst) finally falls short of the Christian ideal (in the Man of Ross). It is possible to argue that the later work of these satirists shows a movement toward God rather than toward pessimism and Juvenalian conventions. The pessimism of their satires is not a veering toward Manicheian dualism but an increasing insistence on the spiritual side of Augustinian Christianity: those aspects that have no counterpart in (or are a reaction against) the classical ethos.

These works also hint at a shift in emphasis that was beginning to take place from the audience, in whom Swift is ordinarily most interested, toward the poet himself, from rhetoric to metaphysics, from persuasion to symbol-making. The Juvenalian satirist of the *Verses* offers a suggestive resemblance to the poets like Gray and Collins who pictured themselves withdrawn from society and as having a somehow special relationship to God. They derive from the seer, the divinely-inspired bard who looms large over Milton's epic, and who also at times owes something to the Juvenalian pose, though drawing on Virgilian melancholy as well:

> though fall'n on evil days,
> On evil days though fall'n, and evil tongues;
> In darkness, and with dangers compast round,
> And solitude ... (Bk. VII, ll. 25–28).

Milton's blindness and isolation in the middle of a hostile London of victorious Belials becomes, or at least gives sanction to, Swift's deafness, sickness, and exile in Ireland.

These are no doubt some of the elements that made Romantic critics look back with interest to Swift's work and read madness and other Romantic preoccupations into it. In his early and mature satires it was possible to study explorations of the evil in the human mind, and in his late ones his own sensibility. In the vatic figure who curses in *The Legion Club* Swift is perhaps unconsciously moving toward the view expressed by Joseph Warton: "WIT and SATIRE are transitory and perishable, but NATURE and PASSION are eternal."[62] And his satirist offers one path to the Byronic hero, another exile and upholder of some ideal (though a private one), who like Astrea has fled his native habitat and cries:

> I have not loved the world, nor the world me;
> I have not flatter'd its rank breath, nor bow'd
> To the idolatries a patient knee,
> Nor conn'd my cheek to smiles, nor cried aloud
> In worship of an echo; in the crowd
> They could not deem me one of such: I stood
> Among them, but not of them, in a shroud
> Of thoughts which were not their thoughts . . .[63]

Conclusion: The Fiction of Whig Satire

The fiction employed by Addison and Steele in *The Spectator* (1711–12) is an eighteenth century version of Horace's circle of Maecenas: a club, a social microcosm, an England in little, of which the reader is meant to think he is a part. Mr. Spectator, the taciturn but observant persona of the papers, is obsessed by the idea of clubs, all kinds of clubs: clubs for the fat or the lean, for the happy or the morose, even for the ugly and the maimed. The only deep-dyed villains are those who, in Dr. Johnson's phrase, are "unclubbable," like the young Crusoe-type (No. 11) who disencumbers himself of the native girl who has saved his life by selling her into slavery. Here for a moment we are back in the world of Tory satire, but such moments are rare in *The Spectator.*

---

[62] *An Essay on the Genius and Writings of Pope* (1756; 1806 ed.), I, 330.
[63] *Childe Harold's Pilgrimage,* Canto III, stanza 113, ed. Samuel C. Chew (New York: Odyssey Press, 1936).

The structure of individual papers is extremely Horatian, whether following the *sermones* or the *epistolae;* in the former the folly is explored in the thesis (though usually with fewer examples than Horace permitted himself) and the good or wise course of action rather abstractly stated in the antithesis. But extended over many papers, in a random series of encounters, members of the Spectator Club tend to take on a more independent life than Horace permitted his characters. They become rounded creations through sheer exposure; and their erratic, even inconsistent, presentation creates a kind of verisimilitude—as a person's attitude to his friends may change from day to day. One of the fictional assumptions of *The Spectator* is that these are real people; their reality is part of Addison's and Steele's plan. They wish to make their characters as lifelike as possible, to make the readers think of them as real people, and thus, when they go to the polls, ask themselves which they would rather have governing them. For the unique place of *The Spectator* in a study of satiric fictions depends largely on its mixture of intentions: one of these was to attack as a romance the Tory myth, reflected at this time in the Tory ministry of Harley and St. John and in Swift's *Examiner*.

In *Spectator* No. 2, which introduces the Club, Steele (the author of this paper) already knows exactly how he wishes to use it, and to make his purpose less obvious but surer of fulfilment he scatters his characterizations of Sir Roger de Coverley and Sir Andrew Freeport among several others. But in typical Horatian fashion, the Tory Sir Roger's character comes first. To begin with, there is his ancestry, one of the important points of the Tory myth. The Golden Age in the past, the wisdom of ancestors, the age-old duties and paternal benevolence of the landed gentry, about which Swift writes so glowingly, here are reduced to the only fact of importance that can be discovered of Sir Roger's ancestors: his great-grandfather invented a dance (the Sir Roger de Coverley). Next there is the Tory's adherence to the good old ways, which in Sir Roger amounts to mere singularity of behavior—the very characteristic the Tories accused the Whigs of fostering. His actions "are Contradictions to the Manners of the World," Steele writes in ironic praise, "only as he thinks the World is in the wrong. However," he adds, "this Humour creates him no Enemies, for he does nothing with Sowrness or Obstinacy . . ."[64] Concession is one of *The Spectator*'s chief devices.

Sir Roger's temperament is the next consideration: he was jilted by a widow he courted, and only then was he "very serious for a Year and a half." He is himself a justice, an example of the Tory claim of paternal interest, responsibility based on own-ership of land; and we are told that "he fills the Chair at a Quarter-Session with great Abilities, and three Months ago gain'd universal Applause by explaining a Passage in the Game-Act." Steele's trick of combining a flamboyant universal with a squalid particular quietly labels Sir Roger the hunting squire of Whig propaganda. In short, Sir Roger is "rather beloved than esteemed." People are "glad of his Company," but they would never trust their government to such a man.[65]

If the first person to be described, in terms of the old con-ventions of status (that is, Sir Roger would *expect* to come first), is the country gentleman, "The Gentleman next in Esteem and Authority among us," we are told with the same ironic praise, is the lawyer, who "knows the Argument of each of the Orations of *Demonsthenes* and *Tully,* but not one Case in the Reports of our own Courts." Tradition for him is not Common Law but the eloquence of ancient Greeks and Romans, quite irrelevant to his cases in eighteenth-century London. "His Familiarity with the Customs, Manners, Actions, and Writings of the Ancients, makes him a very delicate Observer of what occurs to him in the present World. He is an excellent Critick, and the Time of the Play is his Hour of Business. . . ." He is a lover of the ancients who applies their wisdom to theater-going and conversation but

[64] My text for *The Spectator* is Donald F. Bond's (Oxford: Clarendon Press, 1965).

[65] Cf. John Aikin, "On the Humour of Addison and the Character of Sir Roger de Coverley," *Monthly Magazine,* IX (1800), 1–2; and C. S. Lewis has developed the idea persuasively in his essay, "Addison," in *Essays on the Eighteenth Century Presented to D. Nicholl Smith* (Oxford: Clarendon Press, 1945), pp. 2–3.

not to the very social duties that Demosthenes and Cicero would have insisted upon.

Opposed to these representatives of the old and useless is the Whig Sir Andrew Freeport, the London merchant, known for his "indefatigable Industry, strong Reason, and great Experience." He is not particularly lovable, but he gets things done; people can trust him with the government of their affairs.

All of the points made about Sir Roger in this paper—including his courtship of the widow—are developed in later papers, much as Sterne promises and eventually tells us in *Tristram Shandy* about Uncle Toby's courtship of the Widow Wadman and other adventures. The realistic effect is accomplished in each case by unfolding the character's past in relation to a present situation, in the same way that we gradually through contact become acquainted with the various facets of a friend's personality. If Sir Roger is made to be a character who has a past and continues to reveal himself in time, as opposed to the static types in character books from which he descends, he is also regarded by Mr. Spectator with great affection. That Mr. Spectator admires eccentricity only partly explains the fact that over half of Sir Roger's appearances contain hardly a grain of satire. Seen at a distance, and for a shorter period, Sir Roger would appear to be a fool; but the reader's intimacy with him is as great as Mr. Spectator's, and he agrees with Mirabell's comment on Milliamant's faults, that "they are now grown as familiar to me as my own frailties, and, in all probability, in a little time longer I shall like 'em as well."

Nevertheless, at intervals, the more effective because of their separation, the Whig interpretation of Sir Roger emerges out of the love and friendship. Even in the lovable episodes Sir Roger, the "friend," may be used to get at less lovable Tory country gentlemen, like him uneducated and mere huntsmen, "of no manner of use but to keep up their Families, and transmit their Lands and Houses in a Line to Posterity" (No. 123). Sir Roger's friend Will Wimble, a younger son of the nobility, another "good" man, "hunts a Pack of Dogs better than any Man in the Country, and is very famous for finding out a Hare"; but

Mr. Spectator marvels that "so good an Heart and such busy Hands were wholly employed in Trifles; that so much Humanity should be so little beneficial to others, and so much Industry so little advantageous to himself." His "is the case of many a younger Brother of a great Family, who had rather see their Children starve like Gentlemen, than thrive in a Trade or Profession that is beneath their Quality" (No. 108).

At other times the reader notices a slight asperity in references to Sir Roger's "blunt way of saying things, as they occur to his Imagination, without regular Introduction, or Care to preserve the appearance of Chain of Thought" (No. 109). But then, occasionally, the overtones of Sir Roger's significance are allowed play. In No. 116 (by Eustace Budgell) the description of his hunting is suggestive: "Sir *Roger,* being at present too old for Fox-hunting, to keep himself in Action, has disposed of his Beagles and got a Pack of *Stop-Hounds.* What these want in Speed, he endeavours to make Amends for by the Deepness of their Mouths and the Variety of their Notes...." After this almost allegorical excursus into the subject of Tories whose bark is worse than their bite, Mr. Spectator quotes Pascal to the effect that it takes brainless fools to "throw away so much Time and Pains upon a silly Animal, which they might buy cheaper in the Market." Then he distinguishes between the man who "suffers his whole Mind to be drawn into his Sports, and altogether loses himself in the Woods" (Sir Roger) and the indolent man who avoids all exercise (Pascal, he points out, died young for this reason). One pole is the brainless but healthy Sir Roger and the other the sickly but astute Pascal. Implicit between these extremes is the man who intends to "hunt twice a Week" and prescribes "the moderate Use of this Exercise" to all his friends. (Of Sir Andrew we are told later, in No. 232, that he "divides himself almost equally between the Town and the Country," combining the best of business with the pleasure, relaxation, and paternalism of Sir Roger's country life.)

Everything is conveyed by inference, approximation, and concession. Mr. Spectator, when he takes his leave of Sir Roger, uses himself as an opposite extreme to Sir Roger in order to suggest the golden mean which is his ideal; he concludes that "the Country is not a Place for a Person of my Temper, who does not love Jollity, and what they call Good-Neighbourhood" (No. 131). Then in No. 174 (by Steele) the matter is brought to an issue by confronting Sir Roger with Sir Andrew, making Sir Roger the aggressor and giving Sir Andrew the last word, which serves to sum up the impression we have gradually gathered about Sir Roger and Toryism. Mr. Spectator may call such arguments part of "a constant, though friendly, Opposition of Opinions," but Sir Andrew brings the matter down to "keeping true Accounts" as opposed to "Hospitality," by which he means "to drink so many Hogsheads" (or "what they call Good Neighbourhood"); business and its rewards versus "the Chase" whose "only Returns must be the Stag's Horns in the great Hall, and the Fox's Nose upon the Stable Door"; and the man "who has got [his estate] by his Industry" versus the man "who has lost it by his Negligence." Once again the reflection is less on Sir Roger himself, "the good old Knight," than on the tradition-corrupted views he transmits and the worse knights who lose their estates by their negligence.

As these examples suggest, *The Spectator's* satire exploits the balanced syntax of parallel and antithesis in two ways: to infer the absent ideal of behavior by stating opposite extremes, as when we are told of the Tersetts that "their Fortune has placed them above Care, and their Loss of Taste reduced them below Diversion" (No. 100); or to qualify censure through concession, as when Mr. Spectator says that Sir Roger "left me at a Loss whether I was more delighted with my Friend's Wisdom or Simplicity" (No. 109). The latter complicates character, and we end (as in the case of Leonora in No. 37) "with a mixture of Admiration and Pity," much as Pope does at the end of his portrait of Atticus. How admirable, Mr. Spectator concedes, that Leonora devotes herself to innocent and serious subjects like books, but how sad that she has not been guided by books that "enlighten the Understanding and rectify the Passions, as well as those which are of little more use than to divert the Imagination."

There is no virulence in the portrait of Sir Roger de Coverley, only the inference that, though good hosts and drinking companions, the Tories are incompetent, simple-minded old men who have lived beyond their usefulness. Mr. Spectator *loves* Sir Roger, "that good old Man," and in spite of his follies, Sir Roger is accepted as part of the club, absorbed into the group, in effect forgiven, he is so harmless and lovable. The club (England) has room for Tories as well as all other elements of the nation.

Moreover, and this is the important point, Addison and Steele deny that this *is* satire. They stop frequently in both *Tatler* and *Spectator* to excoriate satire—or at least satire written by Tories. Addison more than once equates satire and lampoon and calls satire a violent weapon in the hands of a violent man (as opposed to a gentleman). But one wonders about his motives when he writes: "I once had gone through [that is, written] half a Satyr, but found so many Motions of Humanity rising in me towards the Persons whom I had severely treated, that I threw it into the Fire without even finishing it" (No. 355). Does his remark in reality reflect upon the immorality or on the ineffectiveness, or even the inappropriateness, of such vituperation and lampoon? Steele explicity distinguishes in *Tatler* No. 242 (of October 26, 1710) between what he calls "true Satyr" and false: true satire is good-natured and general, false is malicious and personal. The great satirists of the past, Horace and Juvenal, he asserts, wrote out of good nature, "without Bitterness towards their Persons," but satire as it was being practiced in his own day (i.e., by Tories) was "aimed at particular Persons" and informed by personal malice. In *Spectators* No. 23, 35, 451 Addison also equates satire with invective as well as lampoon. "I cannot," he insists repeatedly, "but look upon the finest Strokes of Satire which are aimed at particular Persons, and which are supported even with the appearance of Truth, to be the Marks of an evil Mind, and highly Criminal in themselves" (No. 451). This is not the place to go into the theories of comedy that were beginning to seek a distinction between the ridiculous and the ludicrous, in the process downgrading satire;[66] but only to point out that Addison's and Steele's doctrine of "true" and "false" satire can be regarded as another satiric weapon with which to discredit their opponents, the Tory satirists.

If they had sought common ground, Swift, Addison, and Steele would have agreed that the important question is one of decorum, as expressed by Steele in *Tatler* No. 242:

> *Horace* was intimate with a Prince of the greatest Goodness and Humanity imaginable, and his Court was formed after his Example: Therefore the Faults that the Poet falls upon were little Inconsistencies in Behaviour, false Pretences to Politeness, or impertinent Affectations of what Men were not fit for. . . . *Juvenal* on the other Hand lived under *Domitian*, in whose Reign every Thing that was great and noble was banished the Habitations of the Men in Power. Therefore he attacks Vice as it passes by in Triumph, not as it breaks into Conversation. . . . Morality and Virtue are every where recommended in *Horace*, as became a Man in a polite Court, from the Beauty, the Propriety, the Convenience, of pursuing them. Vice and Corruption are attacked by *Juvenal* in a Style which denotes, he fears he shall not be heard without he calls to them in their own Language with a bare-faced Mention of the Villanies and Obscenities of his Contemporaries.

"In the Days of *Augustus*," Steele adds, "to have talked like *Juvenal* had been Madness, or in those of *Domitian* like *Horace*." *The Spectator*'s tone of quiet reasonableness therefore expresses a world view antithetical to that of the Tories, for whom, as C. S. Lewis has noticed, "every enemy . . . becomes a grotesque. All who have, in whatever fashion, incurred their ill will are knaves, scarecrows, whores, bugs, toads, bedlamites, yahoos. . . ." We may not, however, wish to go as far as Lewis' conclusion: "It is good fun, but it is certainly not good sense; we laugh, and disbelieve";[67] for this is exactly the point of the *Spectator*'s contrasting moderation. The conservative position is always on the defensive—it *is* a defensive position, even during periods of apparent victory. Swift's *Examiner* can afford to appear middle-of-the-road, tolerant, amusing during the years

---

[66] See Stuart Tave, *The Amiable Humorist* (Chicago, Ill.: University of Chicago Press, 1960).

[67] Lewis, *Essays on the Eighteenth Century*, p. 2.

of the Tory Ministry; but very soon the note of urgency returns —Marlborough is more dangerous than comic, he cannot, like Sir Roger, be tolerated. The Whigs can, in theory, afford to tolerate everyone because this is, after all, one of their tenets going back to the first Earl of Shaftesbury (Achitophel) and the Glorious Revolution. Whig satire thus points up the gross exaggeration—the symbolizing, the poeticizing—of the Tory satires, reminding the reader of the vanity and impotence in their threats and warnings. At the same time it suggests to the reader a sense of confidence in the Whigs' approaching and inevitable victory and the order and security that will ensue.

By claiming not to write satire—and in fact by writing what we would call comedy; by loving and accepting the Tories as private persons while totally discrediting them as public servants —Addison and Steele create as rhetorically effective a satire as can be imagined. A reader of the *Spectator,* drawn into its sympathetic world, might well think twice about voting for a Tory M.P. It is arguable, however, that this satire does not fire the imagination or recruit the reader's ardent support for a cause (an apparently doubtful or hopeless one) as the Tory satire sometimes does. The element of heroism is absent. The *Spectator*'s is a satire of the confident, but it is not meant to work in violent situations such as that of Wood's half-pence, where the reader is called upon to arise and do something out of the ordinary. It lacks the representational interest of the great Tory satires—of those very bedlamites and Yahoos mentioned by Lewis, seen with an intensity and passion that raise them to the level of universal symbols and high art.

Both Whig and Tory satire are, of course, Augustan not only in the assumption of satiric decorum but in their tendency to proceed by concession, imitation, and realistic portrayal, and to avoid absolutes in evil.[68] For the Tories, however, the middling

[68] The Whigs also, of course, used many of the basic Augustan-Tory devices, e.g., the imitation of the enemy. An anonymous Whig (possibly Steele or one of his friends) published a pamphlet called *Essays Divine, Moral, and Political: By the Author of the 'Tale of a Tub'* (1714), which purports to be Swift's self-revelations (the epigraph is "Out of thy own Mouth will condemn Thee, O thou Hypocrit"). Thus "Swift" reveals himself to be an unbelieving hypocrite

quality portrayed is part of the danger, while for the Whigs it is part of the amusement. The Tory villain is isolated by his selfishness and sufficiency, but also by his powerlessness, and the madness of Dennis, the castration of Curll, and the death of Partridge are only the extremes of isolation to which the Tory villain drives himself (or, the *Spectator* would say, is driven by the Tory satirists). Tory satire is preoccupied with situations of isolation and withdrawal from normal society; the evil agent and the satirist share this withdrawal—the one from a sound, the other from a contaminated society. Neither satirist nor villain is clubbable in the *Spectator* sense. The *Spectator* avoids those isolating and easily recognizable satiric conventions of madness, purges, and whippings; in fact, it abominates isolation, gathering into its fold Whigs, Tories, and other types who bear no direct relation to politics at all but carry their own distinctive interpretations of experience (a very different group from the all-Tory Scriblerus Club). If Swift's version of reality led to a great emphasis on states of consciousness or attitudes in his villains and observers, there was no recognition that different points of view are necessary to fill out the spectrum of experience.

Indeed, the members of the Spectator Club, far from being representatives of normative social values against which to judge Sir Roger's oddities, are all, on closer inspection, withdrawals or dropouts of society. Each is in some sense as alienated as William Wood or the "Dean": Mr. Spectator cannot communicate with anyone outside his club; Sir Roger and Will Honeycomb are anachronisms, neither of whom has outgrown the Restoration world of his youth; Captain Sentry has withdrawn from the army, where merit suffers and only political ingenuity is rewarded; the parson is too debilitated to serve any parish, the lawyer too preoccupied with the stage to plead cases; and even Sir Andrew—it is implied—retires to his club from a world where merchants are not given their proper due. All the other clubs mentioned by Mr. Spectator—for ugly, lean, or fat peo-

---

in religion, a cynic in morality, a Hobbesian-Mandevillian egoist in politics. In practice, Addison and especially Steele used the most effective propaganda required to meet a particular situation.

ple—are for similarly un-normative people. The club of eccentrics is Addison and Steele's image of the Whig social unit; these humor-characters, whose eccentricities would have been ridiculed by the Tory satirists, or whose idealism would have led to a Tory withdrawal into dignified exile, are examples of the freedom to be oneself and the heterogeneity of society advocated by the Whigs.

With the Spectator Club we have come full circle from the moderns Swift shows praising their own deformities to the Whigs who understand and enjoy each other in terms of their deformities. Whig satire, then, eliminates the satiric villain by absorbing him into the club, cherishing him as a "character," and turning the whole cast into rather good sorts whose follies or peculiarities are largely points of view detached from actions with consequences. When they are connected, as when Mr. Spectator visits Sir Roger's country house, the acts are in themselves neutral or admirable. (As Horace would say, there is nothing wrong with the chase, unless it usurps all other activity.) Only the point of view, the attitude, is wrong. But whereas Swift augments the point of view with monstrous projects and proposals, sometimes materialized, Addison and Steele will have none of them. In general they direct their different points of view toward some folly, which is tangential to the viewers if not wholly outside them.

Our study of how satiric fictions operate ends in the 1740's. But if we were to look ahead to the second half of the century, we would notice two roads taken by satirists, whether in verse or prose. One, following from Swift's last works and Pope's formal satires, employed the conventional object-eye relation, covering with richness of rhetoric a poverty of fiction. As far back as Butler's *Hudibras,* we can observe the reduction of satiric fiction to a frame on which the satirist hangs verbal satire; the fiction literally disappears in the elaboration of detail, for which it only serves as a means. In Pope's satires it is only with the greatest difficulty that the reader makes out the action or plot of *The Dunciad*'s Book I, and when he has discovered the plot of all four books, it is still the elaboration, the couplet and all it contains, that projects Pope's satire. This as opposed to Swift, in whose *Tale of a Tub,* a work very like *Hudibras* and with even less over-all plot, certain large symbols and relationships stand out of a sort one never finds himself remembering in Butler or Pope. But the tendency of all satire, we have seen, is to resolve into a vituperative or ironic speaker: so with Pope, and the later Swift.

After Pope's death there were no major satires that were unabashedly satires, except for the works of Charles Churchill. Although he did not call them by name, they were essentially formal satires which have become (as his detractors claimed) a farrago of formless rhetoric less like Pope's satire than like the elder Pitt's speeches in the House of Commons—or later Junius' tirades. Churchill's satires repeated the tired old fictions, some of them inherited from Pope, others much older: the session of the poets, the court of Dulness (or Famine), the mock-pastoral—but these fictions are mere pretexts for the spectacular cleverness of the detail. Even Fielding, when he wrote "satire" as such used the most conventional fictions—the invasion of Dulness, the battle of ancients and moderns, the boat crossing the River Styx, and the journey.

In danger of being replaced by its opposite, or alternative, panegyric, satire adjusted itself to the new literary assumptions —or was infiltrated—and so was transformed, for example purified into melancholy meditation. There were certain emphases in satire itself that allowed for the easy metamorphosis. Interest in the character of the satirist, in point of view, in the proper vantage point for showing up folly, permitted a fulcrum to studies of consciousness. The change could take place on a number of such fulcrums: that of satire-comedy (comedy being an element in satire, and so becoming the whole), or Juvenal-melodrama, or indignation-emotion. Even the Christian idea of evil offers opportunities for a slippery descent from satire into pelagianism; and the ideals of classicism could be interpreted by a Tory or by a Whig each in his own way without leaving the camp of the ancients.

But while satire as satire tended to shrivel into personal lampoon or oratory, it survived in partly satiric or nonsatiric works through the agency of its fictions. Fielding, Smollett, and Sterne explored the possibilities of using old satiric fictions within the developing form of the long prose narrative, the novel—and in the process created new ones, which, however, emerging in a new context, lost some of their purely satiric direction. At its best, satire became part of a new form, in which the tradition stayed alive. At its worst, it dwindled into a local effect, disappearing into sentimental, doctrinal, or other kinds of novel. Or, more interestingly, satire was domesticated, reduced to one element in a larger work, placed, and criticized, or merely used as decoration. There were various sources or models for the placing of satire. Manly in *The Plain Dealer* was only one example of Restoration comedy's use of raw satire, and Swift's Gulliver, placed and judged in terms of larger truths, a more recent example—leading to the satirists who appear as characters in so many eighteenth and nineteenth century novels.

The Augustan satirists, culminating in Swift, constructed the kind of satiric fiction, based on illusion and pseudo-realism, a preoccupation with relationships and responsibility, that could lend itself to this kind of accommodation. In some ways *Gulliver's Travels* was a definite technical advance over *Robinson Crusoe,* showing a greater control of realistic resources (e.g., the persona); and much as the Spanish picaresque novelists and Defoe were two sides of a coin, the one attacking the image of gross reality, the other accepting and celebrating it, so Swift and Richardson almost fit together. To read *Gulliver's Travels* and *Robinson Crusoe,* or *A Tale of A Tub* and parts of *Clarissa* is to find a single closely felt world. Satirists like Swift are delicate antennae of society who detect an evil, or rather project a hypothetical image of its potential, which often becomes a precursor of the real thing and perhaps helps writers to better understand the new form. For the novel to emerge, techniques had to be introduced that attacked and laid bare reality as well as celebrating it.

INDEX

designer: Gerard A. Valerio
typesetter: Monotype Composition Co.
typeface: Caslon Olde Style
printer: Universal Lithographers
paper: 60 lb. Perkins & Squier R
binder: Moore and Company
cover material: G.S.B. s/711